MALORY'S ORIGINALITY:

A Critical Study of *Le Morte Darthur*

MALORY'S ORIGINALITY

A Critical Study of
Le Morte Darthur

EDITED BY

R. M. LUMIANSKY

THE JOHNS HOPKINS PRESS
BALTIMORE

This book has been brought to publication with the
assistance of a grant from The Ford Foundation.

With appreciation to
TULANE UNIVERSITY,
*where opportunity to carry out
these studies was provided.*

FOREWORD

This book presents a commentary on *Le Morte Darthur* which, in the authors' opinions, more fully illuminates Malory's literary aims and techniques than any criticism so far available. In several instances hitherto unused source materials are brought to bear upon Malory's work, and throughout new analyses of his purposes are offered.

From one point of view this book can be called a collection of essays by diverse hands. It differs considerably, however, from the usual collection of that sort. The various studies were prepared by a group of people working for the most part in one place, and working systematically upon selected segments of a single book. Also, the various studies were conducted with a single approach and methodology. Though no effort has been made toward uniformity of expository style in the various essays, our hope is that the end result represents a generally unified analysis and argument.

The text of Malory's book which we have used is that to be found in Eugène Vinaver (ed.), *The Works of Sir Thomas Malory* (Oxford: The Clarendon Press, 1947), three volumes with consecutive pagination. This edition is referred to throughout the footnotes as *Works*, followed by page numbers. A slightly altered reissue of this edition appeared in 1948. Our understanding is that Professor Vinaver is now preparing a revision of the three-volume edition.

The authors' faculty affiliations are as follows: Miss Dichmann, University of Southwestern Louisiana; Mr. Guerin,

Centenary College of Louisiana; Mr. Lumiansky, Duke University; Mr. Moorman, University of Southern Mississippi; Mr. Rumble, Wayne State University; and Mr. Wright, Texas Christian University.

Several parts of this book appeared earlier in learned journals. These parts are included here, in revised form, with permission of the editors concerned: Chapter II, *PMLA* for 1950; Chapter III, *MLN* for 1953; Chapter VI, *PMLA* for 1956; Chapter VII, *Mediaeval Studies* for 1957.

DECEMBER, 1963 THE EDITOR

ABBREVIATIONS

The following is a list of abbreviations of journals used in the footnotes.

BBSIA   *Bulletin Bibliographique de la Société Internationale Arthurienne*

CE   *College English*

EETS-ES   *Early English Text Society-Extra Series*

EETS-OS   *Early English Text Society-Old Series*

ELH   *English Literary History*

JEGP   *Journal of English and Germanic Philology*

MLN   *Modern Language Notes*

MLR   *Modern Language Review*

MP   *Modern Philology*

PMLA   *Publications of the Modern Language Association of America*

RES   *Review of English Studies*

SATF   *Société des Anciens Textes Français*

SP   *Studies in Philology*

TSE   *Tulane Studies in English*

CONTENTS

xi

MALORY'S ORIGINALITY:

A Critical Study of *Le Morte Darthur*

INTRODUCTION

BY R. M. LUMIANSKY

One of our most valuable narrative legacies from the late Middle Ages—an era of great interest in good storytelling—is the Arthurian legend. Among the numerous individual medieval writings which present aspects of this legend, *Le Morte Darthur*—completed by Sir Thomas Malory in "the ninth yere of the reygne of King Edward the Fourth" (1469–70) [1]—holds a very important place as the outstanding English book of the fifteenth century. For almost five centuries it has exerted wide influence among English and American authors, and it has received regular attention from both general readers and specialized students.

Until recently, a primary debt for the availability of *Le Morte Darthur* was owed to William Caxton, who first published it. Caxton's colophon reads as follows:

> Thus endeth thys noble and joyous book entytled le morte Darthur, notwythstondyng it treateth of the byrth, lyf, and actes of the sayd kyng Arthur, of his noble knyghtes of the rounde table, theyr marvayllous enquestes and adventures, thachyevyng of the sangreal, and in thende the dolorous deth and departyng out of thys world of them al. Whiche book was reduced into englysshe by syr Thomas Malory, as afore is sayd, and by me devyded into XXI bookes, chapytred and enprynted and fynysshed in thabbey Westmestre the last day of July, the yere our own lord MCCCCLXXXV. Caxton me fieri fecit. [2]

Whether or not Malory gave the book the title *Le Morte Darthur* is not clear; but that Caxton meant it to have this title, despite its relating much more than the death of Arthur, is clear. The structural division of the manuscript from which

[1] *Works*, p. 1260. The "ninth yere" is between March 4, 1469 and March 3, 1470.

[2] *Ibid.* Punctuation mine. E. Vinaver (*Malory* [Oxford, 1929], pp. 10-15) interprets the colophon differently.

Caxton printed the book is also not clear; but Caxton leaves no doubt that it was he who divided the material into "twenty-one bookes whyche conteyne the somme of fyve hondred and seven chapytres. . . ." [3] All editions of *Le Morte Darthur* except the most recent (1947) derive from Caxton's work.[4]

In 1934 a great event occurred in connection with *Le Morte Darthur:* W. F. Oakeshott discovered in the Fellows' Library of Winchester College a fifteenth-century manuscript of Malory's work, in the handwriting of two scribes.[5] This manuscript, which lacks a gathering of eight leaves at each end, differs considerably from that which Caxton must have used; but it, like that from which Caxton presumably worked, seems a copy twice removed from Malory's composition: [6]

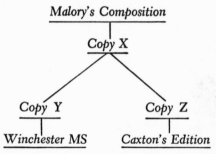

The discovery of the Winchester manuscript obviously furnished important new material for the presentation and assessment of Malory's work. Thus, Arthurian scholars eagerly awaited the appearance of Eugène Vinaver's edition, for which both the Winchester manuscript and Caxton's edition were used.

[3] *Works*, p. cxv, Caxton's Preface.

[4] For the latest listing of these editions see Thomas C. Rumble, "A Survey of the Editions and Criticism of Sir Thomas Malory's *Morte Darthur*," (Master's thesis, Tulane University, 1950).

[5] Microfilm copies of this manuscript may be obtained from the Microfilm Division of the Library of Congress. Reference should be made to positive film reel 1207.

[6] *Works*, pp. lxxxvi–xci.

This critical edition appeared in three volumes in 1947. For it, Vinaver decided upon a structural arrangement which makes immediately clear the eight main divisions of Malory's work; these divisions Vinaver called "Tales." The five longest of these "Tales" he further divided into logical sub-sections. In our opinion Vinaver's arrangement is for any reader much more effective than Caxton's. Also, fruitful consideration of such matters as Malory's thematic purposes, the relationship of structure to theme, the comparative evaluation of the text against its sources, and the functions of the individual divisions becomes far more easily manageable for a critic than was the case with earlier editions. As the Table of Contents for the present study indicates, the eight chapters which follow this Introduction match Vinaver's division of the work into eight "Tales."

Study of the Winchester manuscript led Vinaver to a second and a more startling general conclusion about Malory's work. He maintained in 1947, and has continued to maintain, that Malory intended to write and did write eight separate romances or "Tales" rather than a single unified book.[7] Thus he named his edition *The Works of Sir Thomas Malory*. The chief evidence used by Vinaver to support this view is furnished by the *explicit* at the end of each of the "Tales" except the last in the Winchester manuscript. Caxton seems to have deleted all except the last of these *explicits*, an indication to Vinaver that Caxton was attempting to make one book, in the modern sense, of eight separate "Tales." In the years since the appearance of the 1947 edition, the reaction of scholars on both sides of the Atlantic to this theory of separate romances has been mixed. For example, R. H. Wilson of the University of Texas, a highly respected student of Malory's work, has pointed to cer-

[7] *Ibid.*, pp. xxix–xxxv; "Le Manuscrit de Winchester," *BBSIA*, III (1951), 75–82; *The Works of Sir Thomas Malory* (1 vol.; London, 1954), p. vi; *The Tale of the Death of King Arthur* (London, 1955), p. vii; *King*

tain inconsistencies in the theory; and, more recently, a group of British scholars have made clear their inability to accept fully Vinaver's contention.[8] As will appear in the body of this book, the authors of the present study are convinced that Malory wrote a single unified book rather than eight separate "Tales"; for that book we have used Caxton's title, *Le Morte Darthur*. Whether or not Malory started his writing with the idea of producing a series of separate narratives and later shifted to the idea of a unified book—a situation that we do not believe existed—is not pertinent for this study, which is concerned with Malory's final intention for his work, insofar as it can now be determined.

Given our view of the unity of Malory's work, a primary purpose in each of the chapters which follow is to show the function of the given "Tale" as a part of *Le Morte Darthur* as a whole. Thus the initial chapter stresses preparations and foreshadowings found in the "Tale of King Arthur," and the final chapter the summarizings and retrospections found in the "Tale of the Death of Arthur." The intervening chapters emphasize the connections of the given "Tale" both forward and backward within Malory's book. This examination of *Le Morte Darthur*, we feel, makes indisputably apparent its general unity in theme, structure, and characterization.

The regular method for our examination of *Le Morte Darthur* is detailed comparison of its divisions with their probable sources; upon such comparison we base our interpretation of Malory's work. Each of the eight chapters includes a concise

---

Arthur and His Knights (Boston, 1956), pp. xii–xiii; and R. S. Loomis (ed.), *Arthurian Literature in the Middle Ages* (Oxford, 1959), pp. 541–52.

[8] R. H. Wilson, "How Many Books Did Malory Write?" *University of Texas Studies in English*, XXX (1951), 1–23; R. M. Lumiansky, "The Question of Unity in Malory's Morte Darthur," *TSE*, V (1955), 29–39; J. A. W. Bennett (ed.), *Essays on Malory* (Oxford, 1963); and R. S. Loomis, *The Development of Arthurian Romance* (New York, 1963).

statement of the probable source relationship for the "Tale" under consideration. Perhaps some introductory comment will be helpful concerning our conception of source study in general and Malory's use of sources in particular. The first essential in source study is, of course, the comparison of one piece of writing with an earlier piece; from such comparison the scholar concerned may maintain that the author of the later piece used the earlier piece as source. In the case of *Le Morte Darthur*, the reader should bear in mind that we are not able to point to the exact versions of the sources Malory used. Thus there must be a degree of tentativeness about statements as to just what Malory took from his sources, what is original with him, and what alterations of source materials he effected. Nevertheless, when a scholar establishes the kind of probable source relationship mentioned above, he has added a new fact in the field of literary history. In the instance of *Le Morte Darthur* a tremendous amount of work by a number of able scholars has established the source situation described in this book. But the reader should be aware that further study of Malory's sources is going on steadily. Consequently, at any time a different source relationship from that currently accepted may be established for a given segment of Malory's work.

The chief advantage of source study, however, is that it furnishes a valuable approach for the assessment of a literary work. Once a student can believe—as a result of factual comparison—that Malory used the alliterative *Morte Arthure* as source for his "Tale of King Arthur and the Emperor Lucius," he can then examine Malory's handling of this source with an eye for patterns which point toward that interpretation of the "Tale" which Malory intended. In such an examination we must observe what Malory borrowed *verbatim* from the source, what he altered, what he omitted, and what he added. The fundamental assumption is that in each of these aspects of his work Malory was consciously aware of his handling of the source. He controlled the source; it did not control him, for he could have handled it in an infinite number of ways had he so desired. Accordingly, as we shall see in detail in Chapter II, we may observe in connection with the "Tale of King Arthur and the Emperor Lucius" and the alliterative *Morte* that Malory borrowed episodes in which Gawain plays a leading role in the source, that he omitted Gawain's name from these episodes, and that he added Lancelot's name; these facts represent strong evidence that as he wrote this "Tale" Malory, unlike the author of the alliterative *Morte*, intended us to understand Lancelot's military position in Arthur's society as more important than Gawain's.

We should also bear steadily in mind that the matter of source relationship is not just a question of comparable words, lines, or passages. Rather, it must also include consideration of theme and structure of the pertinent literary pieces. But such comparison cannot lead to absolute certainty in our conclusions. In effect, we are trying to follow the workings of an author's mind as he wrote; such an effort can hardly yield completely objective data, for the workings of minds—especially writers' minds—are likely to be extremely complex and to vary considerably from time to time and from writer to writer. All we can do is to set forth the conclusion which we find defensible on the basis of the observable facts; someone else may arrive at a wholly different conclusion from the same facts. In such a situation the burden rests squarely upon the interested reader to choose between the conflicting views.

With such cautions in mind, we can profit immeasurably from careful study of Malory's sources in trying to interpret *Le Morte Darthur*. And we shall be on safe ground so long as we do not expect the sources to answer conclusively and completely all aspects of the problem. In the last analysis, *Le Morte*

Darthur, not its sources, is at the center of our interest. As will appear from the following chapters, the large conclusion which we have drawn from our study of the text and the sources of *Le Morte Darthur* is that although Malory borrowed a great deal from his sources, his handling of these borrowings resulted in a highly original literary work. Our emphasis upon Malory's originality may seem unwarranted to those readers accustomed to the earlier view of Malory as simply a "translator" and "redactor." But, in our opinion, the following chapters demonstrate his originality not only in the segments of his book for which he appears to have had no source, but also in his careful shaping of his borrowed materials on almost every page of his retelling of the Arthurian story.

Theme.

A final matter calls for brief comment here. A number of inconsistencies occur in *Le Morte Darthur*; for example, a knight who is killed at one point in the book will later reappear in sound health.[9] In quite a few instances we have found that these matters are—for one reason or another—seeming rather than real inconsistencies, once Malory's probable purposes are made clear. However, cases remain which do not yield to such explanation. Our view of these cases is that they simply show need for minor revision, a benefit which was not accorded the book. In contrast with the extensive body of evidence for the careful planning which must have gone into Malory's work, the few inconsistencies do not suggest any intention other than coherent unity. Because of the size and nature of *Le Morte Darthur*, and the difficult conditions under which we think it was written, it is surprising that more inconsistencies did not occur.

[9] E. K. Chambers, *Sir Thomas Malory* (The English Association, Pamphlet No. 21, 1922), pp. 4–5, and "Malory," *English Literature at the Close of the Middle Ages* (Oxford, 1945), pp. 191–94.

CHAPTER I

"THE TALE OF KING ARTHUR":
BEGINNINGS AND FORESHADOWINGS

BY THOMAS L. WRIGHT

The source of Malory's "Tale of King Arthur" is an Old French romance known as the *Suite du Merlin*.[1] This romance was a branch of the Pseudo-Robert de Borron Prose Cycle, a thirteenth-century recasting of the Vulgate Cycle. Though it remains incomplete, the Borron Prose Cycle has been partly

---

[1] The *Suite du Merlin* survives in three major MS. versions (all fragmentary) and a number of shorter fragments. The French sources against which Malory's text has been compared in this study of "The Tale of King Arthur" are as follows:

1. Manuscript: The Cambridge MS. of the *Suite du Merlin* (British Museum Add. 7071, ff. 159–342). Cited hereafter as Camb. This MS. contains versions of the rebellion of the kings and the Balin story which are missing or incomplete in the Huth *Merlin*.

2. Edition: The Huth *Merlin* (British Museum Add. 38117), available in the following edition: Gaston Paris and Jacob Ulrich, (eds.), *Merlin, roman en prose du XIIIe siècle* (Société des Anciens Textes Français: Paris, 1886). Cited hereafter as Huth. All quotations in Old French are from this edition unless otherwise designated.

3. Edition: H. O. Sommer (ed.), *Lestoire de Merlin*, Vol. II in *The Vulgate Version of the Arthurian Romances* (Washington, 1908). Cited hereafter as VM.

4. Edition: H. O. Sommer (ed.), *Die Abenteuer Gawains, Ywains, und le Morholts mit den drei Jungfrauen* (MS. B. N. fr. 112), in *Beihefte zur Zeitschrift für romanische Philologie*, XLVII (1913). Cited hereafter as Sommer. This MS. carries the story beyond points where both the Huth and Cambridge MSS. break off.

5. Other sources are cited where they are relevant to the present study.

reconstructed since it was first identified by Gaston Paris in his edition of the Huth MS. of the *Suite du Merlin*.[2] Miss Fanni Bogdanow has recently described the cycle as follows:

> A long romance beginning with the *Estoire del Saint Graal* and followed by the *Suite du Merlin* and the Post-Vulgate versions of the *Queste* and the *Mort Artu*, was written after the Vulgate Cycle and the First Version of the Prose *Tristan*, but before the *Palamedes*. This work, which used to be called the "pseudo-Robert de Borron cycle," but which I should prefer to call the *Roman du Graal*, deals with the rise and fall of Arthur's kingdom, the *roiaume aventeureux*, and derives much of its material from the earlier cyclic compositions.[3]

The new title *Roman du Graal*, suggested by Miss Bogdanow, would aptly define the most important characteristic of the Borron Prose Cycle as far as Malory is concerned: it is an extensive romance of the Grail. This means that although the Borron cycle retells much of the traditional material of the Vulgate Cycle, it differs significantly from its earlier model. The Borron cycle's account of the origins of the Round Table, for example, is not the same as that in the romances of Chrétien de Troyes and his "continuators." It is the version originated by Robert de Borron, who in his poems *Joseph d'Arimathie* and *Merlin* likened Arthur's Round Table to Joseph's table of the Grail and to the table of the Last Supper.[4] Robert's poems be-

---

[2] Huth *Merlin*.

[3] Fanni Bogdanow, "The Character of Gauvain in the Thirteenth-Century Prose Romances," *Medium Aevum*, XXVII (1958), 154–61. Miss Bogdanow comments more extensively on the *Suite du Merlin* in her article "The *Suite du Merlin* and the Post-Vulgate *Roman du Graal*," in R. S. Loomis (ed.), *Arthurian Literature in the Middle Ages* (Oxford, 1959), pp. 325–35.

[4] The text of Robert's poems may be found in W. A. Nitze (ed.), *Le Roman de l'estoire dou Graal* (Paris, 1927). On Robert de Borron's work, cf. U. T. Holmes, *A History of Old French Literature* (New York, 1937), pp. 292–93. J. D. Bruce gives an analysis of Robert's *Estoire dou Graal* in *The Evolution of Arthurian Romance* (Baltimore, 1923), I, 230–37.

came, in prose renderings, the basis of the Pseudo-Robert de Borron Cycle of romances, and the tenor of the whole cycle is influenced by them. Here the brotherhood of knights is no longer a grouping of chivalric athletes, but a spiritual comradeship embraced in anticipation of the return of the Grail.[5] The Borron Prose Cycle apparently included also post-Vulgate versions of the *Queste del Saint Graal* and the *Mort Artu*. The surviving Spanish and Portuguese versions of these branches of the cycle indicate that its emphasis was on the Grail quest, and that the *Mort Artu* was rigorously shortened.[6] It is this *Mort Artu* which, as J. D. Bruce observed, depicts the most dolorous of Arthurian endings with Mordred's hun-like pillage of a vanquished land.[7]

Even if Malory had known all of the Pseudo-Robert de Borron Prose Cycle, he would not have been likely to use it as a model for his book: it emphasized the Grail adventures and its conclusion underlines the Round Table's failure rather than its glory. Above all, the existing fragments of the cycle indicate that no *Lancelot* romance figured in the plan.[8] What Malory encountered in the French branch of the Borron cycle from which he prepared the opening division of *Le Morte Darthur* was a work essentially unlike the romance he planned to write. The *Suite du Merlin* followed Robert de Borron's *Merlin*, relating the birth and deeds of Merlin up to the coronation of Arthur; from there it supplied a "continuation" (the *Suite*) of ad-

[5] Cf. Alexandre Micha, "La Table Ronde chez Robert de Boron et dans la 'Queste del Saint Graal,'" in *Les Romans du Graal au XIIᵉ et XIIIᵉ siècles* (Editions du Centre National de la Recherche Scientifique: Paris, 1956), pp. 119–33.

[6] The Spanish version is available in Adolfo Bonilla y San Martin (ed.), *El Baladro del Sabio Merlin: Primera Parte de la Demanda del Sancto Grial* in *Libros de Caballerias*, Nueva Biblioteca de Autores Españoles (Madrid, 1907). See also Bruce, *Evolution*, I, 472–77.

[7] Bruce, *Evolution*, I, 473.

[8] Bruce does not believe that a *Lancelot* was actually included in the Borron Prose Cycle (*Ibid.*, I, 475), a view with which Miss Bogdanow seems to concur in her account of the cycle ("The *Suite du Merlin*").

ventures of knights such as Balin, Gawain, and Pellinor, interwoven with the stories of Arthur's victories over the rebel kings, Morgan le Fay's treachery, and Merlin's infatuation with Nyneve. In addition, much of the *Suite* is conditioned by the idea that the Grail adventures impend as the central event of Arthurian history. On Merlin's instruction, Uther Pendragon founds the Round Table in preparation for the Grail mysteries that are prophesied; [9] the tale of Balin and the Dolorous Stroke anticipates the theme of the Wounded King and the Waste Land in the *Queste del Saint Graal*; [10] Arthur's establishment of the Round Table after his wedding is attended by miraculous signs such as the names emblazoned on the seats,[11] while the Siege Perilous awaits the coming of the best knight of all— obviously the Grail knight.[12] Though the *Suite* is situated in a cycle of romances—a fact hinted in its allusions to the *Lancelot*, the *Tristan*, the *Queste*, and the *Mort Artu*—its sustaining theme is the Grail adventure, the chief subject of Merlin's admonitions. Malory was inextricably indebted to this romance for characters and episodes in the "Tale of King Arthur," but a comparison of his version with the *Suite du Merlin* reveals a difference of purpose that is fundamental: Malory aims at a more secular idealism and—with Lancelot as chief protagonist —at a more comprehensive Arthurian history than that foreseen in the *Suite*.

In the Commentary to his edition of *Le Morte Darthur*, Professor Vinaver has described the tapestry-like structure of

---

[9] Huth, I, 94–96; Camb. ff. 185v, col. 2–186v, col. 1; VM, pp. 53–54.

[10] On this aspect of the composition of the *Suite*, cf. Vinaver, *Works*, pp. 1267–77. The Balin episode is discussed on pp. 1273–74. See also Eugène Vinaver, "La Genèse de la *Suite du Merlin*," in *Mélanges de philologie romane et de littérature médiévale offerts à Ernest Hoepffner* (Publication de la Faculté des Lettres et de l'Université de Strasbourg: Paris, 1949), pp. 259–300.

[11] Huth, II, 67–68; Camb. f. 282r, cols. 1–2.

[12] Huth, II, 65; Camb. f. 282v, col. 1.

the *Suite du Merlin,* in which the writer's method is to alternate the major threads of the story in an "interwoven" narrative.[13] The result, as Vinaver notes, is that "adventures were piled up one upon the other without any apparent sequence or design, and innumerable personages, mostly anonymous, were introduced in a wild succession." [14] Any stretch of the French romance may have its sequel at any moment, and none is ever complete; time dissolves in the accumulation of episodes, and so inevitably does the sense of direction and purpose. Rejecting this method, Malory develops the "Tale of King Arthur" as a six-part narrative in which the subdivisions become distinct phases of the story. These subdivisions are marked by the *explicit,* by invented introductions, and by titles which Malory assigns on two occasions ("The Book of Balin" and "The Wedding of King Arthur"). Vinaver supplies titles for the subdivisions as follows:

I. Merlin
II. Balyn le Sauvage or the Knight with the Two Swords
III. Torre and Pellynor
IV. The Death of Merlin and the War with the Five Kings
V. Arthur and Accolon
VI. Gawain, Ywain, and Marhalt

In spite of extensive overlapping among the subdivisions, Malory's procedure suggests to Vinaver that each is a self-contained story, and that the whole "Tale of King Arthur" is an independent work unrelated to Malory's other Arthurian compositions.[15] Believing that Malory knew little of Arthurian romance when he wrote the "Tale of King Arthur," Vinaver also

---

[13] *Works,* pp. 1266–77 (especially p. 1272). See also Introduction, *Ibid.,* p. xlviii ff.

[14] *Ibid.,* p. xlviii.

[15] *Ibid.,* pp. 1273–75. Cf. Introduction, *Ibid.,* p. lvii. Vinaver's view remains unchanged in his article on Malory in *Arthurian Literature in the Middle Ages,* ed. Loomis, pp. 541–52 (see especially p. 544).

cites a number of Malory's departures from his source as evidence that he was ignorant of the main lines of the Arthurian tradition that had evolved in the cyclic romances.[16] These two peculiarities of Malory's work—his structural technique and his apparent failure to perceive the relation between widely separated recurrences of conventional themes—are the basis of Vinaver's theory that the "Tale of King Arthur" is only one of eight independent Arthurian romances.

But the theory of separate romances raises questions that it cannot answer. Vinaver argues that such anomalies of *Le Morte Darthur* as the reappearance of certain knights after their deaths are dispelled when the work is seen as a series of unrelated romances. Of the incongruities, Vinaver writes that "their most significant feature is that they are never found within any one of Malory's romances, but invariably between two different works separated by at least one of the *explicits*."[17] Unfortunately, this claim is inaccurate. The "Tale of King Arthur" contains a number of contradictions which point to an unrevised manuscript and to Malory's susceptibility to occasional confusion and forgetfulness. The sword drawn from the anvil is called Excalibur (19), although another Excalibur is later given to Arthur by the Lady of the Lake; in the quests of Gawain, Ywain, and Marhalt, Gawain's damsel deserts him, and at the end of the story Malory observes that "sir Gawayne had loste his damesel" (178), although the next sentence states—as if she were present—that "the damesell sir Gawayne had coude sey but lytyll worshyp of hym" (178). These incongruities, all found within the "Tale of King Arthur," can scarcely be explained by the theory of separate romances.

More important are Malory's attempts to unify the materials of *Le Morte Darthur*. If the book is a collection of unrelated

---

[16] *Works*, pp. 1273–75.
[17] *Ibid.*, p. xxxii.

romances, why does Malory introduce sourceless retrospective lines denoting chronology within the "Tale of King Arthur"? What explains the cross-references which characterize many of Malory's scenes, particularly those of his own invention? Why does Malory include sourceless anticipations of later events— such as the descent of Balin's scabbardless sword to Galahad— and attempt to link names and to explain far-reaching motivation? [18] Vinaver's insistence, despite all the apparent connections, that nothing is connected seems only to cloud the nature and intent of Malory's work. It is true that Malory is guilty of self-contradictions, that he left his work presumably unrevised with its seams too often visible. But as a composer of Arthurian romance, not merely a compiler, Malory is plainly neither timid nor indifferent: he can finish a story on his own, or turn 500 pages to find the sequel he desires; [19] and his eagerness to identify characters and to connect cause with effect where his source rambles in obscurity marks the effort to achieve coherence that distinguishes his work.

The "Tale of King Arthur" was perhaps Malory's earliest effort to "reduce" a French romance,[20] and it was presumably here that he first encountered the peculiarities of his prose sources—their discursive interwoven structure, their permutations of theme, their reference to other "branches" of Arthurian story. The problem of controlling an episodic pattern of narrative was complicated by Malory's need to achieve consistent characterization and to provide an appropriate chronology. In the "Tale of King Arthur" Malory had to do more than disentangle the interwoven narrative of his model: he had to know the *Suite du Merlin* well enough to avoid its duplications and to shift its principal interest from the foreshadowings of the Grail

---

[18] These questions refer to features of Malory's work which are discussed below.
[19] Vinaver points to such an instance, *Works*, p. lv.
[20] *Ibid.*, pp. xxxv–xl.

to his original account of how Arthurian traditions began. In this process Malory also added fresh material, apparently of his own invention, which included anticipations of subsequent events that are to be found only in *Le Morte Darthur*. Thus he not only rearranged the story but reinterpreted it as well; and it is through these perspectives—not merely his indebtedness to French models—that Malory's work should be viewed. In the following pages the "Tale of King Arthur" is regarded as a version of Arthurian life largely unprecedented, and Malory's originality is traced through his treatment of the main generic features of the *Suite du Merlin:* (1) its structure of alternately developed episodes; (2) its characteristics as a romance of the Grail; and (3) its allusions to other branches of the Arthurian legend.

STRUCTURE AND SEQUENCE

Vinaver's study of the "Tale of King Arthur" demonstrates the contrasts between Malory's method of composition and the digressive pattern of his French source. Where the *Suite du Merlin* allows different themes to break into each other, Malory disentangles them and presents each as a coherent narrative unit. Each of the six subdivisions of the "Tale of King Arthur" illustrates this technique, and, in addition to inventing openings to start off the episodes anew, Malory even assigns titles to two of them as if they were independent tales. Malory's treatment of plot also contributes to this effect. For example, the Dolorous Stroke is not in Malory the punishment for Balin's violation of the Grail sanctuary, but instead the result of his murder of the lady who came to Arthur's court to claim Balin's head. Hence Vinaver is led to observe that "the Dolorous Stroke loses its original significance and acquires a new meaning which can be understood without reference to anything that lies beyond the Balin story proper." [21] Another example is Malory's recasting of the story of Morgan le Fay's treachery. His sixth subdivision, the tale of Gawain, Ywain, and Marhalt, begins with the episode of the magic mantle sent by Morgan to destroy Arthur. Although this material occurs later in the *Suite du Merlin*, Malory uses the episode to motivate the exile of Ywain, Morgan's son, and this event initiates the threefold adventures which follow.

It is self-evident, then, that Malory prefers an orderly presentation of episodes. But as Vinaver sees it, Malory is so intent on this procedure that it delimits and circumscribes his whole approach to the "Tale of King Arthur":

> [Malory] was equally indifferent to anything that the *Tale* might lead up to and to anything in the nature of a sequence within the *Tale* itself; and so instead of treating each theme as a recurrent motif dove-tailed into others, and each episode as a continuation or an anticipation of other episodes, he saw the whole work as an independent production and each division of it as a self-contained entity.[22]

This claim is a hazardous overstatement. Malory's narrative is by no means confined by the shorter unified episodes he constructs, and to stress this aspect of his writing is to neglect some of the most distinctive features of his work. The "Tale of King Arthur," like the *Suite du Merlin*, is in part characterized by the development of recurrent themes. Far from casting off the interweaving method of the cyclic romances, Malory uses it to develop continuity between the individual stories he remodels within the "Tale of King Arthur" and to link the large divisions of *Le Morte Darthur*, drawn from various sources. A case in point is the story of the rebellion of the kings. Arthur's great foe in the rebellion is King Lot, whose forces are defeated in the

[21] *Ibid.*, p. 1274.
[22] *Ibid.*, pp. 1273-74.

opening subdivision of the "Tale of King Arthur"; but this con‑
flict emerges again in the tale of Balin, where King Lot is finally
killed by Pellinor, and where his funeral is the occasion of
prophecies concerning not only Arthur's distant battle at Salis‑
bury but the more immediate treachery of Morgan le Fay which
occupies the fifth subdivision of the "Tale of King Arthur."[23]
In these instances Malory certainly is concerned with the se‑
quence of events and, as will be shown in detail below, he shapes
the events as elements of the destiny that will develop from
Arthur's early experiences.

Another feature of Malory's technique is retrospective nar‑
rative.[24] Not surprisingly, this device is alien to the *Suite du
Merlin*, whose *raison d'être* is to anticipate subsequent ad‑
ventures of the Grail.[25] By nature a romance of preliminaries,
the *Suite* looks toward predestined events. But while he is also
concerned with subsequent history, Malory steadily refers to
events of the recent past; as a result his narrative unfolds in
phases of action that are seen in relation to each other—not as
unrelated tales. The events of a given story may be conditioned
by those in an earlier episode, and the whole narrative thereby
acquires through the movement of time a new dimension.

A close look at this aspect of Malory's work is rewarding. One
pertinent instance occurs at the end of the first subdivision,
when the rebellion of kings has ended with the retreat of
Arthur's enemies at Bedigrayne. Preparing for the recurrence of

---

[23] The slaughter by Arthur's forces at Bedigrayne is stopped by Merlin (*Ibid.*, pp. 36–37); for the final defeat of Lot and the rebels, see *ibid.*, pp. 75–79.

[24] This characteristic device is examined in two articles by Charles Moor‑man, "The Relation of Books I and III of Malory's 'Morte Darthur,'" *Mediaeval Studies*, XXII (1960), 361–66, and "Internal Chronology in Malory's *Morte Darthur*," *JEGP*, LX (April, 1961), 240–49. See also R. M. Lumiansky, "The Question of Unity in Malory's *Morte Darthur*," *TSE*, V (1955), 29–39.

[25] Cf. Vinaver's comments on the origin of the *Suite* cited in note 10 above.

this struggle in the Balin story, Malory specifies, as his source
does not, that the rebels are joined by King Rions and King
Nero, who help prepare for a new assault:

> . . . so they kept hem togydirs the space of three yere and
> ever alyed hem with myghty kynges and dukis. And unto them
> felle kynge Royns of Northe Walis which was a myghty kynge
> of men, and Nero that was a myghty man of men. And all thys
> whyle they furnysshed and garnysshed hem of good men of
> armys and vitayle and of all maner of ablemente that pretendith
> to warre, to avenge hem for the batay[l]e of Bedgrayne. . . .
> (41)

A little later, when King Rions sends a message demanding
Arthur's beard, Malory says that Rions "had discomfite and
overcom eleven kyngis" (54), probably referring to the eleven
original rebels against Arthur. These details, none of which appear in Malory's source, are plainly intended as chronological
links between Arthur's two early battles for his throne.

On at least two occasions in the "Tale of King Arthur"
Malory's reference to past events conditions the meaning of the
issues. One of these is the War with the Five Kings. When
Arthur encounters the invaders, the five kings hold a counsel
in which a knight observes,

> Ye knowe well that sir Arthur hath the floure of chevalry of
> the worlde with hym, and hit preved by the grete batayle he
> did with the eleven kynges. And therefore hyghe ye unto hym
> nyght and day tyll that we be nyghe hym, for the lenger he
> taryeth the bygger he is, and we ever the weyker. And he is so
> corageous of hymself that he is com to the felde with lytyll
> peple, and therefore lette us sette uppon hym or day, and we
> shall sle downe of his knyghtes that none shall helpe other of
> them. (127)

Malory invents this speech, and his terms make it clear that the
rebellion of eleven kings was not inconsequential adventure: it

stands as proof of Arthur's leadership and of the power consolidating in his court. The past is again meaningful to Malory in the tale of Gawain, Ywain, and Marhalt. Besides repeating the pattern of threefold adventures which Malory had previously arranged in the "Wedding of King Arthur," the story's action is an extension of themes developed earlier. Hearing how Sir Hugh and Sir Edward of the Red Castle have extorted land from the Lady of the Roche, Sir Ywain says, "Madam, they ar to blame, for they do ayenste the hyghe Order of Knyghthode and the oth that they made" (177). The oath Ywain refers to is the oath of the knights which Malory invented to conclude the wedding story. It specifies the principles of Arthur's Round Table, and Malory's later reference to it in "Gawain, Ywain, and Marhalt" shows that his stories have a definite bearing upon each other.

Malory's retrospective linking of stories within Tale I is most obvious in the invented summaries at the opening of certain episodes. These are among the lines Vinaver cites to support his claim that Malory's subdivisions are unrelated stories;[26] yet, since chronology is their main burden, it would appear that the intended function of the summaries is to join, not to separate. The Balin episode opens with a reminder of chronological placement: "Afftir the deth of Uther regned Arthure, hys son, which had grete warre in hys dayes for to gete all Inglonde into hys honde; for there were many kyngis within the realme of Inglonde and of Scotlonde, Walys and Cornuwayle" (61). Later the wedding story is introduced with a careful reference to the past rebellion which situates the narrative in terms of Arthurian history:

In the begynnyng of Arthure, aftir he was chosyn kynge by adventure and by grace, for the moste party of the barowns knew nat he was Uther Pendragon son but as Merlyon made hit

26 See Vinaver's comments, *Works*, pp. 1299 and 1318.

opynly knowyn, but yet many kyngis and lordis hylde hym grete
werre for that cause. But well Arthur overcom hem all: the
moste party dayes of hys lyff he was ruled by the counceile of
Merlyon. (97)

Even the account of Merlin's dotage, through its dependence
upon previous events in the wedding story, occurs specifically
within the frame of advancing time:

> So aftir thes questis of syr Gawayne, syr Tor, and Kynge Pelly-
> nore, than hit befelle that Merlyon felle in dotage on the
> damesell that kynge Pellynore brought to courte; and she was
> one of the damesels of the Lady of the Laake, that hyght
> Nyneve. (125)

The variety and number of Malory's retrospective additions
within the "Tale of King Arthur" hardly seems accidental. Nor
is their purpose far to seek. It is through these original cross-
references that Malory's blocked subdivisions become related
units of narrative. Their arrangement itself is determined by
Malory's straightening out of the entangled themes of his
French source, and they record the movement of time through
actions that are neither simultaneous nor isolated. Moreover,
the meaning of Malory's episodes depends upon their sequence
within the "Tale of King Arthur." Ywain remembers the sworn
oath of Arthur's court, and his actions are so conditioned by it
that they attain a moral relevance for which Malory himself is
responsible. In its own terms Malory's narrative follows a
course from disorder and rebellion to the oath of chivalry, itself
a code that grows out of the wedding quests and is proved in
the adventures that close the "Tale of King Arthur." Such departures from the inherited tradition represented by the source
are not adventitious. They point unmistakably to Malory's
conscious drafting of a new version of Arthurian matter, not to
his making a mere facsimile of the *Suite du Merlin.*

What is most surprising about Malory's alterations of structure and sequence in the "Tale of King Arthur" is the fact that critics have so long ignored the pattern which they imply. Behind them lies a far more dramatic reconstruction of the Arthurian legend than has yet been acknowledged. One notable clue to the working of Malory's imagination is found in the sourceless passage which introduces the third subdivision of the "Tale of King Arthur," the story of Arthur's wedding:

> In the begynnyng of Arthure, aftir he was chosyn kynge by adventure and by grace, for the moste party of the barowns knew nat he was Uther Pendragon son but as Merlyon made hit opynly knowyn, but yet many kyngis and lordis hylde hym grete werre for that cause. But well Arthur overcom hem all: the moste party dayes of hys lyff he was ruled by the counceile of Merlyon. (97)

At first glance, these lines appear to be no more than a summary of well-known happenings in the history of Arthur; but in fact Malory mentions here an event that is to be found nowhere in the Old French sources of *Le Morte Darthur*. This event is Merlin's revelation at King Uther's deathbed that Arthur is heir to the throne: "for the moste party of the barowns knew nat he was Uther Pendragon son but as Merlyon made hit opynly knowyn."

Based upon Malory's own description of the death of Uther Pendragon, this statement points to an important reversal of what Malory found in his French source. In the *Suite du Merlin*, Merlin attends the dying Uther and addresses him "moult bas en l'oreille" as follows: "Rois, tu as faite moult bonne fin, se la conscience est tele comme la samblance. Et je te di que tes fius Artus sera chiés de ton regne apriès toi par la viertu de Jesucrist. Et sera acomplissables de la table reonde que tu as fondee." Uther replies, "Merlins, priíes li [i.e., Artus] pour Dieu que il prit a Jhesucrist por moi." [27] The barons who witness this exchange do not overhear Merlin's remarks, and they are unaware that Arthur is Uther's son. But Malory alters the scene extensively:

> So on the morne alle the barons with Merlyn came tofore the kyng. Thenne Merlyn said aloud unto Kyng Uther,
> "Syre, shall your sone Arthur be kyng after your dayes of this realme with all the appertenaunce?"
> Thenne Uther Pendragon torned hym and said in herynge of them alle,
> "I gyve hym Gods blissyng and myne, and byd hym pray for my soule, and righteuously and worshipfully that he clayme the croune upon forfeture of my blessyng," and therwith he yelde up the ghost. (11–12)

Malory's version of the death of Uther is distinguished from its French counterpart in two ways. First, Arthur is identified as the heir to Uther's throne; since the barons know this, their later refusal to accept Arthur even on Merlin's testimony justifies the attack against them.[28] Second, in *Le Morte Darthur* Merlin has a much more forceful hand in the proceedings. In the question addressed to Uther it is manifest that Merlin assumes a special task—that of bringing about the reign of Arthur. In this respect Malory's treatment of Merlin is by no means a mere copy of earlier traditions; it marks the start of a new version of the legend. In his opening subdivision Malory portrays Merlin in two important offices: he is the agent through whom God's will and "grace" are expressed, and he is an omniscient strategist who leads Arthur to victory over the rebel kings. These functions, it is true, are derived from the French tradition which came to Malory through the *Suite du Merlin*, where Merlin appears as a prophet, semi-priest, shapeshifter, and strategist. But

[27] Huth, I, 131; Camb. f. 198r, col. 2; VM, p. 97.
[28] *Works*, pp. 17–18.

it is Malory, not the French romancers, who creates the role in which Merlin contrives the birth of Arthur and guides him steadily to his throne.

Malory's first significant change occurs in the bargain in which Merlin claims custody of the child who will be conceived as Uther shares Igrayne's bed. In the French version of this episode, Merlin agrees to help Uther attain his desire if he will grant "un don tel que je li demanderoie." [29] Uther agrees to this, and after he has lain with Igrayne Merlin specifies his wish: "Je le te demanc, et voel que tu saces que tu as gaaignié un hoir, et que tu le m'as dounet, car tu ne le dois avoir." [30] In Malory Merlin's demand is known from the start because in his agreement with Uther he prophesies the birth of a child and claims it for himself:

> "Syre," said Merlyn, "this is my desyre: the first nyght that ye shal lye by Igrayne ye shal gete a child on her; and whan that is borne, that it shall be delyverd to me for to nourisshe thereas I wille have it, for it shal be your worship and the childis availle as mykel as the child is worth." (9)

This prophetic bargain is an example of how Malory sometimes anticipates the events of his source; [31] as such, it is strong evidence that Merlin occupied a central position in Malory's plan for his opening narrative. In the *Suite*, admittedly, Arthur's birth is mentioned as Uther and Igrayne lie together, [32] but only in a comment by the author; it is Malory who adds a prophetic purpose to the bargain, thus enlarging Merlin's authority and making Arthur's birth for the first time the main point of the story.

This conception of Merlin as godfather to Arthur influences

---

[29] Huth, I, 109; Camb. f. 192v, col. 1; VM, p. 66.
[30] Huth, I, 112; Camb. f. 193v, col. 1; VM, p. 68.
[31] Cf. the premature reference to Excalibur, *Works*, p. 19, and Vinaver's note.
[32] Huth, I, 111; Camb. f. 192r, col. 2; VM, p. 68.

Malory's handling of other scenes in the "Tale of King Arthur" where the chief function is to identify Arthur and his destiny. Among these is the scene in which King Uther asks Igrayne to reveal the father of her child. In the French, in order to make Igrayne give up the child more readily, Uther urges secrecy and disowns the infant: "Biele amie, gardés que nus hom ne nulle feme ne le sache a cui vous le puissiés celer, car vous en seriés honnie, se on le savoit. Et je voel bien que vous sachiés que cis enfes que de vous naistra n'est pas ne miens ne vostres raisonnablement, ne jou ne vous ne l'arons a nostre oes." [33] Malory, on the other hand, shows Uther proudly proclaiming his child and referring even to Merlin's part in the begetting of Arthur: " 'That is trouthe,' saide the kynge, 'as ye say, for it was I myself that cam in the lykenesse. And therfor desmay you not, for I am fader to the child,' and ther he told her alle the cause how it was by Merlyns counceil" (10). A similar purpose governs Malory's account of Merlin when, despite the miracle of the sword, the rebel barons dispute Arthur's right to the throne. The barons ask Merlin why Arthur was made king, and in the exchange which follows Malory extracts from his source only the facts about Arthur's conception, to which he adds a sourceless and quite arbitrary prophecy of Arthur's ascendancy:

> "Nay," said Merlyn, "after the deth of the duke more than thre houres was Arthur begoten, and thirtene days after kyng Uther wedded Igrayne, and therfor I preve hym he is no bastard. And, who saith nay, he shal be kyng and overcome all his enemyes, and or he deye he shalle be long kynge of all Englond and have under his obeyssaunce Walys, Yrland, and Scotland, and moo reames than I will now reherce." (18)

Here Malory's plan for *Le Morte Darthur* seems implicit in Merlin's speech. Against the charge of bastardy, Merlin offers

---

[33] Huth, I, 121; Camb. ff. 195r, col. 2–196v, col. 1; VM, p. 74.

himself as the authority on Arthur's rights, and the assertion that Arthur "shalle be long kynge of all Englond"—invented by Malory—underlines the point. Such a forecast of Arthur's reign has no parallel in Malory's French model.

Malory also ventures other changes in the portrayal of Merlin, many of them keyed to the idea that Arthur comes predestined to his throne. Merlin's appeals to divine sanction in the *Suite du Merlin,* and his interpretations of divine will, become in *Le Morte Darthur* compelling directives because the distinction between Merlin and God is more tenuous. Indeed, Malory's version of Pendragon's death is remarkable in part for the collaboration suggested there: "loke ye al barons be bifore kynge Uther to-morne, and God and I shall make hym to speke" (11). Elsewhere, particularly in the account of the sword in the anvil, Malory carefully emphasizes Merlin's control of events. When King Uther dies, leaving the realm "in grete jeopardy long whyle," Malory reports: "Thenne Merlyn wente to the Archebisshop of Caunterbury and counceilled hym for to sende for all the lordes of the reame and alle the gentilmen of armes that they shold to London come by Christmas" (12). And Merlin is obeyed: "So the Archebisshop by the advys of Merlyn send for alle the lordes and gentilmen of armes" (12). In the French, on the other hand, when Merlin is asked for advice after Uther's death, he replies, "Signour, je ne sui mie Dius que je doie tel affaire conseillier ne que je fois eslire roi ne gouvrenour." [34] Again, according to Malory, the archbishop's guarding of Arthur at the sword trials is "by Merlyons provydence," whereas at this point in the *Suite* Merlin has departed to visit his "Master Blaise" of Northumberland.[35] This characterization of Merlin as the spokesman of God is a singular innovation in the Arthurian legend: it suggests a new pattern of causes, a new

---

[34] Huth, I, 132; Camb. f. 199v, col. 1.
[35] Huth, I, 133; Camb. f. 199v, col. 2; VM, p. 80.

ground upon which the epic adventures are played, and it casts
a new meaning on the reign of Arthur. When King Arthur
comes out to seek accord with the rebel barons, the advice which
Merlin gives him, interpolated by Malory, is unequivocal:
"Fere not, but come oute boldly and speke with hem; and
spare hem not, but ansuere them as their kynge and chyvetayn,
for ye shal overcome hem all, whether they wille or nylle" (18).
Malory thus projects Arthur's reign itself as a destiny ordained
by God and established through Merlin, an event distinct in its
own promise—no longer, as in his source, mainly a preparation
for the recovery of the Grail.

Arthur's claim to his crown is confirmed by his victory over
the eleven kings. Here, using Merlin as military adviser and
tactician for Arthur, Malory turns the episodic narrative of his
source into a realistic and coherent account. Malory advances
his own point of view at the outbreak of the rebellion; he avoids
the French report that Merlin set fire to the tents of the enemy
by enchantment,[36] stating instead that "Merlyn vanysshed
aweye and came to kynge Arthur and bad hym set on hem
fiersly" (18). This shift from magic to hard advice exemplifies
Malory's attitude toward the rebellion and Merlin's role in it.

Merlin's strategy for King Arthur has three phases: the en-
listment of allies, the surprise attack on King Lot, and the division of the allied forces which enables them to win the Battle
of Bedigrayne. Although Malory found these details in his
French source, in every instance he alters his source material to
heighten Merlin's prominence and to improve the story's
coherence. An example is Merlin's advice that Arthur appeal to
Ban and Bors for help. In the French Merlin suggests the invita-
tion of Ban and Bors to England in order to make an alliance;
they are to accompany Arthur to "Carohaise" where he will aid
King Leodegrans, and afterwards they will help Arthur against

[36] Camb. f. 206v, col. 1; VM, p. 93.

his own enemies.[37] But Malory dispenses with King Leodegrans until later and assigns a more explicit and forthright motive in Merlin's speech: if Ban and Bors will help Arthur, he in turn will help them against King Claudas (20). Such a plan is typical of Malory's Merlin, who shows earlier in dealing with Uther Pendragon that he has a firm grasp of ends and advantages. In this case also the Merlin-Arthur relationship is different from anything in Malory's source.

Malory's version of the midnight attack on the rebel kings is similarly marked by his own additions and modifications. In the French, King Lot has a dream that forewarns of a great battle and of danger centered in the nearby forest. His soldiers are wakened to advance upon the enemy, but Merlin, aware of Lot's movements, warns Arthur to hasten to an attack: "Et Merlins commande a haster la gent le roy artus qui bien savoit le convine des autres." [38] In Malory's arrangement, this episode becomes another example of Merlin's strategy: "Than by counceile of Merlion, whan they wyst which wey the an eleven kynges wolde ryde and lodge that nyght, at mydnyght they sette uppon them as they were in their pavilions" (27). In the *Suite du Merlin*, it is true, Arthur's forces surprise the rebels, but the rebels are warned by King Lot's dream and have already begun to search for the enemy: "Et il dient quil seiuent bien de uoir qui auront par tans bataille grant & merueilleuse si se leuerent & esueillierent tous les commandent a monter & a chaualchier tout le pais enuiron." [39]

The decision which wins the battle of Bedigrayne is another of Malory's inventions. When the midnight attack is over, the surviving rebels take refuge on the other side of a "stronge passage" (in the *Suite*, "une riviere") and Merlin presents a new plan of action:

---

[37] Camb. f. 208v, col. 1; VM, p. 97.
[38] Camb. f. 219r, col. 1; VM, pp. 113–14. Camb.: "la vocine de eux."
[39] Camb. f. 219r, col. 1; VM, p. 113.

"Now shall ye do by myne advice," seyde Merlyon unto the three kyngis, and seyde: "I wolde kynge Ban and Bors with hir felyship of ten thousand men were put in a woode here besyde in an inbusshemente and kept them prevy, and that they be leyde or the lyght of the day com, and that they stire nat tyll that ye and youre knyghts [have] fought with hem longe. And whan hit ys daylyght, dresse youre batayle evyn before them and the passage, that they may se all youre oste, for than woll they be the more hardy whan they se you but aboute twenty thousande, and cause hem to be the gladder to suffir you and youre oste to com over the passage." (27; Vinaver's emendation)

The French version of this plan is less dramatic. In the *Suite* Merlin directs Arthur to attack the rebels at a ford in the stream, while Ban and Bors attack them from the rear:

> Ie vous dirai fait merlins que vous en feres . vous en ires par decha al passage dun gue ou il sont bien arreste plus de . m . & vous uous combateres illuec a els si les feres a vous entendre . & li rois bans & son frere sen iront par deuers la forest si les assaudront par deriere la forest & vous par deuant.[40]

What distinguishes these two plans of battle is not their soundness or efficacy—Arthur is successful in both cases—but the fact that Malory's version rests upon a dramatic use of battle psychology rather than a less artful trust in surprise and the weight of numbers. In the French, the pressure of simultaneous attack from the rear brings down the rebels; in Malory it is the late onslaught of Ban and Bors—delayed until Arthur's men are exhausted and victory seems in the balance—that first disheartens the rebel leaders and then routs them with fresher strength. Independent of his source, Malory achieves a climactic moment in his narrative (marked by the alliterative phrase, "Than brake the bushement of kynge Banne and Bors," [31]), having set through Merlin's counsel the pattern of Arthur's victory.

[40] Camb. f. 220v, col. 1; VM, p. 114.

In King Lot's reaction to the sudden appearance of King Bors, Malory exhibits the real force of Merlin's psychology:

> Whan kynge Lotte had aspyed kynge Bors, he knew hym well, and seyde,
>
> "Jesu defende us from dethe and horryble maymes, for I se well we be in grete perell of dethe; for I se yondir a kynge, one of the moste worshipfullyst men, and the best knyghtes of the worlde be inclyned unto his felyship." (32)

This reaction serves also to bring King Lot into the foreground of the narrative. For in Malory's version the central antagonists in the rebellion of the kings are Merlin and King Lot; theirs are the individual wills at conflict for the throne of England, while Arthur himself is little more than a valiant knight serving his own destiny. Malory's King Lot is meant to be impressive. Hence Malory does not attribute to King Lot the frightening dream of floods and destruction which in the French rouses the rebels to arms; [41] in *Le Morte Darthur* this dream occurs instead to the King of the Hundred Knights, doubtless because such alarm would seem unnatural in Malory's determined King Lot. Similarly, Malory assigns to Lot an amazed response, quoted above, when Ban and Bors enter battle; but there is no sign of yielding in Lot's comment, only surprise and apprehension. Later, seeing the victory fade, King Lot proposes new measures in a speech invented by Malory:

> Than all the eleven kynges drew hem togydir. And than seyde Lott, "Lordis, ye muste do othirwyse than ye do, othir ellis the grete losses ys behynde: for ye may se what peple we have loste and what good men we lese because we wayte allweyes on thes footemen; and ever in savyng of one of thes footemen we lese ten horsemen for hym. Therefore thys ys myne advise: lette us putte oure footemen frome us, for hit ys nere nyght. For

[41] Camb. f. 219v, col. 2; VM, p. 113.

thys noble kynge Arthure woll nat tarry on the footemen, for they may save hemselff; the woode ys nerehonde. And whan we horsemen be togydirs, looke every of you kyngis lat make such ordinaunce that none breke uppon payne of deth. And who that seeth any man dresse hym to fle lyghtly, that he be slayne; for hit ys bettir we sle a cowarde than thorow a coward all we be slayne." (35)

Rebel though he is, King Lot gains heroic stature in Malory's treatment: he is a noble enemy whose misfortune is to cast himself against predestined events. Finally it is through the fate of King Lot that the rebellion against Arthur is put down; and both Merlin and Lot, in a last play against each other, attain the fullest expression of their natures. Malory arranges this denouement carefully; nonexistent in his French sources, it displays his most creative treatment of structure and sequence. It begins when the early battle of Bedigrayne is over and the rebels flee to their lands only to find there, in Malory's words, "sorow uppon sorow" (40): their kingdoms are invaded by Saracens and "people that were lawles" (40). Departing from his source at this point, Malory says that the rebels "consented togydir to kepe all the marchis of Cornuwayle, of Walis, and of the Northe" (40). The kings take charge of various cities, and they gain the alliance of King Rions and King Nero, who later lead the insurrection in the "Tale of Balin." Malory writes that "all thys whyle they furnysshed and garnysshed hem of good men of armys and vitayle and of all maner of ablemente that pretendith to warre, to avenge hem for the batayle of Bedgrayne, as hit tellith in the booke of adventures" (41). Thus Bedigrayne and the later fight with King Nero are related battles in *Le Morte Darthur*, each a part of the extensive rebellion against King Arthur.

Merlin's task in the battle with King Nero is to prevent King Lot from joining his ally until it is too late. Arthur meets the forces of King Nero, and Malory reports that "Merlion com to kynge Lotte of the Ile of Orkeney, and helde hym with a tale of the prophecy tylle Nero and his peple were destroyed" (75–76). The situation in the *Suite du Merlin* is otherwise: King Lot is aroused by the reported death of Mordred, and in order to appease Lot, Merlin tells him that Mordred is not dead.[42] Suppressing this motif in the "Tale of Balin," Malory turns back to the earlier narrative of his "Merlin" section, where the battles against King Arthur are interrelated, and where Merlin and Lot are the leading contenders. Malory invents King Lot's lament for Nero's defeat: " 'Alas,' seyde kynge Lotte, 'I am ashamed; for in my defaute ys [many a worshipful man slayne; for and we had ben togyders there hadde ben] none oste undir hevyn were able to have macched us' " (76; Vinaver's emendation). The discussion of what course to take is also Malory's invention:

> "What ys beste to do?" seyde kynge Lotte. "Whether ys me bettir to trete with kynge Arthur othir to fyght? For the gretter party of oure people ar slayne and distressed."
>
> "Sir," seyde a knyght, "sette ye on Arthure, for they ar wery and forfoughtyn, and we be freyssh."
>
> "As for me," seyde kynge Lott, "I wolde that every knyght wolde do hys parte as I wolde do myne." (76–77)

In this exchange there is an echo of the Battle of Bedigrayne, where it was Merlin's strategy to attack the weary enemy with the fresh forces of Ban and Bors. King Lot marches, of course, with no chance of victory; his opposition to the destined reign of Arthur, which Merlin has initiated, cannot succeed. But Malory, regretful that so splendid a knight must be lost to the Round Table, invents a eulogy for King Lot which confirms his heroism:

[42] Huth, I, 254–55; Camb. ff. 258v, col. 2–258r, col. 1.

But allwayes kynge Lotte hylde hym ever in the fore-fronte and dud merveylous dedis of armys; for all his oste was borne up by hys hondys, for he abode all knyghtes. Alas, he myght nat endure, the whych was grete pité! So worthy a knyght as he was one, that he sholde be overmacched, that of late tyme before he had bene a knyght of kynge Arthurs, and wedded the syster of hym. (77)

Because Malory's whole story of the rebellion is in part the record of Merlin's conflict with King Lot, Merlin's delay of Lot with "a tale of the prophecy" is a fitting climax for his role in establishing the reign of Arthur. When Merlin insists that Arthur is Uther Pendragon's son and thus the rightful king of England, his argument is rejected by some of the barons, notably King Lot: "Some of the kynges had merveyl of Merlyns wordes and demed well that it shold be as he said, and som of hem lough hym to scorne, as kyng Lot, and mo other called hym a wytche" (18). After the rebels meet King Arthur and part with "stoute wordes on bothe sydes" (18), Merlin clearly warns the rebels: " 'What will ye do?' seyde Merlyn to the kynges. 'Ye were better for to stynte, for ye shalle not here prevaille, though ye were ten so many' " (18). But again Merlin is scorned: " 'Be we wel avysed to be aferd of a dreme-reder?' said kyng Lot" (18). It is thus ironic that after the bloodshed of the rebellion Lot is finally deceived by the "dream-reader" he proudly scorned. Nor is the irony lost upon King Lot: "Thys faytoure with hys prophecy hath moked me" (76). But Merlin's deception is not a private mockery; rather, it is a necessity peculiar to his situation as the most intermediate of beings. Neither devil, man, nor god, Merlin wears the masks of all three. He is equally capable of the miraculous feats of heroes and gods, or the undignified failings of devils and men. Empowered with extraordinary perceptions, he is also enfeebled, as in his fatal lust for Nyneve, with weaknesses common to men. Merlin's trickery of Lot is like the work of pursuant Furies; but Merlin has no choice, given the misfortune of his ambivalence:

> All that dud Merlion, for he knew well that and kynge Lotte had bene with hys body at the first batayle, kynge Arthure had be slayne and all hys peple distressed. And well Merlion knew that one of the kynges sholde be dede that day; and lothe was Merlion that ony of them bothe sholde be slayne, but of the tweyne he had levir kyng Lotte of Orkeney had be slayne than Arthure. (76)

Merlin is now beyond anger and mockery because he is impressed by his stalwart enemy and reluctant to become, as he must, the medium of Lot's doom.

Several important features of Malory's work in *Le Morte Darthur* are illuminated by his reconstruction of the Merlin legend. While the special and often invented functions of Merlin define the course of Arthur's early days, they also hint that Malory is not merely reproducing a tradition; he is projecting a personal version of the Arthurian world, and he uses Merlin to insist upon its uniqueness. The conflict of Merlin and King Lot, overlapping the first two sections of the "Tale of King Arthur," points to Malory's serious purposes. King Lot attains a tragic level as Malory turns the vengeful warrior of his source into a king of such pride, courage, and dignity that he falls not as a casualty of battle, but of destiny. In short, Malory has produced a narrative of coherent structure and sequence, not a series of issueless adventures.

THE GRAIL THEME

In his third subdivision, "The Wedding of King Arthur," Malory's most impressive departure from the Grail theme of the *Suite du Merlin* is found. This section of the "Tale of King Arthur" and the corresponding pages of the *Suite* tell com-

pletely different stories. The difference is not a matter merely
of structural discrepancies, an area in which Vinaver has demonstrated Malory's vigorous independence of his source,[43] but of
an equally fundamental difference in theme. The *Suite du
Merlin*, which comprises the "Merlin-continuation" of the
Pseudo-Robert de Borron Cycle of prose romances, was apparently part of a plan to imitate the Vulgate Cycle itself, and
the evidence of surviving MSS. indicates that it was to lead up
to a *Queste del Saint Graal* and a *Mort Artu*; these works,
though the French versions are lost, can be found virtually
intact in the Spanish and Portuguese *Demandas*. The *Suite*'s
writer, however, disclaims any intention of including a *Lancelot*
romance, and J. D. Bruce and later students of the *Suite du
Merlin* believe that the Borron cycle never included this branch
of the legend.[44] The *Suite* is unlike the "Tale of King Arthur"
in content and in structure, since it was not followed, as is
Malory's version, by the Roman War and stories of Lancelot,
Gareth, and Tristram, but instead by a Grail romance. Frequently the *Suite* alludes to a *Queste* and a *Mort Artu* as its
sequels,[45] and its episodes are distinctly influenced by the preparation for these two romances.[46] This situation accounts for
many of the divergences of Malory's "Tale of King Arthur" from

[43] *Works*, pp. xlviii–lviii; cf. also Vinaver's note on pp. 1328–29.
[44] Bruce, *Evolution*, I, 458–579 (especially pp. 476–79); cf. E. Vinaver,
"The Dolorous Stroke," *Medium Aevum*, XXV (1957), 174–80, especially note 7, p. 177, citing textual studies of the *Suite*; Vinaver, "La
Genèse de la *Suite du Merlin*," pp. 295–300; Bogdanow, "The Character
of Gauvain," pp. 154–61, and "The *Suite du Merlin*," pp. 325–35.
[45] As Pauphilet notes, romances in the Arthurian prose cycle often refer
to the *Queste del Saint Graal* as "les aventures del graal" and "les perilleuses aventures del roiame de Logres." See A. Pauphilet (ed.), *La Queste
del Saint Graal* (Les Classiques Français du Moyen Age: Paris, 1949), p. i.
For other examples, see the *Suite du Merlin*, Huth, II, 65; M. Dominica
Legge (ed.), *Le Roman de Balain, A Prose Romance of the Thirteenth
Century* (Manchester, 1942), pp. 68–69; and Bogdanow, "The *Suite du
Merlin*," pp. 325–35.
[46] See Vinaver's commentary on the Balin story, *Works*, p. 1274. Cf.
Le Roman de Balain, pp. 68–69.

its source, and particularly for those in the "Wedding of King Arthur."

Malory's rejection of the principal theme of his French source is marked by the contrast between his chivalric code, stated in the "Wedding of King Arthur," and the requirements for Round Table brotherhood described in the *Suite*. Malory's code of chivalry appears at the end of the "Wedding of King Arthur," where, after the adventures of the wedding feast involving Gawain, Tor, and Pellinor, all the Round Table knights take an oath which is to be repeated each year at Pentecost. There is no known source for this passage, and it is generally regarded as Malory's addition to the story, a sort of code expressing his conception of how knights ought to live. The passage is quoted below:

> Thus whan the queste was done of the whyght herte the whych folowed sir Gawayne, and the queste of the brachet whych folowed sir Torre, kynge Pellynors son, and the queste of the lady that the knyghte toke away, whych at that tyme folowed kynge Pellynor, than the kynge stablysshed all the knyghtes and gaff them rychesse and londys; and charged them never to do outerage nothir morthir, and allwayes to fle treson, and to gyff mercy unto hym that askith mercy, uppon payne of forfiture [of their] worship and lordship of kynge Arthure for evirmore; and allwayes to do ladyes, damesels, and jantilwomen and wydowes [socour:] strengthe hem in hir ryghtes, and never to enforce them uppon payne of dethe. Also that no man take no batayles in a wrongefull quarell for no love ne for no worldis goodis. So unto thys were all knyghtis sworne of the Table Rounde both olde and yonge. And every yere so were the[y] sworne at the hygh feste of Pentecoste. (119–20; Vinaver's emendations)

Vinaver notes that this paragraph is "perhaps the most complete and authentic record of M[alory]'s conception of chivalry," [47]

[47] *Works*, p. 1330.

and he points out the similarity of the passage to the didactic treatment of the subject in Caxton's *Order of Chivalry*, published shortly before *Le Morte Darthur*. More important, however, is the fact that there is no similarity between Malory's concept and the type of spiritual chivalry which is operative in the *Suite*'s account of Arthur's wedding. In the *Suite*, the installation of the Round Table at Arthur's court is directly associated with the coming of the Grail adventures. Merlin presides over the ceremony establishing the Round Table, and he makes the occasion significant chiefly because it foreshadows the Grail.[48] Merlin cites attitudes appropriate for the forthcoming spiritual quest and prescribes for the Round Table knights a way of living together as a fraternal order.

"Dès ore mais convient il," says Merlin, "que vous vous entramés et vous tenés chiers comme freres, car pour l'amour et pour la douchour de cele table ou vous serés assis vous naistera es cuers une si grant joie et une si grant amistiés que vous en lairés vos femes et vos enfans pour estre l'un avoec l'autre, et pour user ensamble vos joveneches." [49] Merlin warns them also that the Round Table will not be complete until the coming of "li boins, chis qui metera a fin les perilleuses aventures del roiame de Logres." [50] Later the *Suite* reports that Merlin "les fist tous entrebaisier," [51] and he has the scene blessed by the Archbishop of Canterbury and clergymen who pray "a nostre signour que il dès ore en avant les tenist en boine pais et en boine concorde aussi coume frere germaine." [52]

This procedure is followed by the miracle of the names which

---

[48] Cf. Huth, II, 65–68; Camb. f. 282v, col. 1–282r, col. 2. See also the fragment published by Alexandre Micha in *Romania*, LXXVIII (1957), 37–45, which corresponds to p. 64, line 1 through p. 72, line 13 in Vol. II of the Huth.

[49] Huth, II, 65; Camb. f. 282v, col. 1.

[50] *Ibid.*

[51] Huth, II, 67; Camb. f. 282v, col. 2.

[52] *Ibid.*; Camb. f. 282r, col. 1.

appear in each place as the Round Table knights rise to do
homage to Arthur. While Malory lets it appear that only Merlin
witnesses this miracle, in the *Suite* the names cause excitement
in the court: "Ceste chose tinrent il a grant merveille tout li
sage houme, et disent que se che ne fust chose qui a nostre
signour pleust, ja tel merveille ne fust avenue." [53] The marvel
then, is regarded as a sign of God's approval of the Round Table
order. Arthur too shares the leveling spirituality of these events
when the knights do homage to him: "Et il les rechut comme
ses houmes de par sa terre et coume ses houmes de par la table
reonde. Et il en estoit compains ensi comme le autre, car Merlins
l'i avoit mis pour la bonté de chevalerie qu'il sentoit en lui, et
l'avoit assis droit au commenchement de la table." [54] As Vinaver
remarks,[55] Arthur is here *primus inter pares*, and his sovereignty
is surrendered to the spiritual companionship of the Round
Table.

Inescapably, in the "Tale of King Arthur" Malory has abandoned the principal effect which the Round Table ceremony
had in his source—preparation for the Grail adventure. All of
Merlin's instructions in the *Suite* pertain to the Grail quest; they
are exhortations to piety, peace, and brotherhood; women and
children will be forgotten in the zeal of Round Table fellowship.
But at this early stage in Malory's writing, dedication to the
spiritual test of the Grail would have been irrelevant. He had not
yet introduced his favorites among Arthur's knights—Lancelot,
Tristram, Lamorak—and he had only begun to describe the rise
of Arthur's great court. For Malory, King Arthur's wedding was
not the right occasion for the prolonged anticipation of the
Grail which the *Suite* offered, and he rejected this aspect of his
source, substituting for it his own version of suitable chivalric
ethics.

[53] Huth, II, 68; Camb. f. 282r, col. 2.
[54] *Ibid.*
[55] *Works*, p. 1320. (Cf. *Works*, p. 1050 and Vinaver's note.)

Malory's rules of chivalry tell their own story. They are unlike anything found in the *Suite du Merlin.* Instead of the "pais
et concorde" invoked by Merlin in the *Suite,* Malory's code is
far less placid: it inveighs against murder, treason, outrage; it
appeals for the quality of mercy; it denounces battles taken up
in a "wrongfull quarell" for love and worldly goods. These
precepts convey no hint of religious piety, no promise of mystical
experiences amid the "amour et douchour de cele table." Malory's is not a set of rules for knights approaching, through the
Grail quest, the great spiritual challenge of their careers; rather,
it is a code suitable for an ambitious, high-minded order just
setting out toward adventure. This attitude is suggested in part
by the inclusiveness of Malory's catalogue of knightly virtues.
Instead of circumscribing an aristocratic fraternal group, Malory's view of chivalry includes "ladies, damsels, gentlewomen,
widows," and in its effects embraces not a select company of
knights but the whole of society. At the oath-taking of the
knights in Malory there is no recognized sign of God's special
favor: Malory depicts a society of untried ideals, one which faces
an initial, rather than a final, venture. Malory's story, like that
in the *Suite,* records the blessing of the Round Table by the
"Bysshop of Caunturbiry"; but it omits all reference to the
"boins chevaliers," Galahad, described in the *Suite* as "chis qui
metera a fin les perilleuses aventures del roiame de Logres." [56]
In Malory's book the "adventures of Logres" are to be understood in relation to the adventure-seeking Round Table society
itself—they are incipient, faltering tests of prowess, and they
are secular. Arthur and his knights have yet ahead of them the
conquest of Rome and the romantic adventures of Lancelot and
Tristram; the perils of the Grail are not at hand.[57] As we shall
see, Malory does carefully foreshadow in the "Tale of King

[56] Huth, II, 65; Camb. f. 282v, col. 1.
[57] The *Suite* states that the Grail adventure is far distant (Huth, II, 66;
Camb. f. 282v, col. 2), but this does not modify the point that the
Suite's purpose here is to prepare for the Grail story.

Arthur" the adventures of the Grail quest. But his concern here in the "Wedding of King Arthur" is with other matters.

Malory's emphasis on the knights and their code is gained through his divergence from the "interwoven" structure of the *Suite du Merlin*. In the *Suite*, the Round Table ceremony occurs before Arthur's wedding, before the arrival of Tor to ask for knighthood, and before the arrival of King Pellinor at court. Since this is true, the ceremony itself has at best only a vague connection with the subsequent adventures of Gawain, Tor, and Pellinor. Of the three quests, only Gawain's is said by Merlin to have any bearing on the Grail theme: "sachiés que ceste aventure poés vous bien tenir a une des aventures del saint graal." [58] Only once does any of the characters encountered by the three questing knights refer to the wedding feast of King Arthur, and this too occurs in Gawain's adventure, as he meets two brothers fighting. "Nous venions," explains one of them, "orendroit entre moi et lui d'un mien chastiel qui est près de chi, et aliens a Camalaoth pour veoir la feste del roi et de la roine." [59] Finally, at the end of the third quest—Pellinor's—Arthur implies that he regards the three episodes as related adventures, but he does not expressly associate them with either the wedding feast or the Round Table-Grail motif: "Je n'oi onques parler de gent a cui il avenist si bien coume a vous trois compaignons qui de chaiens meustes ensamble; car il n'i a chelui, Dieu merci, qui ne soit revenus assés sains et assés haitiés et qui n'ait menee sa queste a chief et a sa volonté." [60] Since the question of Tor's parentage, the dubbing of the new knights, and the seating of Pellinor at the Round Table are all subjects which, in the *Suite*, intervene between Arthur's wedding and Gawain's first adventure, the French narrative establishes

---

[58] Huth, II, 96; Camb. f. 290v, col. 1.
[59] Huth, II, 82; Camb. f. 286v, col. 2.
[60] Huth, II, 127; Camb. f. 298v, col. 1.

no formal connection between the wedding and the three adventures. All of these incidents, however, are supposed to be interconnected anticipations of the Grail quest.

Malory, on the other hand, brings together all three of the protagonists of the wedding quests at the start of his story. Next he makes the adventures of Gawain, Tor, and Pellinor immediately follow the wedding feast itself, and he then adapts the adventures so that they lead up to the oath of chivalry as the last event in the story.[61] Thus in *Le Morte Darthur* the wedding, the Round Table ritual, the three adventures, and the code of the knights are all elements which Malory interrelates to gain the effect of coherent sequence. The climax of the "Wedding of King Arthur," in structure and in theme, is the code of chivalry itself, toward which the three adventures and the coming of the Round Table to Arthur's court have led as if by a destined plan.

Malory's process of fitting the wedding adventures into the theme of a new Arthurian order is simply that of adding to them details relevant to the chivalric code itself. Their incidents prefigure the oath later taken by all Round Table knights. An example of this procedure is Gawain's quest, which in the *Suite* resembles the episode of the Dolorous Stroke in being, as Merlin claims it is, a forerunner of the Grail adventures; [62] yet even in the *Suite* it never has any clear bearing on the Grail legend. In this respect the "Tale of King Arthur" improves on

[61] Here is the order of events in the *Suite*: (1) the wedding, (2) the knighting of Tor and Gawain, (3) the arrival of King Pellinor on the day after the wedding, (4) the rancor of Gawain, (5) the announcement of the quests by Merlin. In *Le Morte Darthur* Pellinor arrives on the morning of the wedding; then comes the dubbing of Tor and Gawain, followed by the wedding and the feast at which the adventures begin. Malory telescopes the time in his version, and he mentions the passage of time again only at the end of Tor's quest, where he says, in an original addition, that Tor returned to Camelot "on the third day by noone" (113). Malory thus achieves an effect of greater coherence.

[62] Huth, II, 96; Camb. f. 290v, col. 1.

the quest, for Malory has dropped the Grail relationship, and instead allows Gawain's adventures to lead as a sort of *ex- emplum* to one of the main items in the code of chivalry—the injunction "to gyff mercy unto hym that askith mercy, uppon payne of forfiture [of their] worship and lordship of kynge Arthure for evirmore" (120; Vinaver's emendation). In the *Suite du Merlin*, it is true, Gawain's greatest offense is his lack of mercy toward defeated knights. His crime occurs when he accidentally beheads the nameless lady of Alardyne of the Oute Iles (both are anonymous in the *Suite*) who flings herself over the beaten knight in order to save him. Gaherys says to Gawain with dismay, "Certes ja chevaliers ne deust tel vilonnie faire pour courous ne por haine qu'il euust a homme né." [63] Malory uses this same incident with no major structural alterations; but he assigns to Gaherys a much more rueful speech: "Alas . . . that ys fowle and shamefully done, for that shame shall never frome you. Also ye sholde gyff mercy unto them that aske mercy, for a knyght withoute mercy ys withoute worship" (106). Here, of course, is a darker view of Gawain's accident, and it specifies— in phrasing identical with that of the code of knighthood at the end of Malory's tale—the error in behavior. Malory's rules of chivalry are thus determined empirically, and in Gawain's quest the law of mercy is apprehended.

The judgment of Gawain in the "Tale of King Arthur" re- inforces this idea. When Gawain returns to court in the *Suite*, he is first praised by Merlin [64] and then directed to the judgment of Guinevere and her ladies for penitence. But Malory pointedly omits all of Merlin's praise and his assurances of a promising career for Gawain, and subjects him at once to the judgment

---

[63] Huth, II, 89; Camb. f. 288v, cols. 1–2.

[64] Huth, II, 96; Camb. f. 290v, col. 1. Huth: "il l'a moult mieus fait que vous ne cuidiés, car il a bien sa queste achievee." Camb.: "il a moult mes- fait plus que vus ne quidies e si a bien sa queste acheve."

of a "quest of ladies." The respective judgments from the *Suite* and *Le Morte Darthur* are as follows:

> . . . esgardons nous que vous orendroit jurés sor sains que ja mais tant que vous viverés ne meterés main en damoisiele pour chose que elle vous die ne fache se vous ne veés peril de mort. Et encore volons nous que se la damoisele vous requiert aide ne secours que vous aidiés, ne ja ne soit de si estrange lieu ne si mesconnue, se che n'est encontre vostre hounour.[65]

> They juged hym for ever whyle he lyved to be with all ladyes and to fyght for hir quarels; and ever that he sholde be cur- teyse, and never to refuse mercy to hym that askith mercy. (108)

While the *Suite* omits the issue of mercy, Malory adds it to his version, thereby holding the central error of Gawain's quest in the foreground of the narrative.

Malory's additions to the quest of Sir Tor also increase the pertinence of the story. In both the *Suite* and the "Tale of King Arthur" Tor's quest is a moral success; it is the sort of achieve- ment expected of those who come of high lineage, and, ac- cordingly, in the *Suite* King Pellinor is revealed as Tor's father after all the quests are finished.[66] Having disclosed Tor's parentage before describing the quests, Malory adds details to the quest itself which dramatize Tor's innate grasp of chivalry. When the damsel, for instance, demands the head of Abelleus, whom Tor has defeated, Tor himself pleads for the knight. But the lady is firm, and after it is too late Abelleus begs that Tor overrule the lady's demands as an act of mercy. At this point Malory adds to Tor's remarks a justification for his decision: "for erewhyle *when I wolde have tane you to mercy* ye wolde none

<hr>

[65] Huth, II, 99; Camb. f. 290r, cols. 1–2.
[66] Huth, II, 131–34; Camb. ff. 299v, col. 1–300v, col. 1.

aske, but iff ye had the brachett agayne that was my queste"
(112; italics mine). This comment explains why Tor does not
render mercy despite his sympathy for Abelleus: he is not—
like Gawain—unmerciful, but instead bound by his earlier
promise to the lady. With Tor, Malory creates in effect a foil
for the unyielding Gawain.

Like Gawain, Pellinor has troubles on his quest, the chief one
being that through negligence he is instrumental in causing the
suicide of his own daughter, whom Malory calls Alyne (119).
On his return to court, Pellinor is reprimanded by Guenevere:

> "A, kynge Pellynor," seyde quene Gwenyver, "ye were gretly
> to blame that ye saved nat thys ladyes lyff."
>
> "Madam," seyde kynge Pellynore, "ye were gretely to blame
> and ye wolde nat save youre owne lyff and ye myght. But, salf
> youre displesure, I was so furyous in my queste that I wolde
> nat abyde, and that repentis me and shall do dayes of my lyff."
> (119)

Vinaver seems to misread Pellinor's answer to Guenevere, ob-
serving that it "is clearly incompatible with the code of chivalric
behaviour: a knight, he says, would be *gretely to blame* if he did
not think of his own safety, a notion worthy of a Dinadan." [67]
But no real incompatibility exists, because Pellinor is addressing
the queen rather than referring to himself. He means that any
person who takes his life is blameworthy. Pellinor's only fault
is having been too "furious" in his quest to stop and help the
damsel who proved to be his own daughter. From this fault he
is not exonerated; but Pellinor's remark on the evil of suicide,
invented by Malory, must certainly be intended to moderate
his guilt.

All of these changes which relate the wedding adventures to
the oath of chivalry point to one of the major qualities of Mal-

---

[67] *Works*, p. 1328. Vinaver is answered by R. T. Davies, "Was Pellynor
Unworthy?" *Notes & Queries*, New Series, IV (1957), 370.

ory's presentation: his concern with the meaning of the story.
Gawain's adventure at the wedding feast exemplifies the un-
chivalric behavior condemned in Malory's list of rules at the
close of the wedding story. The other adventures have a similar
bearing on the code of chivalry, Tor's as an example of successful questing and Pellinor's as another instance of failure.
Through their contrasts with each other the episodes of adventure are the medium of a thematic interplay which resolves
itself in the code. The idea common to both the adventures and
the code is that chivalry is an acquired ideal, a mode of life
which the Round Table knights must master through experience. Nothing comparable to this idea is to be found in the
Suite du Merlin. Where his source wanders in a profusion of
incidents mysteriously associated with the Grail, Malory supplies
his own theme of emerging order in Camelot.

Elsewhere in the "Tale of King Arthur" Malory does retain
the Grail theme of his source, and he handles it with the same
purposeful freedom he exhibits in the "Wedding of King
Arthur." The most elaborate example of this procedure is the
tale of Balin, where in Malory's arrangement Balin's experiences
foreshadow the coming of Galahad more explicitly than they
do in the extant versions of his source. Vinaver has attempted to
show that Malory's explanation of the Dolorous Stroke severs
the *Suite*'s intended connection between Balin's adventures and
the Grail romance. In the French, the Dolorous Stroke is a punishment for Balin's violation of the Grail sanctuary, and it serves
as a prelude for the themes of the Blighted Land and the
Maimed King which occur in the *Queste del Saint Graal*. Malory's explanation is more limited: the Dolorous Stroke punishes
Balin for killing the lady who claims his head at Arthur's court.
"As a result," Vinaver argues, "the Dolorous Stroke loses its
original significance and acquires a new meaning which can be
understood without reference to anything that lies beyond the

Balin story proper." [68] But this, certainly, is an overstatement
for in the *Suite du Merlin* the Dolorous Stroke is never explained
at all, and Malory has done no more than supply an explanation
—and hence a coherent meaning—where one was lacking in his
source. What is more, he goes further than Vinaver admits
toward relating the tale of Balin specifically to the Grail quest.
His account of the *result* of the Dolorous Stroke, for example,
is not to be found in the extant versions of his source:

> And kynge Pellam lay so many yerys sore wounded, and myght
> never be hole tylle that Galaad the Hawte Prynce heled hym
> in the queste of the Sankgreall. For in that place was parte of
> the bloode of oure Lorde Jesu Cryste, which Joseph off
> Aramathy brought into thys londe. And there hymselff [lay]
> in that ryche bedde. And that was the spere whych Longeus
> smote oure Lorde with to the herte. And kynge Pellam was
> nyghe of Joseph his kynne, and that was the moste worship-
> fullist man on lyve in tho dayes, and grete pité hit was of hys
> hurte, for thorow that stroke hit turned to grete dole, tray and
> tene. (85–86)

It is especially noteworthy that in this explanation Malory
describes Joseph of Arimathea himself lying "in that ryche
bedde," an obvious reference to the bed included without source
authority [69] in Malory's earlier description of the Grail chamber:
"abedde [a bed] arayed with cloth of golde, the rychiste that
myght be, and one lyyng therein" (85).

But Malory's most exact connection of the Balin story with
the Grail quest is found in a forecast whose validity in *Le Morte
Darthur* would be hard to discredit. At the end of the Balin
story Malory writes:

> Than Merlion lette make a brygge of iron and of steele into
> that ilonde, and hit was but halff a foote brode, 'and there

[68] *Works*, p. 1274.
[69] Cf. *Ibid.*, p. 1313.

shall never man passe that brygge nother have hardynesse to
go over hit but yf he were a passynge good man withoute
trechery or vylany.' Also the scawberd off Balyns swerde
Merlion lefte hit on thys syde the ilonde, that Galaad sholde
fynde hit. Also Merlion lette make by hys suttelyté that Balynes
swerde was put into a marbil stone stondynge upryght as
grete as a mylstone, and hoved allwayes above the watir, and
dud many yeres. And so by adventure hit swamme downe by
the streme unto the cité of Camelot, that ys in Englysh called
Wynchester, and that same day Galahad the Haute Prynce
com with kynge Arthure, and so Galaad brought with hym the
scawberde and encheved the swerde that was in the marble
stone hovynge uppon the watir. And on Whytsonday he en-
chevyd the swerde, as hit ys rehersed in THE BOOK OF THE SANK-
GREALL. (91–92)

This statement was suggested by a similar one at the end of
the Balin story in the *Suite du Merlin*.[70] However, there is
nothing in the source resembling Malory's specific additions.
Merlin's prophecy in the *Suite* states that Lancelot will inherit
Balin's sword, but to Lancelot's name Malory adds "other ellis
Galahad, hys sonne" (91). Malory further adds that "the scawberd off Balyns swerde Merlion lefte hit on thys syde the ilonde,
that Galaad sholde fynde hit" (91–92). Accordingly, in Malory's "Quest of the Holy Grail"—many pages distant in *Le
Morte Darthur*—Galahad arrives at court with an empty scabbard which fits Balin's sword in the stone (862); and, to prepare for this event as early as the "Tale of King Arthur," Malory
also adds to the forecast in the Balin story the point that
"Galaad brought with hym the scawberde" (92). The whole
prophecy is finally corroborated by the speech of Galahad in the
"Quest of the Holy Grail" which [71] is Malory's attempt to link
these distant divisions of *Le Morte Darthur*:

[70] Huth, II, 59–60; Camb. f. 280r, cols. 1–2.
[71] *Works*, p. 1533.

Now have I the swerde that somtyme was the good
knyghtes Balyns le Saveaige, and he was a passynge good
knyght of hys hondys; and with thys swerde he slew hys
brothir Balan, and that was grete pité, for he was a good
knyght. And eythir slew othir thorow a dolerous stroke that
Balyn gaff unto kynge Pelles, the whych ys nat yett hole, nor
naught shall be tyll that I hele hym. (863)

As the wedding story and the story of Balin attest, Malory i
by no means unaware that the Grail legend is the primary bur
den of his French source. Using the *Suite du Merlin* as a source
book to implement, rather than to determine, his Arthurian
scheme, Malory is equally capable of suspending the Grail motif
as he does in the "Wedding of King Arthur," or of stressing its
connection with his narrative, as in the Balin episode. In this
way Malory dealt with the problem of theme which he en
countered in the source of the "Tale of King Arthur"—that of
disengaging the narrative from its original significance, but not
from its allusiveness.

ALLUSIONS

As part of the Borron cycle of romances which centered upon
the Grail legend, the *Suite du Merlin* contains numerous al
lusions to other branches of Arthurian romance. In particular,
it anticipates events of the *Queste* and the *Mort Artu*; but in
addition there are allusions to the prose *Tristan*, the prose *Lancelot*, and to an unknown work, the *Conte del Brait*, though
presumably the last three never formed part of the Borron
cycle itself.[72] Allusiveness was one of the characteristics of Mal-

[72] Bruce, *Evolution*, I, 458–79, 480–82; see also Bogdanow, "The *Suite
du Merlin*," pp. 325–35.

ory's source for the "Tale of King Arthur," and, far from being baffled by this trait, Malory retains it as a means of unifying *Le Morte Darthur*. In general, Malory relies on three types of allusions: those borrowed from the *Suite du Merlin* and altered to suit his own purposes, those he invents himself, and those reproduced from the *Suite* with no significant alterations.

Malory's use of allusion to correlate widely separated episodes in *Le Morte Darthur* has been shown above in the Balin story's forecast of Galahad and the Grail quest. Among many other examples, only those which have no source authority will be considered here. Some of these amount to little more than inclusion of names, as when Merlin identifies King Pellinor by use of this sourceless prediction: "he shall have two sonnes that shall be passyng good men as ony lyvynge: save one in thys worlde they shall have no felowis of prouesse and of good lyvynge, and hir namys shall be Percyvall and sir Lamorake of Walis" (52). To the list of King Lot's sons who come to court with their mother Malory adds the name Gareth, unknown outside *Le Morte Darthur*: "And thydir com unto hym kynge Lottis wyff of Orkeney in maner of a message, but she was sente thydir to aspye the courte of kynge Arthure, and she com rychely beseyne with hir four sonnes, Gawayne, Gaheris, Aggravayne and Gareth, with many other knyghtes and ladyes, for she was a passynge fayre lady" (41). When King Arthur first encounters Pellinor, who pursues the Questing Beast, Malory interpolates this identification: "Whos name was kynge Pellynor that tyme folowed the questynge beste, and afftir hys dethe sir Palomydes folowed hit" (43). Of a different sort is Malory's version of the allusion concerning Perceval's sister which he found in the adventures of Balin. In the *Suite* Balin's lady is required to give a dishful of her own blood to save the lady of a castle; when this fails and Balin and the lady depart, the

Suite states that Perceval's sister will "acompli l'aventure dou
chastiel." [73] Malory is much more specific. He not only alludes
here to the "Sankgreall" itself, but supplies the outcome of the
adventure as the *Queste* describes it: "And as hit tellith after
in the Sᴀɴᴋɢʀᴇᴀʟʟ that sir Percivall hys syster holpe that lady
with hir blood, *whereof she was dede*" (82; italics mine).

Malory's allusions are not always on so small a scale. Those
which attain consistency and concreteness of detail as well as
breadth establish this type of cross reference as one of Malory's
main resources in unifying *Le Morte Darthur*. At two points
in the "Tale of King Arthur" Malory does his most original
work with allusions. One of these is the sourceless passage which
serves to sum up the triple adventures of Gawain, Ywain, and
Marhalt at the end of the "Tale of King Arthur." It also forms
the general conclusion of the whole "Tale." Malory's habit, of
course, was to close his subdivisions with brief summaries; but
the conclusion of this final subdivision is more extensive than
usual, either because the source broke off at the end of Gawain's
adventure with Pelleas and Arcade (Ettard), or, as seems more
likely, because the continuation of the source did not suit Malory's purposes.[74] In any event, the short, routine adventures of

[73] Huth, II, 15–19; Camb. ff. 268v, col. 2–269v, col. 2.
[74] Both the Huth and Cambridge MSS. of the *Suite du Merlin* break
off after the adventure of Gawain, Pelleas, and Arcade. A fuller version
of the story is found in a fragment in MS. B. N. fr. 112, edited by H. O.
Sommer under the title *Die Abenteuer Gawains, Ywains, und le Morholts
mit den drei Jungfrauen* in *Beihefte zur Zeitschrift für Romanische Philologie*, XLVII (1913). Since this fragment is a branch of the Borron Prose
Cycle, it is here considered as a part of the *Suite du Merlin* (cf. C. E.
Pickford, *L'Evolution du roman arthurien en prose vers la fin du moyen
âge* [Paris, A. G. Nizet, 1960], p. 66). How much of the story contained
in MS. 112 Malory had before him is unknown; it would seem that Malory
was familiar with much, if not all, of the material represented in this fragment. This view is supported by F. Whitehead, "On Certain Episodes in
the Fourth Book of Malory's *Morte Darthur*," *Medium Aevum*, II (1933),
199–261, which cites a number of parallels between Malory's text and the
fragment in MS. 112. In subsequent notes references to "Sommer" indicate Sommer's edition of this fragment.

ʼwain and Marhalt are sourceless and appear to be inventions
ıf Malory to demonstrate the skills and valor of the two knights
ınd to round off the series of adventures.[75] Having himself pro-
ʼided the last two sets of adventures, Malory ends the tale with
ın account of a high feast in which his principal object is to
ıake leave of his recent protagonists by means of brief comments
ın their subsequent careers:

> So agayne the feste of Pentecoste cam the Damesell of the
> Laake and brought with hir sir Pelleas, and at the hyghe feste
> there was grete joustys. Of all knyghtes that were at that justis
> sir Pelleas had the pryce and sir Marhaute was named next.
> But sir Pelleas was so stronge that there myght but few
> knyghtes stonde hym a buffette with a spere. And at the next
> feste sir Pelleas and sir Marhalt were made knyghtes of the
> Rounde Table; for there were two segis voyde, for two knyghts
> were slayne that twelve-monthe.
>
> And grete joy had kynge Arthure of sir Pelleas and of sir
> Marhalte, but Pelleas loved never after sir Gawayne but as he
> spared hym for the love of the kynge; but oftyn-tymes at justis
> and at turnementes sir Pelleas quytte sir Gawayne, for so hit
> rehersyth in the booke of Frensh.
>
> So sir Trystrams many dayes aftir fought with sir Marhaute
> in an ilande. And there they dud a grete batayle, but the laste
> sir Trystrams slew hym. So sir Trystrams was so wounded that
> unnethe he myght recover, and lay at a nunrye half a yere.
>
> And sir Pelleas was a worshypfull knyght, and was one of
> the four that encheved the Sankgreal. And the Damesel of
> the Laake made by her meanes that never he had ado with sir
> Launcelot de Laake, for where sir Launcelot was at ony justis
> or at ony turnemente she wolde not suffir hym to be there
> that day but yf hit were on the syde of sir Launcelot. (179–80)

The main interest of these lines lies in the fact that, however
nuch they may resemble Malory's ordinary summarizing, they

[75] The adventures devised by Malory for Ywain and Marhalt are discussed
xtensively in the article by Whitehead, "On Certain Episodes."

accomplish a great deal more. The real function of the résumé is not to draw a curtain and close off the view, but to anticipate through allusion some later developments in the story and to suggest that further episodes are to follow.

The difference between terminating the story of "Gawain, Ywain, and Marhalt" and suspending temporarily the histories of its personnel is illustrated by Malory's remarks about Tristram and Marhalt. Apparently Malory intends in his summary to mention the chief characters whose adventures he has related —Gawain, Pelleas, Marhalt, the Damsel of the Lake. But the summary of Marhalt's career curiously emphasizes only Tristram, while Marhalt's name barely comes to the surface in a phrase: "So sir Trystrams many dayes aftir fought with sir Marhaute in an ilande. And there they dud a grete batayle, but the last sir Trystrams slew hym. So sir Trystrams was so wounded that unnethe he myght recover, and lay at a nunrye half a yere" (179). True, the events thus described do look ahead to Marhalt's death; but all the action is Tristram's, and the final sentence concerns no one else. The result here is an obvious incongruity, since Malory has at no previous point made Tristram the subject of his narrative. It would be easy, of course, to explain away this odd synopsis by recalling Malory's evident haste and his frequent imprecision with details. Yet the events described suggest that the passage was written with care: the point that Tristram "lay at a nunrye half a yere" is sourceless, but all the other details of Tristram's fight with Marhalt form an accurate précis of the story as it appears later in *Le Morte Darthur* and in Malory's French source.[76]

In the *Suite du Merlin* there are, to be sure, allusions to the death of Marhalt which Malory could have known even though

---

[76] *Works*, pp. 377–83; Eilert Löseth, *Le Roman en prose de Tristan, le roman de Palamède et la compilation de Rusticien de Pise. Analyse Critique d'après les manuscrits de Paris* (Paris, 1890), sec. 28.

they occur in passages he does not reproduce. For instance, the list of knights who defeat Gawain is followed in the *Suite* by this comment: "Et sachent tout cil qui cest conte lisent que le Morhous dont ie parole chi fu cil Morhous que Tristrans li nies le roi March occhist en l'isle Sanson pour le treuage qu'il demandoit de Cornvaille." [77] It is conceivable that Malory could have constructed his synopsis of Marhalt's death by using details such as these from his French source. However, two items suggest Malory's independent and prior knowledge of the Tristan legend. First, the seemingly accidental emphasis on Tristram in the summary indicates both Malory's awareness of Tristram's importance and his desire to maintain an accurate emphasis in retelling the Tristan story. Second, the remark that Marhalt's death occurs "many dayes aftir" his reception at Arthur's court, while typical of Malory's prophetic statements elsewhere, cannot be set aside as an effort to disguise a mere ignorance of the Tristan matter; rather, it agrees with the allusions to the Tristram romance which are the basis of Malory's sourceless episode about Marhalt and the giant Taulurd. Malory describes the latter situation as follows:

> And so within sevennyght his damesel brought hym to an erlys place. His name was the erle Fergus that aftir was sir Trystrams knyght, and this erle was but a yonge man and late com to his londis, and there was a gyaunte fast by hym that hyght Taulurd, and he had another brother in Cornuayle that hyght Taulas that sir Trystram slewe whan he was oute of his mynde. So this erle made his complaynte unto sir Marhaute that there was a gyaunte by hym that destroyed all his londis and how he durste nowhere ryde nother go for hym. (175)

As in the case of Tristram's fight with Marhalt, here again Malory accurately anticipates an episode in the Tristan story to

[77] Huth, II, 240; Camb. f. 327v, col. 2; Sommer, p. 9.

which he turns later in *Le Morte Darthur*.[78] The episode with
Taulurd, aside from filling out the adventures of Marhalt, contains several features characteristic of Malory's attempt to unify
diverse romances. There is, for example, no authority in the
French tradition for Taulas's having a brother named Taulurd.[79]
Malory's claim that the two giants are brothers and his invention of a similar name for Marhalt's opponent suggest a self-
conscious *departure* from the Tristan material: if Malory had no
intention of retelling the Tristram story later, he would also have
no need to keep the relationships and the sequence of events
distinct in this early adventure of Marhalt. Yet such distinctions
are a particular concern of Malory's in the Taulurd episode.
Again, although Fergus has no part in the incident with the
giant Taulas in either the French *Tristan* or Malory's version of
it, Malory is careful to say that Earl Fergus is "aftir" (i.e., after-
ward) Tristram's knight, and that now he is "but a yonge man
and late com to his londis." Doubtless a similar motive inspired Malory's recording of names in the list of knights who
defeat Gawain.[80] The ranking of Tristram next after Lancelot
in this survey is probably, like the Taulurd story and the anticipation of Marhalt's death, a part of Malory's effort to project a
place for the Tristram story within *Le Morte Darthur*. Similarly,
the remoteness of Marhalt's death "many dayes aftir" and the
stress on Fergus's youth are details which seem to outline in *Le
Morte Darthur* a loose but nonetheless definite time scheme for
the Tristram story.[81] They also serve to conclude "Gawain,

[78] *Works*, pp. 499–500.

[79] Löseth, *Le Roman en prose de Tristan*, sec. 103.

[80] *Works*, p. 162; *Suite du Merlin*, Huth, II, 240; Camb. f. 327v, cols.
1–2; Sommer, p. 9.

[81] Vinaver has pointed out that at the time of Tristram's battle with
Marhalt in the French prose *Tristan*, Arthur's rule has not yet begun (*Le
Roman de Tristan et Iseut dans l'Oeuvre de Thomas Malory* [Paris, 1925],
p. 158). Whitehead notes that in *Le Morte Darthur* Arthur's rule is already established, so that in the "Tristram" division Marhalt can logically

Ywain, and Marhalt" as part of an extended work, rather than as the end of a self-contained romance.

The remaining summaries with which Malory closes "Gawain, Ywain, and Marhalt" have the same function of anticipative reprise which operates in the summary of Marhalt's career. As in the case of the Tristram-Marhalt fight, Malory's recapitulation of the histories of other characters in "Gawain, Ywain, and Marhalt" is hardly more than a pose, and the synopses have an extensive relevance that should not be ignored. Thus Malory neglects to mention Ywain, presumably because he had no further plans for this character in *Le Morte Darthur*; but Marhalt, Pelleas, Gawain, and the Damsel of the Lake are all characters who interest Malory and who later appear so frequently that their presence creates an effect of continuity.

The main purpose of the lines concluding "Gawain, Ywain, and Marhalt" is to imply that there are further adventures in Arthur's court and to arouse the reader's interest in them—an effect Malory achieves deliberately, not by accident. For an example of finality, as opposed to allusiveness or anticipation, one need only turn to the ending Malory supplies as he breaks off the story of Gawain and Ettard and turns to the affairs of Marhalt: "So this lady Ettarde dyed for sorow, and the Damesel of the Lake rejoysed sir Pelleas, and loved togedyrs durying their lyfe" (172). In the last phrase Malory resorts to the customary ending of the fairy tale: "and they lived happily ever after." However terse, it is an ending; it hints of no further incident, and it implies finality.[82]

---

be a knight of the Round Table ("On Certain Episodes," p. 210). In Löseth's compilation the point is made that at the time of the Tristram-Marhalt fight Arthur's rule has just begun (*Le Roman en prose de Tristan*, sec. 28). Cf. Lumiansky, "The Question of Unity," pp. 29–39; T. C. Rumble, *The Tristan Legend and Its Place in the Morte Darthur*, unpublished dissertation, Tulane University (1955), pp. 150 ff.; Moorman, "Internal Chronology," pp. 240–49.

[82] Cf. the conclusion of the "Tale of Gareth" (*Works*, p. 363), where

But Malory's later views of Pelleas and his lady in the same story are another matter altogether. They bear a distinct resemblance to his earlier treatment of Marhalt and Tristram. In connection with Lancelot, Pelleas is referred to without being named, while Lancelot's name appears three times in the statement: "And the Damesel of the Laake made by her meanes that never he had ado with sir Launcelot de Laake, for where sir Launcelot was at ony justis or at ony turnemente she wolde not suffir hym to be there that day but yf hit were on the syde of sir Launcelot" (179–80). There can be little question of where the emphasis is intended in this comparison: Malory introduces Lancelot into the summary arbitrarily. Although Lancelot has had no part in "Gawain, Ywain, and Marhalt," he is to become the greatest knight of the Round Table, and his eminence is predicted earlier in the "Tale of King Arthur" when Merlin and Nyneve see "yonge Launcelot" on their travels (125–26). In the summary closing "Gawain, Ywain, and Marhalt" the implied relationship between Pelleas and Lancelot joins in the Round Table court two characters never before associated with each other in Arthurian romance and thereby welds together diverse branches of Arthurian fiction which formerly were independent.[83] In the "Tale of King Arthur" there is perhaps no clearer example of the unifying process.

Yet the Pelleas-Lancelot relationship has a further significance. It is meant to contrast with the touchy disaffection of Pelleas's later relations with Gawain: ". . . but Pelleas loved never after sir Gawayne but as he spared hym for the love

Malory again employs the fairy-tale ending, having established within the tale numerous relationships with other divisions of *Le Morte Darthur*. On the relationships, see Wilfred L. Guerin, *The Functional Role of Gareth in Malory's Morte Darthur,* unpublished M.A. thesis, Tulane University (1953), pp. 60–123.

[83] The branches here connected are the prose *Lancelot* of the Vulgate Cycle and the later Post-Vulgate Grail romance (*Roman du Graal*) which contains the Pelleas story (in MS. 112).

of the kynge; but oftyntymes at justis and at turnementes sir Pelleas quytte sir Gawayne, for so hit rehersyth in the booke of Frensh" (179). Here again Malory's story does not end; further incidents are implied, and the taut relationship of Pelleas and Gawain is a continuing state.[84] But, like Marhalt in the shadow of Tristram, Pelleas is not himself the real topic of Malory's comments; rather, he is a convenient figure through whom Malory indicates the fatal contrast between Gawain and Lancelot. Presumably it was with this end in mind that Malory changed the hour and the nature of Gawain's increase of strength in "Gawain, Ywain, and Marhalt," agreeing not with the *Suite du Merlin* but with his own "Tale of the Death of Arthur" and its sources.[85] At the end of "Gawain, Ywain, and Marhalt," then, both Pelleas and Marhalt are overshadowed by the greater knights and the greater themes which will dominate *Le Morte Darthur*.

At a second point in the "Tale of King Arthur," Malory's allusiveness becomes a method of ordering themes which in later pages of *Le Morte Darthur* underlie the tragedy besetting the Round Table. The occasion is the passage interrupting the tale of Balin to describe King Lot's death and interment.[86] King Lot is killed in battle by Pellinor, who temporarily disappears. Lot's funeral is attended by his wife, Morgause, and his sons, Gawain, Aggravain, Gaheris, and Gareth, as well as by Arthur, Merlin, and Morgan le Fay and her husband, King Urience. Honoring Arthur's victory over the rebel kings, Merlin erects a splendid memorial featuring statues of the kings bearing

[84] Malory lists Pelleas as one of the knights who defeat Gawain (*Works*, p. 162).
[85] Cf. R. H. Wilson, "Malory's Early Knowledge of Arthurian Romance," *University of Texas Studies in English*, XXIX (1950), 33–50; and R. M. Lumiansky, "Gawain's Miraculous Strength: Malory's Use of *Le Morte Arthur* and *Mort Artu*," *Etudes Anglaises*, X (1957), 97–108.
[86] *Works*, pp. 77–79.

tapers, with a statue of Arthur above them, his sword drawn
in triumph. Merlin prophesies that the tapers will be extin-
guished after his death and after the adventures of the "Sankgreall," and that Balin will give the Dolorous Stroke, bringing
down "great vengeance." He also warns Arthur to guard the
scabbard of Excalibur, which defends him from wounds, and
Malory inserts a summary of Morgan le Fay's theft of the scabbard for her lover, Accolon. Merlin's final prophecy, closing
the funeral episode, is that Arthur's son Mordred will oppose
him in a battle at Salisbury. The source of this ominous scene
is the *Suite du Merlin*,[87] but Malory's alterations transform it
into a prophetic tableau more explicit than anything found in
the source. Some of Malory's explanations and prophecies are
invented, others adapted from his source; all of them reflect
the apparent aim of establishing links with later episodes in *Le
Morte Darthur*.

The first of these prophetic motifs occurs at the end of
Malory's sourceless eulogy of King Lot, and explains Lot's enmity toward King Arthur: "And for because that kynge Arthure
lay by hys wyff and gate on her sir Mordred, therefore kynge
Lotte helde ever agaynste Arthure" (77). In the *Suite*, Lot is
angry not because of Arthur's incest, but because he thinks
Arthur has slain Mordred in the May Day massacre of infants.[88]
Seemingly Malory changes Lot's motivation in order to suppress
Arthur's part in the infanticide; but it is equally significant
that his invented explanation of the conflict with King Lot
neither excuses nor justifies King Arthur. Instead, it emphasizes
the unnatural circumstance of Mordred's birth, expressly involving King Arthur in the strife that troubles Lot's tragic
house [89] and ends in the disaster with Mordred at Salisbury
Plain.

[87] Huth, I, 259–65; Camb. ff. 259r, col. 2–260v, col. 1.
[88] Huth, I, 254–55; Camb. f. 258v, col. 2.
[89] For instances of this strife, cf. *Works*, pp. 102, 158, and 612.

Lot's death is followed by the prophecy of Gawain's vengeance on King Pellinor, who, fighting for Arthur, "bare the wyte
of the dethe of kynge Lotte" (77). There is confused authoriza-
tion for this prophecy in the surviving MSS. of the *Suite du
Merlin*,[90] but none expresses so exact a chronology as Malory
does, nor such clear identifications: "sir Gawayne revenged the
deth of hys fadir the ten yere aftir he was made knyght, and slew
kynge Pellynor hys owne hondis" (77–78). It is Malory who
makes this prophecy seem so conclusive. Again, after creating
Lot's ornate tomb, Merlin prophesies in the *Suite* that his own
death will occur on the same day as the Dolorous Stroke, which
will herald the start of the Grail adventures;[91] but Malory cor-
rects this prophecy in *Le Morte Darthur*, casting Merlin's death
and the Grail adventures in their proper order, and predicting
the Dolorous Stroke separately (79). Balin's fated stroke thus
becomes a cause of "grete vengeaunce" (78) in *Le Morte
Darthur*, not a cause of the Grail adventures, and through
Malory's deliberate alteration it is connected with the vengeance of Lot, of Gawain, even of Mordred, in the foreboding
episode of King Lot's death and burial. Further, Malory invents
the prophecy which follows the Morgan-Accolon parenthesis:
". . . Merlion tolde unto kynge Arthure . . . that there sholde
be a grete batayle besydes Salysbiry, and Mordred his owne
sonne sholde be agaynste hym" (79). The origin of this prophecy is a passage at the end of the *Suite*'s first tale of Morgan and
Excalibur in which Merlin foretells the death of Sagremor—
Mordred's foster father—at the battle of Salisbury.[92] Malory
patently makes this prophecy refer instead to King Arthur, and
with it he concludes his series of motifs foreshadowing the whole
hapless course of King Arthur's time.

One further question remains concerning the pattern of

[90] Huth, I, 261; Camb. ff. 259r, col. 2–260v, col. 1.
[91] Huth, I, 264 (lines 15–26); Camb. f. 260r, col. 1.
[92] Huth, I, 274; Camb. f. 263v, col. 1.

allusions at King Lot's burial: What function among the
prophetic motifs did Malory conceive for his sourceless anticipation of the Morgan-Accolon affair? Malory's summary itself
indicates that he saw a particular meaning in Morgan le Fay's
betrayal of Arthur's confidence. He writes that *"for grete trust*
Arthure betoke the scawberde unto Morgan le Fay" (79; italics
mine), a conception perhaps modeled upon the *Suite's* explanation that Arthur gives his sword to Morgan "pour la fiance qu'il
avoit en li." [93] But in *Le Morte Darthur* King Arthur's trust is
exceptional because it exists not between lord and vassal, but
between members of the same family, brother and sister. Accordingly, when Morgan attends Lot's funeral, Malory explains
that "ther com thydir kynge Uryens, sir Uwaynes fadir, and
Morgan le Fay, hys wyff, *that was kynge Arthurs syster*" (78;
italics mine), while the *Suite* only observes that "li roi Uriiens i
vint et Morgue sa feme." [94] The kinship of Arthur and Morgan
is stressed again in the parenthesis about Morgan and Accolon:
"for grete trust Arthur betoke the scawberde unto Morgan le
Fay, *hys sister*. And she loved another knyght bettir than her
husbande kynge Uriens, othir Arthure. And she wolde have had
Arthure *hir brother* slayne . . ." (79; italics mine). Malory's use
of the appositives *hys sister* and *hir brother* points to the un-
naturalness of Morgan's intended fratricide. This is also the
inference which Malory adds to his tale of "Arthur and Accolon." When Morgan's plot is at last discovered, King Arthur
voices his disillusionment in an invented comment which re-
peats Malory's earlier point of view: "God knowyth I have
honoured hir and worshipped hir more than all my kyn, and
more have I trusted hir than my wyff and all my kyn aftir"
(146). The Morgan-Accolon episode represents, then, a failure
of confidence among members of Arthur's own family and

court, and in this respect the motif has its place among the other foreshadowings of destiny at the interment of King Lot. In the prophetic funeral scene Malory has taken up the foreshadowings in his source, remodeled them, and added others of his own devising to form a design of themes that will extend the full distance of Arthurian history in *Le Morte Darthur*. The Dolorous Stroke brings vengeance to all knights, as it does to Balin, whose sword "pleased hym muche" (63); the Grail adventures will "com amonge you and be encheved" (78), reaching an end though not a victory; feuding befalls the sons of King Lot and Pellinor as Gawain seeks revenge for "the deth of hys fadir" (77); Morgan "wolde have had Arthur hir brother slayne" (79) through her mistrust and treachery; and in "a grete batayle besydes Salysbiry, Mordred hys own sonne" (79) will be against King Arthur. Even Guenevere is involved, for Arthur does not value her confidence: he has trusted Morgan above "my wyff and all my kin aftir" (146). Each of the themes invoked at Lot's funeral pronounces upon Malory's Arthurian world a separate element of its doom; like faults in the earth, each further unsettles the Round Table ideal until eventually it is lost in the upheavals at Benwick and Salisbury.

Like its French source, the "Tale of King Arthur" is a narrative supported by numerous allusions which broaden its perspective and link it to the body of Arthurian matter. But, as we have seen above, it is Malory's particular aim to draw the Arthurian themes together into new patterns of order and coherence.

CONCLUSION

Any extensive literary reworking of traditional materials calls for an estimate based upon its new terms and its particular qualities. Malory's treatment of inherited matter in the "Tale of

King Arthur," which has here been described as "largely unprec- edented," likewise gives rise to unavoidable questions about *Le Morte Darthur* as a whole. What is the nature of the book Malory wrote? Does he move toward a type of medieval tragedy, or does he attempt a heroic strain within the frame of ro- mance? What is the meaning of the Arthurian story to Malory? Perhaps the earliest distinction Malory achieves in *Le Morte Darthur* is that, unlike its sources, the "Tale of King Arthur" deals with Uther-Merlin-Arthur history not as phenomenon but as predestiny. In Malory's hands Logres is transformed from a battle-doomed kingdom where fortunes are determined by blind prophecy into a nation that shapes itself under the particular burden of a code of chivalry.

The shortcomings of the Arthurian code, and of the society which follows it, are to be found in the code's limitations. It is too inflexible and too static; it cannot embrace enough of the contingencies inherent in the human situation. Indeed, though it may at first inspire order and impose justice, it becomes finally the weakest aspect of Camelot because the Arthurian demonology which it expresses is weak. The knights are aware of giants of evil; otherwise there would be no code to combat them. But visible demons are most quickly toppled, and the code is ineffective against other demons that move men from within: it fails to articulate the need of accommodating large disparities, of compromise, of expanding tolerance. As *Le Morte Darthur* unfolds, the Arthurian characters will move in a system of order which ultimately fails them, and which turns the struc- ture of their society into chaos again. Malory's type of progress from disorder to coherence and thence to disorder again is not in itself unique in Arthurian literature. The *Suite du Merlin* achieved in the Grail quest a truly central motive which of- fered a sense of direction, an exceptional goal, an extraordinary challenge to test the moral sinew of a battle-proven court. But this test was spiritual and not social, a contest with the divine rather than the human, whereas it is above all else the struggle of man with himself that lies at the heart of *Le Morte Darthur*. For Malory the quest of the Grail will be less important than what it implies, in failure, about chivalric men. The "Tale of King Arthur" serves as Malory's preparation and earliest illustration of this kind of human struggle.

Malory's idea of kingship is no less unusual than his code of knighthood. Late in *Le Morte Darthur*, Mador de la Porte expresses this idea when he accuses Guenevere of treason in the Poisoned Apple story: " 'My gracious lorde,' seyde sir Madore, 'ye muste holde me excused, for thoughe ye be oure kynge, in that degré ye ar but a knyght as we ar, and ye ar sworne unto knyghthode als welle as we be' " (1050).[95] The equality which Arthur shares with his knights is apparent later when the Round Table is disrupted by the factions siding with Lancelot against Arthur: " 'And now hit ys fallen so,' seyde the kynge, 'that I may nat with my worshyp but my quene muste suffir dethe, and was sore amoved' " (1174). Again: "And ryght so was hit ordayned for quene Gwenyver: bycause sir Mordred was ascaped sore wounded, and the dethe of thirtene knyghtes of the Rounde Table, thes previs and experyenses caused kynge Arthur to commaunde the quene to the fyre and there to be brente" (1174). In Malory's source it is the barons, not Arthur, who condemn the queen to death. Malory's reversal of this procedure forces upon Arthur a delicate choice in which, pointedly enough, the preservation of the Round Table outweighs loyalty to one's queen.[96] As we have seen, Arthur's dilemma in this later instance

[95] This statement and the two that follow (p. 1174) are Malory's additions. Cf. Vinaver's notes on the passages cited.

[96] Cf. *Works*, p. 1184: "And much more I am soryar for my good knyghtes losse than for the losse of my fayre quene; for quenys I myght have inow, but such a felyship of good knyghtes shall never be togydirs in no company" (sourceless).

is the same kind that others of his knights have faced since the
founding of the order. Had Pellinor but stopped in his hasty
quest at Arthur's wedding feast, he could have prevented the
suicide of his own daughter—and even though he is unaware of
this condition, Pellinor is held responsible. His son Tor, likewise, must choose between appeals for vengeance and for mercy,
one from an offended lady, the other from a defeated knight; he
is reduced to dealing his justice on a "first-come" basis and obeys
the lady's wish. The code of chivalry, even after it is sworn and
established, is insufficient to mediate cases such as these. Worse,
it has a creaking stiffness in the amendments which Malory
later adds. One example is this: "For the custom was such at
that tyme, that all maner of [s]hamefull death was called treson"
(1050). Thus when Sir Patrise is killed even the queen will be
hastily put to the stake for a murder of which she is innocent,
and the death of the Maid of Astolat will certainly darken
Lancelot's record—to say nothing of the deaths of Lanceor and
Columbe in their adventure with Balin (68–72; 568). But nowhere is the issue more dramatically set forth than in the
astonishing cry of Lamorak, who, as Gaherys cuts off his
mother's head, accuses Balin le Sauvage of killing King Lot:

> "A, sir Gaherys, kynght of the Table Rounde! Fowle and
> evyll have ye done, and to you grete shame! Alas, why have ye
> slayne youre modir that bare you? For with more ryght ye
> shulde have slayne me!"
>
> "The offence haste thou done," seyde sir Gaherys, "nat-
> withstondynge a man is borne to offir his servyse, but yett
> sholdyst thou beware with whom thou medelyst, for thou
> haste put my bretherne and me to a shame; and thy fadir
> slew oure fadir, and thou to ly by oure modir is to muche shame
> for us to suffir. And as for thy fadir, kynge Pellynor, my
> brother sir Gawayne and I slew hym."
>
> "Ye ded the more wronge," seyde sir Lamerok, "for my fadir

slew nat your fadir: hit was Balyn le Saveage! And as yett my fadyrs deth is nat revenged." (612) [97]

Here indeed is the utterance of demons raging within—wild accusation, misdirected revenge, filial treachery, the breakdown of coherence itself, with no appeal to any code above the elemental law of feud.

The limited relevance and efficacy of the code presented in the "Tale of King Arthur" weakens the whole structure of Arthurian life, and this fact becomes evident in the equivocation of good men and the mistrust of everyone. No one can be believed—neither King Mark, whose letters press truth into the service of falsehood (616-17), nor Morgan le Fay, whose unreliable but truthful warnings attest the perversion of value and order in Camelot (617). In the end nothing is left of the court whose ambition earlier soared while its attainment held fast to the earth: Arthur is transported to Avalon, the knights are dispersed, the aim and meaning of Camelot's life are disrupted.

When one looks forward to the remaining sections of *Le Morte Darthur*, with the themes initiated in the "Tale of King Arthur" well in mind, he can see that what will endue the *Morte Darthur* with its tragic character is the sense of wasted potential; what will relieve it of mere futility is the idea, urged by Malory, that even in the smoke of ruin the men and women involved understand what they have lost. This point will be put forward by Malory in his scene of Lancelot's visit to Guenevere, where the queen acknowledges that "thorow the and me ys the f[lou]re of kyngis and [knyghtes] destroyed" (1252; Vinaver's emendations).[98] Arthur himself, aware that he has epitomized the chivalry of England, will complain of the

---

[97] Sourceless; cf. Vinaver's note on this passage.
[98] The figure is typically Malory's. Cf. *Works*, pp. 117–18 and p. 127. Vinaver notes that Malory expands the remorse expressed in the source: *ibid.*, p. 1640.

strife with Lancelot: "me sore repentith that ever sir Launcelot sholde be ayenste me, for now I am sure the noble felyshyp of the Rounde Table ys brokyn for ever" (1174). And the meaning of the fall of the ideal Round Table will be unmistakable in Arthur's remark to Bedivere as he is rowed to Avalon:

> Than sir Bedwere cryed and seyde,
>
> "A, my lorde Arthur, what shall becom of me, now ye go frome me and leve me here alone amonge myne enemyes?"
>
> "Comforte thyselff," seyde the kynge, "and do as well as thou mayste, for in me ys no truste for to truste in." (1240) [99]

The sense that a time of greatness has eluded the grasp of men will also be the theme of Ector's threnody for Lancelot, where each superlative is cut by the reminder that what was had is lost, and not likely to return: "And thou were the godelyest persone that ever cam emonge prees of knyghtes, and thou was the mekest man and the jentyllest that ever ete in halle emonge ladyes, and thou were the sternest knyght to thy mortal foo that ever put spere in the reeste" (1259).[100] None of Malory's sources makes the same evaluations, and in none do the characters move, as in *Le Morte Darthur,* toward an understanding of their own history. To provide the foundation for this great theme, and to make clear its presence even in the earliest days of the Round Table, is the purpose underlying Malory's highly original presentation in the "Tale of King Arthur."

[99] Sourceless; cf. *ibid.,* p. 1637.

[100] Sourceless; Vinaver cites a similar elegy for Gawain from the alliterative *Morte Arthure (Ibid.,* p. 1646).

CHAPTER II

"THE TALE OF KING ARTHUR AND THE EMPEROR LUCIUS":
THE RISE OF LANCELOT

BY MARY E. DICHMANN

I

The re-evaluation of Malory's work which followed the appearance of Professor Vinaver's edition showed clearly that the
second division—"The Tale of King Arthur and the Emperor
Lucius"—merited closer attention than it had previously received. Since it appeared that Caxton had reduced Tale II to
about half its length in the Winchester manuscript, the relationship of this "Tale" to its source and to the whole body of
Malory's work needed reconsideration. The main source had
long been identified as the alliterative *Morte Arthure*, an
anonymous fourteenth-century poem which survives in the
unique Thornton manuscript.[1] This manuscript, generally considered corrupt, is almost certainly a different version of the

[1] *Morte Arthure, or The Death of Arthur*, ed. E. Brock, EETS-OS, No. 8
(London, 1871); I have used numbers in parentheses for reference to lines
in this edition. For recent discussion of this poem, see William Matthews,
The Tragedy of Arthur (Berkeley and Los Angeles, 1960) and R. S. Loomis
(ed.), *Arthurian Literature in the Middle Ages* (Oxford, 1959), pp.
521–26.

poem from that which Malory knew; [2] nevertheless, it is helpful in a study of Malory's use of source materials. Such a study can, of course, throw much light upon his ultimate literary purposes.

The *Morte Arthure* is a long poem; the Thornton manuscript contains 4,346 lines. Its verse form is the four-stressed, alliterative line, and its style is robust, direct, and action-packed. It glories in deeds of strength and courage, and it gives far more space to detailed and bloody accounts of battles than to worship of ladies or to descriptions of knightly courtesy. The poem opens with Arthur already securely established in the kingship, as lord both of the British Isles and of large territories on the continent. The action begins on New Year's Day, when messengers arrive from the Emperor Lucius of Rome to demand that Arthur journey there to pay the homage and tribute owing since the time of King Uther. Arthur entertains the messengers at a feast and then sends them back to Lucius with his answer: instead of visiting Rome to pay homage, he will invade the lands of the Emperor. In this undertaking Arthur has the support of many thousands of knights, whose strength and splendor strike terror into the hearts of the messengers.

Both rulers prepare for war, each assuming personal command of his armies. Before leaving Britain at the head of his invasion force, Arthur proclaims Mordred his viceroy and consigns to him the care of both the kingdom and the Queen. Mordred is unhappy about this assignment, preferring to join

[2] The fact that "The Tale of King Arthur and the Emperor Lucius" contains many alliterative passages not paralleled in the Thornton MS attests the probable existence of a lost version of the *Morte Arthure*. A discussion of this hypothetical lost version may be found in an article by Tania Vorontzoff, "Malory's Story of Arthur's Roman Campaign," *Medium Aevum*, VI (1937), 99–121, and in an article by Eugène Vinaver and E. V. Gordon, "New Light on the Text of the Alliterative Morte Arthure," *Medium Aevum*, VI (1937), 84–85. Vinaver summarizes these longer discussions; see *Works*, pp. 1360–61.

the campaign, but Arthur is adamant. Aboard the ship from Sandwich to Barfleet, Arthur dreams of a fight between a dragon and a huge black bear, from which the dragon emerges victorious. The interpretation of the dream is that Arthur will overcome either a giant or the tyrants who oppress his people. Arthur's first act after disembarking is to fight and overcome a giant who has been killing the inhabitants of the land.

Having disposed of the giant, Arthur then begins his campaign against Lucius. In the course of the war, there take place the events familiar to the readers of heroic poetry: urgent pleas for help by those whose lands have been ravaged, exchange of challenges between King and Emperor, skirmishing and taking of prisoners, single combats and full-scale battles. Most of these happenings are blood-drenched. At last, after the loss of many brave knights on both sides, Arthur meets Lucius on the field of battle and kills him. Pursuing his advantage, he then presses on into Italy to establish his mastery of all Europe with the proud boast that he will be crowned by the Pope at Christmas. At this climactic point in the story, the usefulness of the poem to Malory ceased; he ended here his narrative of the Roman war.

This brief summary of the first 3,218 lines of the Thornton *Morte Arthure* indicates a close parallel between the action of Malory's "Tale" and that of the Middle English poem. The similarity does not mean, however, that this poem—or the postulated lost version—is the only source which Malory used. Malory may have known many Arthurian writings: for example, Geoffrey of Monmouth, Layamon, Wace, and other earlier pieces both French and English. In fact a study of "The Tale of King Arthur and the Emperor Lucius" yields more evidence to support than to refute the belief that before writing the story of the Roman war Malory had knowledge of some Arthurian

matter besides the alliterative poem.[3] Although the version of
the *Morte Arthure* with which Malory was acquainted was probably fuller than that preserved in the Thornton manuscript,
we need not assume that every incident in "The Tale of King
Arthur and the Emperor Lucius" not included in the Thornton
manuscript must have appeared in the lost version. A case in
point is the passage describing the behavior of certain young
knights after the Roman ambassadors have delivered to Arthur
the terms of Lucius' demands:

> Than somme of the yonge knyghtes, heryng this their message,
> wold have ronne on them to have slayne them, sayenge that
> it was a rebuke to alle the knyghtes there beyng present to
> suffre them to saye so to the kynge. And anone the kynge
> commaunded that none of them upon payne of dethe to
> myssaye them ne doo them ony harme. (186–87)

Malory's use of this incident, related by Wace but not found
in the Thornton manuscript, argues as easily for his familiarity
with the work of the Anglo-Norman poet as for his having used
a hypothetical lost *Morte Arthure* which contained it.[4] Since
the wording and the cadence of the passage do not suggest an
alliterative poem as source,[5] we may more reasonably assume

[3] Vorontzoff, "Malory's Story," p. 121, n. 1: "Malory seems to retain . . .
the characteristic set phrases indicating transition: 'Now leave we . . . and
speak we' etc., or 'Now turn we to' which he found in his French sources
('or laisse le conte a parler de ... et retourne a parler de')." Although this
evidence of Malory's acquaintance with French Arthurian romances before
writing "The Tale of King Arthur and the Emperor Lucius" is not conclusive, it suggests such knowledge.
[4] *Ibid.*, pp. 103–4. Miss Vorontzoff mentions that Wace relates this incident, but does not credit the *Roman de Brut* with being Malory's immediate source. Instead, she postulates a sequence of lost MSS, which
carried the incident down into the lost *Morte Arthure* where it was read
by Malory.
[5] Alliterative passages which echo the phraseology of the *Morte Arthure*

that Malory here borrowed directly from Wace than conjectur
that he found the passage in a lost *Morte Arthure*.[6] Both textua
evidence and logic therefore suggest that Malory knew other
Arthurian romances when he "reduced" the *Morte Arthure* into
his "Tale of King Arthur and the Emperor Lucius."

Through comparison of this "Tale" with the *Morte Arthure*,
we shall see numerous evidences of Malory's originality in treating the material. The main conclusion to which this evidence
points is that Malory so adapted the *Morte Arthure* as to fit
Tale II into his over-all plan for *Le Morte Darthur*.[7] The discussion which follows will stress three matters: (1) Malory's
structural alterations; (2) his changes in characterization of
Lancelot and Arthur; and (3) his important shifts in emphasis
in presenting Tristram, Gawain, Bors, Kay, and Bedivere.

---

are to be found throughout "The Tale of King Arthur and the Emperor
Lucius."

[6] This assumption is further supported by Malory's account of the
initial battle with Lucius; like Wace, Malory credits Bors with being the
first British warrior to seek combat with the Romans, whereas the *Morte
Arthure*, following Layamon, gives the adventure to Gawain.

[7] The unity of *Le Morte Darthur* is not universally accepted. In his edition of the Winchester manuscript, Vinaver explains and defends his now
famous theory that Malory's tales were not intended to present a unified
history but are separate romances (see *Works*, pp. xxx–xxxv). J. A. W.
Bennett in his review of Vinaver's edition, *RES*, XXV (1949), 161, accepts the theory with qualifications; a review by R. H. Wilson, *MP*,
XLVI (1948), 136, tentatively rejects it, but remarks that Vinaver's in-
ferences have made it impossible any longer to assume the unity of
Malory's work without a careful re-examination of the tales; Mary E.
Dichmann in "Characterization in Malory's *Tale of Arthur and Lucius*,"
PMLA, LXV (1950), 877–95, argues against the separate romances
theory; and Helen I. Wroten in her 1950 University of Illinois dissertation, "Malory's *Tale of King Arthur and the Emperor Lucius* Compared
with its Source, the Alliterative *Morte Arthure*," presents cogent arguments for the unity of the work (summarized in *Microfilm Abstracts*, XI
[1951], 127–28). In *English Literature at the Close of the Middle Ages*, Oxford History of English Literature (Oxford, 1945), II, ii, 190–91, Sir Edmund Chambers, who had some knowledge of Vinaver's conclusions before the publication of *Works*, rejects the theory.

II

The most obvious structural change which Malory made in adapting the plot of the *Morte Arthure* to "The Tale of King Arthur and the Emperor Lucius" is his omission of the last 1,128 lines of the poem. The reason for the omission is, of course, clear enough when one considers that Malory was at this point near the beginning of his version of the whole Arthurian story. The last episode of the *Morte Arthure* brings the Arthurian story to a rapid close without mention of the Grail quest and the adultery of Lancelot and Guenevere, material which Malory was to treat in detail before giving his account of the great battle at Salisbury and of Arthur's death.

The portion of the *Morte Arthure* which Malory omits relates the story of Arthur's downfall and death. Just as Arthur has reached the crest of victory and has made arrangements to be crowned by the Pope, he has a fearsome dream, which is interpreted to mean that he is about to suffer a change of fortune. This change comes about very soon when he receives word from Britain that Mordred has seized his kingdom and married Guenevere, who has borne the false viceroy a child. Arthur rushes home to subdue the traitor and, after fierce encounters during which Gawain and other brave knights are killed, meets Mordred in their last battle. Arthur kills Mordred in hand-to-hand combat, but only after he himself has received a mortal wound. Arthur's death does not occur immediately: he has time to remove himself to a manor house near Glastonbury and seek the attentions of a physician before realizing that he is fated to die. When the realization comes to him, he prepares himself to depart this world: he asks for the services of a priest, names

Sir Constantine his heir, and commands that Mordred's children be slain. He dies soon thereafter and is buried at Glastonbury, lamented by the remnants of his noble court.

That Malory in Tale II ignored this portion of the *Morte Arthure* can best be explained by the theory that he had more extensive plans for his Arthurian presentation than he could execute if he followed closely the course of events in the poem. These plans must have included the incorporation into his own Arthurian narrative of material which, by logic and chronological probability, could have taken place only after the Roman war. Otherwise, it would have been more reasonable for him to have retold the whole story of the *Morte Arthure*.

An equally significant structural change in Malory's adaptation of the *Morte Arthure* concerns his treatment of Mordred and Constantine. In the alliterative poem Mordred is left as an unwilling regent in Britain upon Arthur's departure for the Roman war. In "The Tale of King Arthur and the Emperor Lucius" he is not mentioned at all, though his birth and the prophecy of his evil-doing were duly noted in the preceding "Tale of King Arthur." Presumably Malory felt that the time of the Roman war was too early for Mordred to enter into the action of the story; he wanted Mordred's villainy to mature slowly and did not wish to invest him with importance so early in Arthur's history. We should also note that Malory borrowed the knight whom the dying Arthur of the *Morte Arthure* designates as his heir, Sir Constantine, to be co-regent with Sir Baudwen of Bretagne during the king's absence in the campaign against Lucius. This is the Sir Constantine who, according to Malory, "aftir was kynge aftir Arthurs dayes" (195).

These changes from the source are too important to be accidental. They point inescapably to the conclusion that Malory must have written "The Tale of King Arthur and the Emperor Lucius" as part of a larger whole.[8]

III

The chief figures in *Le Morte Darthur* are Arthur and Lancelot, the two characters most changed in "The Tale of King Arthur and the Emperor Lucius" from their portrayal in the *Morte Arthure*. The most plausible reason for the changes is that Malory had in mind a large, over-all plan for his whole work into which he wanted to fit the appearances of these two knights in Tale II. Thus he toned down the stern, warlike character of Arthur to suit the requirements of the ideal of kingly courtesy and aggrandized the character of Lancelot in order to prepare him for his pre-eminent role in *Le Morte Darthur*. Lancelot probably presented the more difficult problem. Since he is mentioned only six times in the *Morte Arthure*,[9] a specific place had to be made for him in "The Tale of King Arthur and the Emperor Lucius."

Malory's aggrandizement of Lancelot begins with the first sentence of "The Tale of King Arthur and the Emperor Lucius":

Hyt befelle whan kyng Arthur had wedded quene Gwenyvere and fulfylled the Rounde Table, and so aftir his mervelous knyghtis and he had venquyshed the moste party of his enemyes, than sone aftir com sir Launcelot de Lake unto the

[8] In *The Tragedy of Arthur* (pp. 172–73) Matthews discusses Malory's omission of the last quarter of the alliterative poem. Although he suggests that Malory may have wished to elaborate the history of Arthur and consequently could not kill his hero, he seems to suggest that the chief reason for the omission was the repugnance which Malory felt for the moral ideas presented in the last part of the poem.

[9] *Morte Arthure*, lines 368, 1720, 1999, 2073, 3638, and 4266. It should be noted that lines 3638 and 4266 occur in the section of the poem not used by Malory.

courte, and sir Trystrams come that tyme also, and than kyng
Arthur helde a ryal feeste and Table Rounde. (185)

In naming Sir Lancelot second only to the king among the
members of the Round Table, Malory sets the pattern that he
uses throughout *Le Morte Darthur*, the pattern of Lancelot's
supremacy.[10] He did not, it should be noted, find this pattern
ready-made in the *Morte Arthure*; the poem makes no mention
of Lancelot until he appears as a member of the king's council,
pledging with the others his loyalty to Arthur in the coming
war with Rome. In the *Morte Arthure* it is Gawain who is, aside
from Arthur, the indisputable hero.

At the council meeting which Arthur calls after the arrival
of the Roman ambassadors to demand that Arthur pay tribute
to Rome, Malory follows the *Morte Arthure* in his description
of Lancelot's behavior, but changes the emphasis to suit his
own characterization of the hero. In the *Morte Arthure*, Lancelot makes the same kind of speech as the other knights who
offer their support to the king:

> "By oure Lorde," quod sir Launcelott, "now lyghttys
>   myne herte!
> I loue Gode of this loue this lordes has avowede!
> Nowe may lesse mene haue leue to say whatt theme
>   lykes,
> And hafe no lettyng be lawe, bot lystynnys thise
>   wordez;
> I salle be at journee with gentille knyghtes,
> On a jamby stede fulle jolyly graythide,
> Or any journee be-gane to juste with hym selfene,
> Emange alle his geauntez genyuers and other,
> Stryke hym styfflye fro his stede, with strenghe of
>   myne handys,

---

[10] Even in "The Tale of King Arthur," which covers the years before
Lancelot was old enough to prove himself as a knight, Malory mentions
his future prowess (162, 179–80).

ffor alle tha steryne is stour, that in his stale
    houys!
Be my retenu arayede, I rekke bott a lyttille
To make rowtte in-to Rome, with ryotous knyghtes!
With-in a seuenyghte daye, with sex score helmes,
I salle be seene on the see, saile whene the
    lykes." (368–81)

By condensing this speech and slightly changing it, Malory alters Lancelot's stereotyped battle-boast into the bold, ardent
promise of a very young man:

Than leepe in yong sir Launcelot de Laake with a lyght herte
and seyde unto kynge Arthure, "Thoughe my londis marche
nyghe thyne enemyes, yet shall I make myne avow aftir my
power that of good men of armys aftir my bloode thus many I
shall brynge with me: twenty thousand helmys in haubirkes
attyred that shall never fayle you whyles our lyves lastyth."
(189–90)

A comparison of the two passages quoted above shows the skill
with which Malory vitalizes the figure of "young" Lancelot.
Adding a significant detail to Lancelot's statement—the fact
that his lands border on Lucius' domain (and would, therefore,
be vulnerable to attack) [11]—he makes Lancelot's offer of assistance to his king a more daring act and a greater indication
of his personal loyalty than it is in the *Morte Arthure*. Malory
also multiplies the number of men whose services Lancelot
promises to Arthur from "sex score helmes" to twenty thousand. By these slight changes, Malory's Lancelot is individual-
ized; the conventional warrior becomes a bold and devoted

---

[11] In a note on Lancelot's speech, Vinaver remarks that "it is not clear
to what lands Lancelot is referring" (*Works*, p. 1367). If Malory is here
allowed knowledge of the whole Arthurian legend, however, it would be
clear that he means to designate Lancelot's own country in France border-
ing on Lucius' domain.

youth, whose courage and initiative foreshadow a noble future.[12]

Later in the story Malory gives Sir Lancelot an important role in adventures in which he plays no part in the *Morte Arthure*. After Arthur has crossed to France and has had his first encounter with Lucius' forces, he summons several of his chief knights to convoy the Roman prisoners to Paris. In the *Morte Arthure*, the king gives Sir Cador command of the company and names eleven knights to accompany him, excluding Lancelot. In "The Tale of King Arthur and the Emperor Lucius," however, Malory is consistent with his policy of accenting Lancelot's importance; he not only adds him to the expedition, but even places him above Sir Cador in command. Having listed the knights whom the king calls to him, Malory says:

> . . . and also [Arthur] . . . called sir Launcelot in heryng of all peple, and seyde, "I pray the, sir, as thow lovys me, take hede to thes other knyghtes and boldely lede thes presoners unto Paryse towne, there for to be kepte surely as they me love woll have. And yf ony rescowe befalle, moste I affye the in me, as Jesu me helpe." (212)

Because Malory has here given Lancelot the place occupied by Sir Cador in the *Morte Arthure*, he finds it necessary to reassign speeches originally made by the latter knight, sometimes giving the entire speech to Lancelot, sometimes allowing Cador

---

[12] *Works*, p. 1367. Vinaver's note on the line, *Than leepe in yong sir Launcelot de Laake with a lyght herte*, shows that he also sees a change in the character of Malory's Lancelot. He makes here much the same statement as was made earlier in his article written in collaboration with E. V. Gordon, "New Light," p. 85: "Logically [Lancelot] . . . should not appear until Book VI, but Malory seems to have already decided to make him the protagonist, and deliberately enhances the prowess and glory won by him in the Roman expedition. We are told several times that Lancelot is still young, having only recently been knighted; yet Malory will not allow him to be eclipsed by Gawain, who in the *Morte Arthure* is far above all other knights."

to voice his agreement, and sometimes splitting the original speech into dialogue. He never lets the reader forget that it is Lancelot who makes the decisions, Lancelot who gives the commands, and Lancelot who is always first to be addressed (212–16). When Arthur's knights are ambushed by the Romans and battle is joined, it again is Lancelot who so distinguishes himself in gallantry that Malory interpolates in the story his own editorial comment:

> And sir Launcelot ded so grete dedys of armys that day that Sir Cador and all the Romaynes had mervayle of his myght, for there was nother kynge, cayser, nother knyght that day myght stonde hym ony buffette. Therefore was he honoured dayes of his lyff, for never ere or that day was he proved so well, for he and sir Bors and sir Lyonel was but late afore at an hyghe feste made all three knyghtes. (216)

Besides suggesting in this comment the life-long honor that Lancelot will enjoy, Malory stresses his probable future greatness in the account of the conversation between Cador and Arthur after the knights had returned to their camp:

> "Sir," seyde sir Cador, "there was none of us that fayled othir, but of the knyghthode of sir Launcelot hit were mervayle to telle. And of his bolde cosyns ar proved full noble knyghtes, but of wyse wytte and of grete strengthe of his ayge sir Launcelot hath no felowe."
>
> Whan the kynge herde sir Cador sey such wordys he seyde, "Hym besemys for to do such dedis." (217)

Lancelot's last active appearance in "The Tale of King Arthur and the Emperor Lucius" is again suggestive of his future greatness; in fact, on this occasion his feats are so notable that he is admired not as a young knight of promise but as a seasoned warrior. The particular adventure in which he is engaged occurs during the final battle with Lucius. The *Morte*

Arthure contains brief mention of the incident, but in Malory's hands it is characteristically elaborated.

> Than sir Launcelot lepe forth with his stede evyn streyght unto sir Lucyus, and in his wey he smote thorow a kynge that stoode althirnexte hym, and his name was Jacounde, a Sarezen full noble. And than he russhed forth unto sir Lucyus and smote hym on the helme with his swerde, that he felle to the erthe; and syth he rode thryse over hym on a rowe, and so toke the baner of Rome and rode with hit away unto Arthure hymself. *And all seyde that hit sawe there was never knyght dud more worshyp in his dayes.* (220; italics mine)

As a result of this passage, we see a Lancelot who has come of age; Malory has completed his development from an eager, newly-made knight to a battle-hardened warrior. Malory's summation of the opinions about Lancelot, given in the italicized sentence at the end of the quotation, shows that the hero has attained full knightly stature. Malory describes him again in the course of the battle, courageously following Arthur in the final rally against Lucius, aiding Sir Lovel to rescue the wounded Bedivere, and pursuing the fleeing Romans to avenge the hurts of Bedivere and Kay (222–24). In the rest of the story Lancelot does not figure until after the final victory when Arthur grants large tracts of the conquered land to him and his cousin Bors (245).

Malory's handling of Lancelot's growth from an untried knight to the acknowledged champion of the battlefield shows careful design, bearing the marks of meticulous and foresighted workmanship. Such care seems to suggest strongly that while writing the story of the Roman wars Malory was thinking of the position Lancelot would have in the coming portions of *Le Morte Darthur*.

Malory's treatment of the character of Arthur is also important to any discussion of the place held by "The Tale of

King Arthur and the Emperor Lucius" in the design of the
entire work. Just as Malory aggrandized the character of Lance
lot, whom the *Morte Arthure* had almost disregarded, so we
find him reshaping the Arthur of the alliterative poem for the
apparent purpose of making his character consistent with that
of Arthur in the other "Tales" of *Le Morte Darthur*. The
changes in his characterization of Arthur are often subtle, but
their direction is always the same: they are calculated to con-
vert the king from the chieftain of the *Morte Arthure*, respected
for his strength and daring rather than loved for his gentleness,
to the chivalric leader, whose courage is tempered by self-
control.

The gain in dignity and manliness which Arthur makes
through Malory's handling is apparent when parallel passages
from the *Morte Arthure* and "The Tale of King Arthur and the
Emperor Lucius" are examined. First, let us look at Arthur's
reaction to the demand of the Roman ambassadors that he pay
tribute to Rome. In the lines from the *Morte Arthure* Arthur's
rage exhibits itself with primitive violence:

> The kyng blyschit one the beryne with his brode eghne,
> That fulle brymly or breth brynte as the gledys;
> Keste colours as kynge with crouelle lates,
> Luked as a lyone, and on his lyppe bytes! (116–19)

In the parallel passage from "The Tale of King Arthur and the
Emperor Lucius," Malory eliminates the manifestation of
Arthur's rage, though not its impact, by concentrating on the
grim immobility of the scene: "Whan kynge Arthure wyste
what they mente he loked up with his gray yghen and angred
at the messyngers passyng sore. Than were this messyngers aferde
and knelyd stylle and durste nat aryse, they were so aferde of
his grymme countenaunce" (185).

A second example of the increased self-control to be found in

Malory's Arthur occurs after Arthur has reached his domains in France. One of his subjects reports to him the evil deeds of a giant who has been preying upon his people. In both accounts Arthur is grieved, but his manner of showing his grief is very different. In the *Morte Arthure* he again gives way to an exhibition of emotion:

> Thane romyez the ryche kynge for rewthe of the pople,
> Raykez ryghte to a tente, and restez no lengere!
> He welterys, he wristeles, he wryngez hys handez!
> Thare was no wy of this werlde, that wyste whatt
>   he menede! (888–91)

Arthur's reaction to the same situation in "The Tale of King Arthur and the Emperor Lucius" shows a manly restraint: "The kynge seyde, 'Good man, pees! and carpe to me no more. Thy soth sawys have greved sore my herte.' Than he turnys towarde his tentys and carpys but lytyll" (199).

The self-control which Arthur exhibits here increases his dignity as a king and a leader of men, for as the truism points out, the ability to command oneself necessarily precedes the ability to command others. Whether or not Malory consciously applied this principle to his study of Arthur's character, he certainly acted upon it in altering the tone of another tempestuous scene in the *Morte Arthure*. In both accounts, as has already been mentioned, a band of knights is assigned to convoy to Paris the prisoners that were taken in the first battle with Lucius' forces. The Romans prepare an ambush for the British knights, but are discovered before they can make a surprise attack. However, in spite of their inferior numbers, Arthur's men decide to join battle with the Romans. The encounter results in victory for the British, but it is a victory that costs the lives of several knights. After delivering the prisoners and returning to the British encampment, Sir Cador reports these facts to

Arthur. In the *Morte Arthure*, the effect on the king is powerful:

> Thane the worthy kynge wrythes, and wepede with
>   his eghne,
> Karpes to his cosyne sir Cador theis wordez,—
> "Sir Cador, thi corage confundez vs alle!
> Kowardely thow castez owtte alle my beste knyghttez!
> To putte mene in perille, it es no pryce holdene,
> Bot the partyes ware puruayede, and powere arayede;
> When they ware stade on a strenghe, thou sulde
>   hafe with-stondene,
> Bot ȝif thowe wolde alle my steryne stroye fore
>   the nonys!" (1920–27)

In contrast to Arthur, Sir Cador restrains his wrath and answers with dignity:

> "Sir," sais sir Cador, "ȝe knowe wele ȝour selfene;
> ȝe are kynge in this kythe, karpe whatte ȝow lykys!
> Salle neuer vpbrayde me, that to thi burde langes,
> That I sulde blyne fore theire boste, thi byddynge
>   to wyrche;
> Whene any stirttez to stale, stuffe thame the
>   bettere,
> Ore thei wille be stonayede, and stroyeded in ȝone
>   strayte londez.
> I dide my delygens to daye, I doo me one lordez,
> And in daungere of dede fore dyuerse knyghttez,
> I hafe no grace to thi gree, bot syche grett wordez;
> ȝif I heuen my herte, my hape es no bettyre."
>
> (1928–37)

Realizing the mistake that he has made in upbraiding Sir Cador, Arthur is forced to retract his words:

> ȝofe sir Arthure ware angerde, he ansuers faire,
> "Thow has doughttily donne, sir duke, with thi
>   handez,

And has donne thy deuer with my dere knyghttez;
ffor-thy thow arte demyde, with dukes and erlez,
ffor one of the doughtyeste that dubbede was euer!
Thare es none ischewe of vs, on this erthe sprongene;
Thow arte apparant to be ayere, are one of thi
 childyre;
Thow arte my sister sone, for-sake salle I neuer!"

(1938–45)

Malory's adaptation of this incident shows Arthur in a much
etter light. He conducts himself with restraint, and he is not
ompelled to retract an unjustified accusation. He is of course
addened when he hears the list of knights who have been
illed, but he does not quarrel with Cador: "Than the kynge
 epte and with a keuerchoff wyped his iyen and sayde, 'Youre
orrage and youre hardynesse nerehande had you destroyed, for
nd ye had turned agayne ye had loste no worshyp, for I calle
it but foly to abyde whan knyghtes bene overmacched'" (217).
Iere is a sympathetic and respected leader, with whose policy
he knights may not always agree, but who will never be repri-
nanded by them for his lack of gratitude or his heedlessness of
 eir welfare.

Malory particularly emphasizes Arthur's sympathetic concern
 r his knights. At the end of the battle in which Lucius is
 illed, many of them are dead or wounded. Malory says:
. . . than relevys the kynge with his noble knyghtes and ren-
 ked over all the feldis for his bolde barouns. And tho that
 ere dede were buryed as their bloode asked, and they that
 yght be saved there was no salve spared nother no deyntés to
 ere that myght be gotyn for golde other sylver" (224). Thus
 r the account of Arthur's activities after the battle follows the
 liddle English poem. Then Malory adds his original humaniz-
 g statement: "And thus he let save many knyghtes that wente
 ever to recover, but for sir Kayes recovir and of sir Bedwers

the ryche was never man undir God so glad as hymself was (224). The poem merely remarks,

> He bydes for the beryenge of his bolde knyghtez,
> That in batelle with brandez ware broughte owte
> of lyfe, (2377–78)

and proceeds immediately with a list of the knights and their places of burial. Such a king may be respected for his generalship, but he is not a figure who could draw to him and hold together the fellowship of the Round Table. It is Malory again who supplies the missing ingredients of Arthur's chivalric greatness.

In accordance with the ideal of chivalry, Arthur should care for the welfare of his humble subjects as well as of his valiant knights. In the *Morte Arthure,* Arthur's attitude toward the common people is kindly, but lacks warmth; in "The Tale of King Arthur and the Emperor Lucius," Malory adds the warmth by giving to the story of the king's battle with the giant a characteristic touch, which shows Arthur's concern for the poor. This change from the source has to do with the person who reports the giant's evil deeds to the king; in the *Morte Arthure* he is called a "templar" (841), but in "The Tale of King Arthur and the Emperor Lucius" he is a "husbandman" (198). This alteration, slight as it is, takes Arthur out of exclusive contact with the nobility and puts him into a protective relationship with the commonalty. Although the *Morte Arthur* (1215–16), like "The Tale of King Arthur and the Emperor Lucius" (205), tells us that at the end of the battle Arthur distributes the treasure won from the giant among the people,[18] the effect is not the same, because the poet has not previously shown a personal tie between the king and his subjects.

The height of Arthur's kingly demeanor is found in the in-

[18] See also Vinaver's notes on this passage, p. 1373.

tructions which he gives to the Roman senators charged with
onvoying the bodies of their dead princes back to Rome after
he slaughter of Lucius and his chief warriors. In the *Morte
Arthure* the speech is definite and threatening:

> "Here are the kystis," quod the kynge, "kaire
>   ouer the mownttez;
> Mette fulle monee that ȝe haue mekylle ȝernede,
> The taxe and the trebutte of tene schore wynteres,
> That was tenefully tynte in tyme of oure elders.
> Saye to the senatoure, the ceté that ȝemes,
> That I sende hyme the somme, assaye how hyme likes!
> Bott byde theme neuere be so bolde, whylles my
>   blode regnes,
> Efte for to brawlle theme for my brode landez
> Ne to aske trybut ne taxe be nakyne tytle,
> Bot syche tresoure as this, whilles my tyme lastez."
>
> $(2342-51)$

n "The Tale of King Arthur and the Emperor Lucius," the
ing's speech is changed in tone from hot anger to grim coolness:

> "Now sey ye to the Potestate and all the lordys aftir that I
> sende hem the trybet that I owe to Rome, for this is the trew
> trybet that I and myne elders have loste this ten score wyntyrs.
> And sey hem as mesemes I have sent hem the hole somme,
> and *yf they thynke hit nat inowe, I shall amend hit whan that
> I com*. And ferthermore, I charge you to saye to them never
> to demaunde trybute ne taxe of me ne of my londes, for suche
> tresoure must they take as happyns us here." (225–26; italics
> mine)

Once again Malory has altered the Arthur of the poem to fit
he conception of the king which is found throughout *Le Morte
Darthur*.[14]

---

[14] In the Commentary (p. 1387) Vinaver points out that the italicized
ne in this quotation was Malory's addition to the speech, but draws no
onclusion.

IV

In addition to molding the character of Arthur into con
formity with his conception of the ideal chivalric king and to
preparing Lancelot for the adventures of his glorious future
Malory also concentrates attention upon other knights in "Th
Tale of King Arthur and the Emperor Lucius" who are late
to play important roles. The most important are Tristram and
Gawain. Since Tristram has no part in the *Morte Arthure*, an
reference which Malory makes to him had to be a consciou
addition and may be cited as proof both of Malory's familiarit
with the French cycles and of his conscious foreshadowing o
succeeding parts of his own story. Tristram is mentioned twic
in "The Tale of King Arthur and the Emperor Lucius": firs
in the introductory paragraph (185), where his name is couplec
with Lancelot's as having arrived at Arthur's court, and later in
the description of the departure of Arthur's forces for the Rc
man war. The second instance is as follows: "And sir Trystram
at that tyme beleft with kynge Marke of Cornuayle for th
love of La Beale Isode, wherefore sir Launcelot was passin
wrothe" (195). In these lines Malory hints at two stories which
will later assume great importance in *Le Morte Darthur*: th
stories of Tristram and Isolde and of Lancelot and Guenevere.[1]

Sir Gawain presented a different problem to Malory from
either Lancelot or Tristram, because he figures as importantl
in the *Morte Arthure* as King Arthur himself. In attemptin
to mold the story of the Roman wars into an episode that func
tions effectively within the completed whole, Malory foun
that Gawain had to be de-emphasized, just as Lancelot had t
be built up. His solution to this problem was to assign t

[15] Gordon and Vinaver in "New Light," p. 85, comment on Malory
anticipation of both Tristram and Lancelot in the story of the Roman wa

another knight some of Gawain's adventures in the *Morte Arthure,* and to have other knights accompany Gawain on expeditions which in the source he had undertaken alone. An example of the first device is found in the account of Arthur's initial battle with Lucius: in the *Morte Arthure* (1368 ff.) Gawain is the first of the British warriors to seek a Roman knight in combat, but in Malory's "Tale" (208) this honor is taken from him and given to Bors.[16] Then in Malory's account of the last battle with Lucius (222–23) Gawain, who leads an attack alone in the *Morte Arthure* (2218 ff.), is accompanied by Lancelot, Lovel, and various other heroes who equal him in might. By these devices, Malory manages to reduce Gawain's importance.

In adapting one incident from the *Morte Arthure,* Malory seems at first glance to have been inconsistent in his treatment of Gawain by adding to the hero's importance instead of subtracting from it. According to the *Morte Arthure* (1557–88), Sir Ewaine FitzHenry is sorely wounded in the first battle with Lucius; Arthur expresses great concern for him, swearing that a Roman senator who has just been captured will be held as a hostage for his recovery. In Malory's version (211), it is Gawain who is sorely wounded and for whom Arthur is concerned. The probable reason for this inconsistency is that in attempting to give unity to his story Malory has merely substituted a well-known name for an obscure one. Both Vinaver and Wilson point out that such substitutions are common in Malory, whose habit it was to concentrate attention on a few names familiar to the reader instead of mentioning numerous unfamiliar ones.[17]

[16] In a note on this passage (p. 1375) Vinaver remarks the fact that the *Morte Arthure* follows Layamon in giving this adventure to Gawain, but that all other versions give it to Bors or Gerin. This, in itself, seems further evidence of Malory's knowledge of the "French books" before he began writing "The Tale of King Arthur and the Emperor Lucius."

[17] Vinaver, *Malory* (Oxford, 1929), pp. 35–36, and R. H. Wilson, "Malory's Naming of Minor Characters," *JEGP,* XLII (1943), 364–85.

Sir Bors is among the lesser characters in Tale II whom
Malory apparently wished to develop for later use. He is, in
deed, an important figure in the total history, playing a large
part in subsequent tales, particularly in the Grail quest, though
he never attains the stature of Lancelot, Tristram, or Gawain.
In Tale II, Malory develops him into a character whose cour
age and knightly behavior the reader will remember.[18] He be
gins the aggrandizement of Bors by making him the first knight
to seek an encounter with a Roman in battle (208), a distinc
tion that in the *Morte Arthure* (1368 ff.) belongs to the heroic
Gawain. He then proceeds to insert Bors into the action of the
story, usually in the company of Lancelot. When, for example,
the knights who are escorting the prisoners to Paris become
aware of the ambush that has been laid for them, both Lancelot
and Cador express their eagerness to fight. Agreeing with
them, Bors also exhorts the other knights. Like Lancelot's, this
speech is an adaptation of part of Cador's speech in the *Morte
Arthure* (1726-37):

> "Ye sey well," seyde sir Borce, "lette us set on hem freyshly,
> and the worshyp shall be oures, and cause oure kyng to honoure
> us for ever and to gyff us lordshyppis and landys for oure noble
> dedys. And he that faynes hym to fyght, the devyl have his
> bonys! And who save ony knyghtes for lycoure of goodys tylle
> all be done and know who shall have the bettir, he doth nat
> knyghtly, so Jesu me helpe!" (214)

Bors' appearances in "The Tale of King Arthur and the
Emperor Lucius" after this speech are Malory's original addi
tions, since he is last mentioned in the *Morte Arthure* when his

[18] Bors (under the name "Boice" and its variants) is mentioned only
five times in the *Morte Arthure*: (1) line 1263, in a list of knights sent as
messengers to the Romans; (2) line 1378, as having killed an enemy; (3)
lines 1426-56, among other knights doing battle with the Romans; (4)
lines 1483-85, as being rescued in battle by Gawain; and (5) line 1605,
in the list of knights who are to convoy the prisoners to Paris. See R. M.
Lumiansky, "Malory's Steadfast Bors," *TSE*, VIII (1958), 5-20.

name is listed among the knights ordered to accompany Sir Cador to Paris with the Roman prisoners. Malory, however, has Bors riding side-by-side with Lancelot and Cador to launch a renewed attack upon the Romans (215). Bors next appears in the company of Lancelot and Clegis, disagreeing with King Arthur's statement that it is folly to fight against great odds (218). Then he takes part in the final battle against Lucius, performing deeds of great prowess (220), which in the *Morte Arthure* (2081–94) are attributed to Lott; and he is mentioned among the knights who pursue the remnants of the fleeing Romans after their final defeat (224). Finally, like Lancelot and Priamus, he is granted a share of the conquered lands by the King (245). Through all these adventures, Malory seems to have developed Bors, just as he did Lancelot, with an eye to his future role in *Le Morte Darthur*.

Another characteristic of Malory's narrative technique in Tale II is his careful conservation of knights who will later figure prominently in other tales. In the *Morte Arthure* both Sir Kay (there called Cayous) and Sir Bedivere are killed in the final battle with Lucius,[19] whereas in "The Tale of King Arthur and the Emperor Lucius" their wounds are severe but not fatal (222–24). This alteration is significant: since there is no reason for keeping them alive insofar as their subsequent participation in the Roman War is concerned, we may conclude that Malory is saving them for the future when their presence will contribute to the advancement of his plot.[20]

V

Consideration of the various kinds of evidence presented above leads inevitably to the conclusion that "The Tale of

[19] *Morte Arthure*, lines 2165–96, for the death of Kay, and lines 2234–41, for the death of Bedivere.
[20] Gordon and Vinaver, "New Light," p. 85. This convincing argument was later discarded by Vinaver in favor of the "separate romances" theory.

King Arthur and the Emperor Lucius" was written to function as one division of a larger whole, specifically *Le Morte Darthur*. Had Malory not been working in accordance with such a general plan, he would not have found it necessary to increase the importance of some characters, minimize that of others, and introduce still others whose presence in "The Tale of King Arthur and the Emperor Lucius" is superfluous, but who must be readied for future episodes. The changes, omissions, and additions that become evident in a comparison of Malory's "Tale" with the *Morte Arthure* are too consistent in their pattern to be accidental. They testify to Malory's originality of purpose and offer sound evidence that from the beginning he knew the direction which his whole work would take.

The chief evidence of Malory's artistic intentions in "The Tale of King Arthur and the Emperor Lucius" lies in his treatment of Lancelot. In his preparation of Tale II, Malory obviously focused his attention on the development of Lancelot for the central role which he was to play in *Le Morte Darthur*, a development which is assumed in the immediately following "Tale of Lancelot."

CHAPTER III

"THE TALE OF LANCELOT":
PRELUDE TO ADULTERY

BY R. M. LUMIANSKY

The "Tale of Lancelot" is the shortest of the eight main divisions of Malory's book. It very clearly shows, however, a high
degree of originality on Malory's part; and all the evidence
points to the conclusion that this originality was motivated by
Malory's conception of the function which this "Tale" would
perform in Le Morte Darthur as a whole. As was demonstrated
in the preceding chapter, a primary purpose of the "Tale of
King Arthur and the Emperor Lucius" was to introduce Lancelot
as the chief knight of the Round Table, with stress upon his,
rather than Gawain's, military prowess. Most of the narrative
progression in Tale III continues this demonstration of Lancelot's fighting ability; accordingly, we see his conquest of Belleus
(259–60), his victory in the tournament for King Bagdemagus
(262–63), his killing of Tarquyn (265–66), his conquest of Perys
de Foreste Savage (270), his killing of the two giants (271),
his rescue of Kay (273), his overcoming of Gawtere, Gylmere,
and Raynolde (276), his defeat of the four knights of the
Round Table (277–78), his saving the life of Melyot de Logrys
(280), his escape from Phelot (284), and his overcoming Sir
Pedyvere (285).

These exploits leave no doubt that Lancelot's courageous ac-

tivity in the war against Lucius truly foretold his coming distinction as a man at arms, and they fully establish Lancelot as
the central hero of *Le Morte Darthur*. But the primary function
which Malory—with his eye toward later developments in his
book—assigned to Tale III is therein to offer the reader a view
of the Lancelot-Guenevere relationship before the beginning of
the adultery. A detailed examination of this view will be presented here after a brief look at the source relationship for Tale III.

Malory's chief source here is the Agravain section of the Old
French prose *Lancelot*.[1] His material up to the point at which
Lancelot leaves King Bagdemagus is based upon successive
episodes in this source; the narrative from that point through
the liberation of Tintagel comes from a much later section of
the *Lancelot*; and the remaining material, except for two episodes, is derived from two other sections of the *Lancelot*.[2] Of the
two remaining episodes, the Phelot adventure has no known
source, and the Melyot adventure parallels a section of the
Perlesvaus. In preparing this "Tale," Malory greatly reduced the
bulk of his source materials. But, more importantly, we should
note that he must have exerted considerable effort in the selection of such widely separated episodes to go into his "Tale."
Then he was able to weave these incidents into a tightly unified
short narrative following the plot-line of Lancelot's activities
from the time he leaves Arthur's court through his return. One
important device he used to unify the various events within the
"Tale" is represented by two of the five references therein to the
Lancelot-Guenevere relationship.

---

[1] H. Oskar Sommer (ed.), *The Vulgate Version of the Arthurian Romances* (Washington, 1912), Vol. V ("Le Livre de Launcelot del Lac").
For studies of Malory's use here of source material, see *Works*, pp. 1398–
1416; and three articles by R. H. Wilson: "Malory and Perlesvaus," *MP*,
XXX (1932), 13–22; "Malory's Early Knowledge of Arthurian Romance," *University of Texas Studies in English*, XXIX (1950), 33–50;
"Notes on Malory's Sources," *MLN*, LXVI (1951), 22–26.

[2] Sommer, V, 87–102, 160–62, 167–68, 204–14, 306–18.

At the beginning of the tale, Malory states that after their return from Rome Arthur and his knights held many "joustys and turnementes," in which various knights won honor; then he continues:

> But in especiall hit was prevyd on sir Launcelot de Lake, for in all turnementes, justys, and dedys of armys, both for lyff and deth, he passed all other knyghtes, and at no tyme was he ovircom but yf hit were by treson other inchauntement. So this sir Launcelot encresed so mervaylously in worship and honoure; therefore he is the fyrste knyght that the Freynsh booke makyth mencion of aftir kynge Arthure com frome Rome. Wherefore quene Gwenyvere had hym in grete favoure aboven all other knyghtis, and so he loved the quene agayne aboven all other ladyes dayes of his lyff, and for hir he dud many dedys of armys and saved her from the fyre thorow his noble chevalry. (250)

This introductory passage of nineteen lines does not match any section of Malory's source. It is obviously his device for connecting the "Tale of Lancelot" with the immediately preceding second large division of *Le Morte Darthur*, the "Tale of King Arthur and the Emperor Lucius." We have seen that in this "Tale" one of Malory's chief alterations of his source, the Middle English alliterative *Morte Arthure*, was to raise Lancelot from a knight who is mentioned casually but six times to the chief position among the knights of the Round Table.[3] It is therefore readily understandable, after Lancelot's outstanding achievements in the second "Tale," for Malory, in the introductory passage for the third "Tale," to call Lancelot "the fyrste knyght." Vinaver strangely interprets this comment to mean that Lancelot was first in chronological mention;[4] the context seems to make clear that Malory here means to point to Lance-

---

[3] Mary E. Dichmann, "Characterization in Malory's *Tale of Arthur and Lucius*," PMLA, LXV (1950), 877–95.
[4] *Works*, 1398.

lot's having attained the first or pre-eminent place among Arthur's knights. This reading is made certain by Malory's next sentence: "Wherefore quene Gwenyvere had hym in grete favour aboven all other knyghtis. . . ." Guenevere has this regard for Lancelot because he is Arthur's oustanding knight, not because he is chronologically the first mentioned.

Further, the implication is that Lancelot set out to prove himself in the "straunge adventures" of the third "Tale" in order to win the approval of Guenevere, whom he already loves. Certainly, this desire for the Queen's approval seems present when, in the course of his various adventures, he tells a number of his conquered opponents to go to the court and "yelde you unto quene Gwenyvere." Malory found in the prose *Lancelot* the idea for this indication of the Lancelot-Guenevere relationship. In the French text Lancelot, after rescuing Kay, overcomes four knights at the bridge—the incident from which Malory develops Lancelot's fight with Gawtere, Gylmere, and Raynolde (275–77); in the old French story, after conquering the fourth knight, Lancelot says: "Dont te commanch ... que tu le iour de pentecoste soies a la cort monseignor le roy artu et illuec te rendras a madame la royne de par keu le senescal et conteras ceste auenture par deuant tous ceuls de laiens" (V, 308). Malory has Lancelot apply this necessity of yielding to Guenevere not only to the knights conquered at the bridge but also to the three knights who attacked Kay (274). There is also in the prose *Lancelot* the incident in which Lancelot forces the knight who cuts off the damsel's head to report to the Queen (V, 161–62, 167–68); from this incident, of course, Malory developed the Pedyvere episode (284–86). It would seem, then, that Malory has used both the opening reference to the Lancelot-Guenevere relationship and Lancelot's ordering a number of the conquered knights to yield to the Queen at the concluding assembly as a chief unifying device for his "Tale of Lancelot."

There are also in the tale three specific conversations, original with Malory, in which various characters refer to Lancelot's and Guenevere's interest in each other (257–58, 270–71, 281). The four queens inform Lancelot of their knowledge that he can love only Guenevere; he replies: "And as for my lady, dame Gwenyvere, were I at my lyberte as I was, I wolde prove hit on youres that she is the treweste lady unto hir lorde lyvnyge." We should note in passing that for this incident Malory so altered his source-passage as to have Morgan le Fay as the dominating character among the queens; this change fits with other appearances of Morgan in Malory's book (10, 429, 504–6, 557, 798).[5] Later, the damsel who has led Lancelot to his successful adventures against Tarquyn and Perys tells Lancelot that she and many others regret the rumor that he loves Guenevere and can love no other lady; Lancelot puzzlingly replies that an adventurous knight such as he cannot be bothered with either a wife or paramours. Finally, in the Melyot episode, Hallewes the Sorceress tells Lancelot as he is leaving the Castel Perilous that she loves him, that she realizes no woman can have him alive except Guenevere, and that she (Hallewes) wishes to have his "body dede . . . dispyte of quene Gwenyvere." To this fearsome disclosure Lancelot simply replies: "Jesu preserve me frome youre subtyle crauftys!"

The total effect of these five indications of a relationship between Lancelot and Guenevere is, I think, easily grasped: Lancelot loves the Queen, and he orders the individuals he conquers to report to her in order to show her that he performs such feats for her sake; she, because of his knightly eminence, holds him "in grete favoure aboven all other knyghtis," but she has as yet given him no indication that she will grant him her love;

[5] *Ibid.*, 1405. For a survey of Morgan's appearances in *Le Morte Darthur*, see R. M. Lumiansky, "Arthur's Final Companions in Malory's *Morte Darthur*," *TSE*, XI (1961), 5–19.

he therefore can maintain stoutly to the four queens that Guenevere is completely true to Arthur; he can feel justified in answering the damsel who led him to Tarquyn and Perys with the half-truth to the effect that he is more interested in adventures than in women; and he can refrain from meaningful comment about Guenevere to Hallewes.

Further, it is not particularly difficult to fit this total effect into Malory's handling of the Lancelot-Guenevere relationship throughout *Le Morte Darthur*. An intentional general pattern of progressive development for this adulterous relationship runs through the book as a whole, and this pattern should be regarded as a pivotal factor in the collapse of the Round Table. Before the "Tale of Lancelot," Arthur sees, loves, and decides to marry Guenevere; Merlin warns Arthur that Lancelot and Guenevere will love each other, but Arthur disregards this warning and weds her (39, 97–98). Also before the third "Tale," we have had one slight indication of Lancelot's love for Guenevere: he is "passynge wrothe" because Tristram is allowed to join Iseult in Cornwall instead of going to fight the Romans, whereas Lancelot must leave Guenevere and go to the wars with Arthur (195). But, after the "Tale of Lancelot," we have the development of the adulterous relationship and its catastrophic effects upon the characters involved and upon the whole society of the Round Table. Thus, within this large pattern, the function of the references in the third "Tale" to the Lancelot-Guenevere relationship is to show the two characters, in their own minds and in the minds of society at large, drawing more closely together in preparation for the adultery, which comes to be a matter of almost common knowledge by the time we reach the fifth "Tale," that of Tristram (425, 430). Further, coming developments in the Lancelot-Guenevere relationship are explicitly and importantly foreshadowed in the introductory passage for Tale III; ". . . and so he loved the quene agayne aboven all other ladyes dayes of his lyff, and for hir he dud many dedys of armys and saved her from the fyre thorow his noble chevalry" (250). In the last two "Tales," as final catastrophe approaches, Lancelot will save Guenevere on three occasions "from the fyre": in the "Poisoned Apple," in the "Knight of the Cart," and in "Tale of the Death of Arthur." That Malory had these three future instances in mind when he wrote the passage just quoted seems almost indisputable.

It is also noteworthy that in the "Tale of Lancelot" two of the five references to the Lancelot-Guenevere relationship are made by supernatural figures—Morgan le Fay and Hallewes—who thereby reinforce the effect of Merlin's earlier prophecy to Arthur. Further, Malory's careful attention to this problem is almost certainly to be observed in his alteration to Tintagel of the name for the castle held by the two giants whom Lancelot kills (272). This name and the mention of Ygraine and Uther carry the reader back to Arthur's being conceived before the marriage of his father and mother (10), a situation which in the book as a whole—like that between Arthur and his sister Morgawse, from which Mordred was born (41)—has immensely important thematic connections with the adulterous relationship of Lancelot and Guenevere.

We have seen, then, that of the five references in the "Tale of Lancelot" to the relationship between Lancelot and Guenevere, four are original with Malory. These references help to unify the "Tale," and they should be viewed as Malory's intentional effort to fit the "Tale of Lancelot" into the progressive development of the Lancelot-Guenevere relationship which runs through *Le Morte Darthur*. Most important is the fact that Malory chose in the "Tale of Lancelot" to change the adultery between Lancelot and Guenevere, which he found clearly stated in the Old French prose *Lancelot* (V, 177–95), to a view of these two characters preceding the commencement of the adulterous relationship. Thus, Malory's presentation of Lancelot in Tale III is by no means characterized by the incoherence with which it has been charged.[6]

Finally, we should note that in Tale III Malory alters his source in order to include Gaheris in place of Gareth. In one part of the prose *Lancelot* used by Malory as source for a part of Tale III, Gaheriet (Gareth) appears; but Malory removes each of his appearances. Thus, in *Le Morte Darthur*, Lancelot finds Gaheris "overthwarte" a horse driven by Tarquin; Lancelot kills Tarquin and releases Gaheris, who frees many of Tarquin's prisoners (265–68). But in the source Terrican's captive is Gaheriet, who later frees Terrican's prisoners (V, 205–8). The point here is that Malory replaces Gaheriet (Gareth) with Gaheris because Gareth is to be the central figure in Tale IV, and therefore at the time of Tale III has to be a youth at home rather than an adventurous knight.[7] Here again we may observe an instance of Malory's meshing an aspect of a given "Tale" with considerations affecting his book as a whole.

---

[6] Vinaver, *Malory*, pp. 46–47.
[7] W. L. Guerin, Jr., "The Functional Role of Gareth in Malory's *Morte Darthur*," (Tulane University Master's thesis, 1953), pp. 97–98.

CHAPTER IV

"THE TALE OF GARETH":
THE CHIVALRIC FLOWERING

BY WILFRED L. GUERIN

The fourth large division of Le Morte Darthur, the "Tale of Gareth," presents the arrival of "the goodlyest yonge man and the fayreste" that the court of Arthur has ever seen. Appearing on Pentecost, at the time when Arthur holds "the Rounde Table moste plenoure," the young man humbly asks for three gifts. For the moment he requests only the first: food and drink for a year. Sir Kay scorns the young man as a "vylayne borne" and mockingly names him "Beawmaynes." [1] But Beaumains is "meke and mylde," and as a kitchen knave he endures Kay's abuse for a year.

When Pentecost is next celebrated, a damsel named Lynet arrives at court to request help for her sister, Lyonesse, whose castle is besieged by the Red Knight of the Red Lands. Beaumains now requests his other two gifts: that he be assigned this adventure and that he be knighted by Lancelot. Lynet is insulted when the kitchen knave is assigned to her, but she has no choice. Beaumains identifies himself to Lancelot as Gareth, brother to Gawain, is knighted, and begins a series of encounters of increasing difficulty, during which Lynet is exceedingly un-

[1] For the meaning of the nickname, see Wilfred L. Guerin, "Malory's Morte Darthur: Book VII," Explicator, XX (1962), 64.

sympathetic toward him. He overcomes six thieves, two knights at a bridge, the Black Knight, the Green Knight, the Red Knight, Sir Persaunt of Inde, and finally the Red Knight of the Red Lands. By his prowess and his gentlemanly qualities, he wins approval from Lynet.

But Lyonesse now requires that he "laboure in worshyp this twelve-monthe" (327) in order to win her love. Subsequent episodes effectively test Gareth's prowess, his determination, and his chastity. He and Lyonesse plan a tournament, the intended result of which is to have Gareth publicly win her as his lady. After the tournament, but before he rejoins Lyonesse, Gareth fights the Brown Knight without Pity, the Duke de la Rouse, and—unknowingly—his own brother Gawain. Lynet stops the final encounter by making the two brothers known to each other. Arthur then arranges for the marriage of Gareth and Lyonesse, which is celebrated by the whole court with great joy and ceremony.

The "Tale of Gareth" presents particular difficulties to the commentator concerned with originality in *Le Morte Darthur*. Though almost every aspect of the "Tale" is somewhat similar to aspects of earlier romances in French, no actual source has been found for Malory's story. As will appear in the next section of this chapter, many scholars have assumed that Malory did have a French source, now lost, for this division of his book. My own view is that Malory borrowed hints for this "Tale" from French romances, but that he is to be credited with great originality for its creation. The analysis offered in the final section of the chapter will suggest reasons for his creation of this "Tale" and an explanation of its place in *Le Morte Darthur*. In brief, it will be my contention that—through its happy picture of the Round Table at the height of its success, and through its preparation of Gareth for the role he will later play in the collapse of the Round Table—the "Tale of Gareth" contributes importantly to the unity of Malory's book.

I

Some scholars, notably H. O. Sommer and Eugène Vinaver, have assumed that Malory was incapable of creating the "Tale of Gareth." Instead, they maintain, he must have had a source, now lost but probably French and similar to analogues that are extant in several languages. Sommer even doubted whether the "Tale" originally belonged "to the Arthurian cycle to which it may have been adapted by Malory, or by some unknown writer before him from some now lost French poem." [2] Vinaver more recently argued that "Although its French source is entirely unknown it is safe to assume that such a source existed and that it was built on the familiar pattern of the thirteenth-century prose novel: a knightly quest successfully brought to its conclusion by a young hero and followed by a brilliant tournament" (1417). He pointed to the similarities between the "Tale of Gareth" and that of La Cote Male Tayle, and said that such details in the "Tale of Gareth" fit a larger pattern, a "mixture of literary reminiscences, among which the romances of Chrétien de Troyes figure prominently" (1417–18). But Malory did not put together these disparate incidents: ". . . the story of Beaumains as a whole must be part of the story of Gaheret as it existed in the French cyclic tradition" (1421); and again, "All these themes must have reached Malory through some French 'romance of Gaheret' the specific form and character of which is entirely unknown to-day except through Malory's adaptation" (1422). This work must have been associated with the Old French prose *Tristan*,[3] from which it may or may not have been detached when it reached Malory. At any rate, Malory "was clearly content to follow it, adding

[2] H. Oskar Sommer, *Le Morte Darthur* (London, 1891), III, 6.
[3] This view is also the essence of Vinaver's article, "A Romance of Gaheret," *Medium Aevum*, I (1932), 157–67.

occasionally a touch of subtle humour or a spirited dialogue, not as an antidote, but as a suitable contribution to the French tale. And so his work may well be said to belong to the French narrative literature of the late Middle Ages . . ." (1424).[4]

The "lost source" theory is of necessity conjectural; studies of known analogues are of greater help in placing Malory's "Tale of Gareth" in perspective. These "Fair Unknown" stories exist both in Continental and in English literature, and include Malory's own story of La Cote Male Tayle, found within the "Tale of Tristram." In 1895, William H. Schofield published a study of four of them, all probably written before 1400,[5] but he did not correlate them with Malory's later work. Robert H. Wilson has since used the results of Schofield's research in a consideration of the "Tale of Gareth," and at the same time has studied the "La Cote" in relation to Vinaver's opinions.[6] Having thus before him a fuller representation of the "Fair Unknown" group, Wilson attempted to show a direct relationship between the "Tale of Gareth" and several of the analogues, rather than a "coincidental agreement with the Fair Unknown group." According to Wilson, Malory used a source which in turn had as its sources "La Cote Male Tayle," "Bel Inconnu," and a now lost, but common, source of "Bel Inconnu" and "Libeaus Desconus"; perhaps there was also some use of the *Erec*. Malory himself, Wilson argued, did not go to any of

[4] E. K. Chambers agrees generally with Vinaver about the probability of a lost French source; see *English Literature at the Close of the Middle Ages* (Oxford, 1945), p. 190. Arguing on the basis of various Celtic analogues, Morton Donner, in a 1956 Columbia dissertation, "The Backgrounds of Malory's Book of Gareth," has also suggested the former existence of a now lost source.

[5] *Studies on the Libeaus Desconus*, Vol. IV in (Harvard) *Studies and Notes in Philology and Literature* (1895). The approximate dates of the four, according to Schofield (pp. 1–2) are as follows: "Le Bel Inconnu" (or "Guinglain"), 1190; "Wigalois," 1210; "Libeaus Desconus," 1350; and "Carduino," 1375.

[6] "The Fair Unknown in Malory," *PMLA*, LVIII (1943), 1–21.

these works but to the one source which was a conflation of them all.[7] Thus, Wilson's argument also assumes a lost source.

In their comparisons of Malory's version with the "Fair Unknown" stories, scholars until recently have neglected one narrative which resembles Malory's story as closely as those just mentioned. While studying the *Suite du Merlin* as represented by MS. B. N. 112, Thomas L. Wright encountered this narrative within a section concerning Gawain, Yvain, and Marhalt.[8] The resemblance is sufficiently strong to suggest that Malory made some use of this story of Gaheriet (the normal French version of Gareth's name). In the first place, the broad outline of the Gaheriet episode resembles Malory's "Tale." The episode begins after Yvain returns to court with the news that Gawain and Marhalt are imprisoned in the Roche aux Pucelles; a final message from Merlin states that they will be freed by Gaheriet, once the latter is knighted. Gaheriet is accordingly knighted, along with his brothers Aggravain and Guerrehes; following this occasion, a wounded knight appeals to Arthur for help against the Red Knight who holds his brother prisoner. Gaheriet volunteers to undertake the adventure, which ends with Gaheriet's liberating Gawain and Marhalt and his returning to court. There are other general similarities between the Gaheriet episode in the *Suite* and Malory's version:

[7] Malory's story has also been compared to *Fergus*, by Guillaume le Clerc, and to the Latin *Historia Meriadoci*. See, respectively, Alexandre Micha, "Miscellaneous French Romances in Verse," in *Arthurian Literature in the Middle Ages*, ed. R. S. Loomis (Oxford, 1959), p. 377; and Loomis's own comments in "The Latin Romances," p. 475 in the same volume.

[8] See his dissertation, "Originality and Purpose in Malory's 'Tale of King Arthur'" (Tulane University, 1960), pp. 279–84. For the French version, see *Die Abenteuer Gawains, Ywains, und le Morholts mit den Drei Jungfrauen*, ed. H. O. Sommer, in *Beihefte zur Zeitschrift für Romanische Philologie* (Halle, 1913), especially pp. 88–134. This tale, a continuation of the Huth *Merlin*, is sometimes cited as *Suite*. For a study of MS. 112, see C. E. Pickford, *L'Evolution du roman arthurien en prose vers la fin du moyen age* (Paris, 1960).

Gaheriet is younger than Gawain and Aggravain; it is prophesied that Gaheriet will die at Lancelot's hands during the battle over Guenevere's honor; Malory's Gareth generally has the same personality traits that the Gaheriet of the *Suite* has, and the less noble Aggravain suffers in comparison with Gaheriet.

Furthermore, Wright calls attention to several specific parallels between the two versions. When Gaheriet is knighted, a damsel appears, in mid-winter, with a mantle of roses for him; Malory's Gareth, newly knighted, receives a horse and elaborate equipment from a mysterious source. Wright also suggests that some of the "Tale of Gareth" may have been borrowed from Malory's own episode of Balin le Sauvage, which, like the episode of Gawain, Yvain, and Marhalt, derives from the *Suite*: for example, both Balin and Gareth, when they first come to Arthur's court, appear poor and certainly are shabbily dressed. The identification of Gareth's mother as Morgause also shows internal borrowing, for although the *Suite*, the source for the first "Tale," keeps her anonymous, both in the "Tale of King Arthur" and in the "Tale of Gareth" she is named. Wright concludes that Malory, in writing his version of the episode of Gawain, Yvain, and Marhalt, suppressed the Gaheriet passages in the *Suite* in order to use them later in the "Tale of Gareth."

This list of similarities can be expanded. For example, both in the French *Suite* and in Malory Gareth seeks as a "gift" the quest which immediately follows his being knighted. In the French, Gaheriet fights a knight who wears "armes aussi vermeilles comme sang" when he first appears in the tale; in Malory, the quest is against the Red Knight of the Red Lands. When Gaheriet sets out he is followed by the envious Aggravain, who wants to overthrow Gaheriet, but instead Aggravain is ignominiously defeated; in Malory, the jealous and scornful Kay follows his former kitchen knave, challenges him, and is promptly wounded and unhorsed. In the *Suite du Merlin,* Aggravain is lectured and scolded by his own squire for desiring such vengeance upon his younger brother; in Malory, Lancelot and Gawain warn Kay not to follow Beaumains. In the French, Aggravain, Gaheriet, and Guerrehes are knighted together; in Malory, at the end of the "Tale of Gareth," all three men marry women who are related to each other. The chaplet of winter roses comes from "l'Isle Faee"; Dame Lyonesse's brother lives on the "Ile of Avylyon," where Lynet practices magical healing on a mysterious knight. Possibly the name "Avylyon" was suggested by the name of the castle (Auarlan) which is Gaheriet's destination in the *Suite.* Of the several parallels in the climactic combats in the two versions, some may well be the result of the virtual formulas for battles—being unhorsed and rendered unconscious, then resuming with swords; littering the field with pieces of armor ("en my le champ grandismes pieces," "grete pecis . . . felle in the fyldes"); suffering the exposure of parts of their bodies ("les chars nues," "their naked sydys"). But the parallels do accumulate, and when the combatants take a rest, in both versions, it is Gareth who calls for resumption of the battle: Gaheriet says, "Vassal, assez no[u]z sommes reposes, ie vous appel de la bataille"; Gareth looks up at Dame Lyonesse "And therewith he bade the Rede Knyght of the Rede Laundes make hym redy, 'and lette us do oure batayle to the utteraunce.' " The spectators "within" and "without" ("qui dehors estoient" and "ceulx dentour la place") pity the knights. In both versions, after Gareth conquers his foe and makes him foreswear vengeance, Gareth does not enter the castle: in the *Suite du Merlin,* the people simply overlook him in their joy at the outcome, and in Malory Lady Lyonesse refuses him admittance. Later in the French, Gaheriet travels with a lady who, in her advice to the knight, bears some slight resemblance to Lynet, the companion of Beaumains. In following her advice concerning the rescue of

Gawain, Gaheriet fights a knight whose equipment and horse are black.

All in all, there are a striking number of parallels between this section of B. N. 112 and Malory's "Gareth," some of which are even verbal. To be sure, the medieval romances were such that parallels of necessity abound, but this instance seems to go beyond conventionality.

II

It seems clear from the preceding discussion that many similarities exist between earlier French romances and numerous aspects of the "Tale of Gareth." But the fact remains that, so far as we know, Malory had before him in the writing of this "Tale" no "source," at least not in the sense that we use in considering the other segments of *Le Morte Darthur*. Consequently, I suggest that in light of the various relationships which the "Tale of Gareth" has to the remainder of *Le Morte Darthur*, we should grant the possibility—even the probability—that this "Tale" is Malory's original creation, with bits taken from earlier romances, specifically to serve certain functions within the book as a whole. These relationships and functions will be discussed below.

As a preliminary we should note Malory's consistency in the spelling of Gareth's name and in the conception of his age. In the *Vulgate Cycle*, the prose *Tristan*, and the English stanzaic poem *Le Morte Arthur*,[9] all used by Malory, Gareth's name is spelled in numerous ways. Frequently Gareth is confused with

[9] See, respectively, the following works: the Index to *The Vulgate Version of the Arthurian Romances*, ed. H. O. Sommer (Washington, 1908–16); Eilart Löseth, *Le Roman en Prose de Tristan, le Roman de Palamède, et la Compilation de Rusticien de Pise: Analyse Critique d'après les Manuscrits de Paris* (Paris, 1891), p. 22; and *Le Morte Arthur*, ed. J. D. Bruce, EETS-ES, No. 88 (London, 1903).

his brother Gaheris, whose name in the manuscripts often resembles Gareth's.[10] But in Malory's version the form for the
younger brother is consistently *Gareth*.[11] Malory also modified
the statements of the French romances concerning Gareth's age.
Possibly for better dramatic effect and for smoother integration
of the "Tale of Gareth," matters to which I shall return, Malory
caused Gareth to be considerably younger than his brothers and
to enter the story after it was well under way.[12] The point at
present is that Malory maintained this pattern throughout his
bulky work, even into the final "Tale," as in Gawain's sourceless
comment concerning the youth of both Gareth and Gaheris
(1176). Similarly, Malory went beyond the French romances by
making Gareth consistently admirable in ideals, personality, and
physical attributes. There can be no doubt about Malory's
desire to give a more clearly etched picture of Gareth than was
present in the French romances.

Such a clarification of the character, and even of the name, of
Gareth facilitated one of Malory's major objectives: to use the
"Tale of Gareth" in the portrayal of Arthur's Round Table at
the height of its power and glory,[13] during the happy period

[10] For Gareth we find these variants: Gaheriet, Gaheries, Ghaheriet,
Gahariet, Gaharies, Ghaharies, Gaheriez; for Gaheris: Guerrehers, Guerre-
hes, Guerrehiers, Gaheret, Guerhes, Guerreet, Guerhees, Guerehes, Gerehes,
Guerrier, Guerrehet, Gaheriet.

[11] The exception is *Garethe*, used on rare occasions in the Winchester
MS.

[12] Though the sources seldom give specific ages (Gauvain is about seventy-
six at the time of his death; see *Vulgate Version*, VI, 344), all references
to the brothers seem to imply that the four legitimate sons are close in
age. Gaheriet also appears to be older than Lancelot and not far from
Arthur's age. In the prose *Lancelot*, he is one of forty knights who go in
quest of a newcomer knight (Lancelot), and subsequently he stands
guard over Lancelot several days before the latter becomes a member
of the Round Table (*Vulgate Version*, III, 228 and 427). Lancelot is
later described as one who "ne peut pas auoir plus haut de .xxv. ans"
(*Vulgate Version*, V, 87).

[13] D. S. Brewer, "Form in the *Morte Darthur*," *Medium Aevum*, XXI
(1952), 20.

before the inevitable decline.[14] It may be well to recall at this
point the oath that Arthur instituted for the members of the
Round Table, for in its principles we find the code by which
Gareth lives and which, in the "Tale of Gareth," he brings to
its clearest manifestation. In the oath, original with Malory,
Arthur charges his knights

> never to do outerage nothir morthir, and allwayes to fle treson,
> and to gyff mercy unto hym that askith mercy, uppon payne of
> forfiture of their worship and lordship of kynge Arthure for
> evirmore; and allwayes to do ladyes, damesels, and jantilwomen
> and wydowes socour: strengthe hem in hir ryghtes, and never to
> enforce them uppon payne of dethe. Also that no man take no
> batayles in a wrongefull quarell for no love ne for no worldis
> goodis. (120)

The oath is presented in the course of the first "Tale"; there and
in the second "Tale" Arthur consolidates his power and gathers
around him knights who are capable of fulfilling most of the
injunctions of the oath. Then, in the "Tale of Lancelot," Lancelot emerges as the protagonist of the developing society.

Once the rise of that society is sufficiently clear, Malory is
ready to show the arrival of young Gareth in the "Tale of
Gareth"—and to exemplify the spirit and the letter of the oath
presented many pages earlier. Thus, Gareth is horrified by the
barbaric deeds of the Red Knight of the Red Lands (320–24);
he befriends Lynet and Lyonesse, "strengthening" the latter in
her rights, and he accuses the Red Knight of forcing his attentions upon her (322); he disavows association with murder
and vengeance, even when his brother Gawain is guilty of them
(360). He also illustrates the positive elements of the oath, as
when he "endured all that twelve-monthe and never dyspleased
man nother chylde, but allwayes he was meke and mylde" (295).

[14] Vida D. Scudder, *Le Morte Darthur of Sir Thomas Malory: A Study
of the Book and Its Sources* (London, 1921), p. 225.

Lynet says, ". . . he is curtyese and mylde, and the moste sufferynge man that ever I mette withall. . . . And at all tymes he gaff me goodly and meke answers agayne" (330). After his climactic victory over the Red Knight of the Red Lands, Gareth grants mercy to those who ask it, although his sense of justice dictates that the Red Knight should die; his yielding to the petitions for mercy represents an advance over the harsher requirement of an avenging justice. Gareth's fulfillment of the oath of chivalry, the timing of his arrival at court, and the respect he is given during the "Tale of Gareth" together show that the Round Table has achieved the flowering of chivalry.

In other ways the "Tale of Gareth" reveals the general happiness of Arthur's court. The story emphasizes color, the charm of magic and myth, the bustle of tournaments, the joys of family ties, and, perhaps most of all, the joys of wedded love. Color, both literal and figurative, stimulates the imagination in Gareth's victories over knights in black, green, red, "inde," red again, and brown. Gareth uses the magically changing color of his armor to confuse the audience at the tournament. This sensuous appeal compares with such episodes as that of the mysterious, light-exuding knight who carries a battle-ax and whose head can be replaced on his shoulders. The wedding feast, the procession of knights paying homage to Gareth, and the accompanying jousts make the close of the "Tale" a panorama of the richness and glory of this era of Arthur's reign.

Of deeper significance for the structural emphasis on the flowering of chivalry is the treatment of love. At one level, it exists in the mutual concern shown by the brothers whom Gareth defeats on his way to the besieged castle. At another, love and respect bring Gareth into varying relationships with Gawain, Arthur, Lancelot, and Morgause. But the height of emotion is in the mixture of passionate love and ideal love that brings together Lyonesse and Gareth. Beginning with Gareth's fighting

the Red Knight of the Red Lands, this love at first seems little
more than the conventional sudden emotion of the courtly
romances, an interpretation strengthened by Lyonesse's request
that Gareth "labor" for a year and by the youthful attempts of
the lovers to meet at night in Gryngamour's castle. But as
Charles Moorman points out, the "Tale of Gareth" is far from
a courtly love romance; instead Malory deliberately makes it
"a commentary upon love and the behavior of lovers, the main
purpose of which is to present a natural, untutored affection,
very different from the artificial, conventionalized *l'amour cour-
tois*." [15] Whatever traces of courtly love there are in the
"Gareth" take on an almost ironic meaning.

> If read in context, Gareth is clearly a commentary on *l'amour
> courtois* and is so placed as to contrast with the adulterous
> affairs of Lancelot and Tristan. The "Tale of Gareth" works
> towards the propositions that the true end of love is marriage,
> not adultery, that young lovers may in fact be fickle, that wise
> maids had best not tarry, and that young lovers sometimes
> need restraining. Gareth is a "vertuous" rather than a "courtly"
> lover. . . . [16]

Thus, when Lynet intervenes to save the love for a fulfillment
different from that of the courtly love tradition, she acts with
a sense of righteousness and "was a lytyll dysplesed; and she
thought hir sister dame Lyonesse was a lytyll overhasty that she
myght nat abyde hir tyme of maryage, and for savyng of hir
worshyp she thought to abate their hoote lustis. And she lete
ordeyne by hir subtyle craufftes that they had nat theire
intentys neythir with othir as in her delytes untyll they were
maryed" (333). That Lynet's efforts are well directed is later
clear when Arthur asks Gareth "whether he wolde have this

---

[15] Charles Moorman, "Courtly Love in Malory," *ELH*, XXVII (1960),
169.
[16] *Ibid.*, p. 171.

lady as peramour, other ellys to have hir to his wyff" (359). Both
Gareth and Lyonesse insist that marriage is their goal; they
explicitly use the words "wife" and "husband"; and Lyonesse
protests that Gareth "is my fyrste love, and he shall be the
laste" (359–60). With their marriage and with those of two
of Gareth's brothers, Malory brings full stress upon the happiness of all concerned. As with the married love of Pelleas and
Nineve in the first "Tale," Gareth's is an index to the noblest
elements of the chivalric ideal—and an effective contrast to the
loves that will later wither the flower of chivalry. But for the
moment, the "Tale of Gareth" shows the Round Table at its
highest point: the oath is being fulfilled, there is a sense of well-
being and security, and a type of happy love is established at
court.

Gareth's role, however, is not limited to the "Tale" which
bears his name. Just as the contrast with other loves and lovers
in *Le Morte Darthur* reaches beyond the "Tale," Malory's treatment of Gareth includes an interplay of personalities which
helps to portray some of Malory's most important figures.
Gareth's role in characterization is more significant than that
of the Gaheriet of the *Vulgate Cycle*, for Gareth not only shows
the complexities of the protagonists but is beloved of the three
great knights of the Arthurian world: Gawain, Tristram, and
Lancelot.

The relationship between Gareth and his older brother is complex but by no means contradictory. He is proud of Gawain,[17]
yet quite capable of speaking out against the latter's faults (699).
This seeming inconsistency has been criticized as an artistic
fault,[18] but is defensible when one recalls that while Gareth
regularly espouses good and shuns evil, he is also faithful to

[17] Both in the "Tale of Gareth" and in the "Tale of Tristram," young
Gareth introduces himself as the "brothir unto sir Gawayne" (299, 696).
[18] See, for example, E. K. Chambers, "Sir Thomas Malory," English
Association Pamphlet No. 51 (January, 1922), p. 6.

friends and relatives. The literary relationship derives from the psychological, for Gareth is a foil to Gawain: his actions and statements consistently point up his brother's faults, as in the contrast between Gawain's vengeance (derived from the sources) and Gareth's hatred of vengeance (apparently original with Malory).[19] These contrasts are emphasized by the many times that Malory causes one brother to refer to the other, using expressions such as "my brother Gareth" or "my brother Sir Gawain." But Malory also uses Gareth to portray certain redeeming qualities in Gawain. For instance, Gawain is shown as capable of a lasting affinity with, and of a paternalistic attitude toward, Gareth, the epitome of all the good qualities of the Gawain clan (e.g., 1184–85). Gawain is magnanimous: though Gareth is a close friend of Lancelot, Gawain looks upon this friendship as something praiseworthy, not as a cleavage in the family. Since Gareth is the mainstay of his family's best traits, Gawain is ennobled by his appreciation of the worth of such a relative.[20] Furthermore, since Gawain appears more like a father to Gareth in *Le Morte Darthur* than in the sources, his grief and his desire for revenge after Gareth's death are more credible. In short, Gareth is used to demonstrate the depth and breadth of Malory's Gawain.

Comparisons between Gareth and his three other brothers

[19] The germ of this hatred may be in Aggravain's violent desire for vengeance against Gaheriet in the *Suite* (*Die Abenteuer*, pp. 88 ff.). For suggestions about Malory's originality here, see *Works*, 698–700 and 1500–1. For other references to vengeance, see 325, 360, and 1162 (and note, 1614). Besides the contrasts that exist in the chastity theme (168–71, 1147), Gawain's rashness is opposed to Gareth's calmness. For Gawain's faults, see 106, 866, 1199–1200, and 1213; for Gareth's virtues, see Scudder, *Le Morte Darthur*, p. 218, and, in the "Tale of Gareth," the numerous passages attesting Gareth's patience, especially his restraint in the fight with the Red Knight of the Red Lands.

[20] Not content with the passages expressing Gawain's grief over the death of Gareth, Malory apparently adds similar passages, such as those on 1185 (where he specifically applies the adjective "good" to Gareth but not to Gaheris), 1189, and 1200.

re of a different sort, consistently advantageous for him and disparaging to them. Like the comparison with Tristram, this relationship was inherited from the French;[21] since it served Malory's purpose to perpetuate the contrast,[22] it underwent little change. It should be noted that while Gaheris does not fare so poorly as do Aggravain and Mordred,[23] he never approaches the level of Gareth. Clearly, Malory considered the family of Gawain as a complex of personality traits, with Gareth at its center, epitomizing more admirable qualities than any of his brothers.[24]

Since the relationship between Gareth and Tristram is not radically different from those between Gareth and the other two important knights, it is not necessary to consider it in detail here, with one exception: the relationship achieves more than characterization, for the "Tale of Gareth," with its appearances of Tristram and knights associated with him, helps to fuse the "Tale of Tristram" into the general scheme of Malory's plot.[25]

[21] Similarities in the relationships can be found in the *Vulgate Version*, I, 280; IV, 358–59, 361; and in *Die Abenteuer*, pp. 88 ff.

[22] Possibly added by Malory are Dinadan's comparison of Gareth and the other brothers (700), and the narrator's comparison in the "Healing of Sir Urry" (1148). Malory causes Gawain particularly to bewail Gareth's death while somewhat overlooking Gaheris' (1184); Malory may be developing here a sketchy speech by Gawain in the stanzaic *Morte Arthur*. In expanding another passage from the poem, Malory similarly stresses Gareth over Gaheris when Gawain, accusing Lancelot to his face, is made to forget Gaheris, though Lancelot remembers both knights: ". . . what cause haddist thou to sle my good brother sir Gareth that loved the more than me and all my kynne?" To this Lancelot replies in part, "And alas, that ever I was so unhappy that I had nat seyne sir Gareth and sir Gaherys!" (1189).

[23] If R. S. Loomis is correct, Gaheris' reputation may compare with Gareth's because the two characters were at one time in literary history one person. See "Malory's Beaumains," *PMLA*, LIV (1939), 656–68. Cf. Scudder, *Le Morte Darthur*, p. 255.

[24] Cf. Scudder, *Le Morte Darthur*, p. 272: "Malory's studies of family groups have a good deal of interest and unconventionality."

[25] Much of the "Tale of Tristram" is retrospective, and therefore the "Tale of Gareth" takes place during the early part of the "Tristram,"

This fusion was important, since Malory was adding to his con
ventionally "Arthurian" sources the formerly separate pros
Tristan.

Of greater significance, however, both for characterization and
for the increased artistry of Malory's plot, is the stress in the
"Tale of Gareth" and elsewhere on Gareth's relationship with
Lancelot. That friendship not only constitutes one of the key
aspects of Malory's characterization, but intensifies the irony of
Lancelot's inadvertent killing of Gareth late in *Le Morte
Darthur.* Unlike the Gareth-Gawain affiliation, which often
points up the differences between the two brothers, the friend
ship between Gareth and Lancelot more consistently shows
similarities. Mutual love, not kinship, is the essence of this
relationship.[26] Lancelot's worth, necessary for Malory's general
purpose, is made clearer by his friendship for and fostering of
the young Beaumains. From the time that Lancelot dubs the
young man to the end of *Le Morte Darthur,* that friendship
prospers. Their affinity and their oneness in ideals and in innate
goodness become more important as the book progresses; to

---

before Gareth appears as a young knight in the latter tale. Consequently,
in the "Tristram" there is evidence of Malory's attempt to keep Gareth
out of those early parts of the "Tale" which would upset the inclusion of
the "Tale of Gareth." Since Gareth appears in the comparable part of the
French source, Malory seems to have deliberately removed all mentions and
appearances of Gareth from the first 320 pages of the "Tristram." For
indications of deletions, compare Malory with Löseth, *Le Roman en
Prose de Tristan,* especially paragraphs 29, 30, 126, 128, 132, 137, 140,
141, 145. For still another deletion, see Vinaver's note (*Works,* 1465). In
one instance Malory changes *Gaheriet* to *Gaheris:* cf. *Works,* 529, with
Löseth, *Le Roman en Prose de Tristan,* paragraphs 128 and 132. Had
Malory not changed the name to Gaheris in this instance, he would have
been faced with the problem of a *vengeful* Gareth fighting Tristram
(532–33).

[26] Malory himself draws early attention to this different relationship: "But
as towchyng sir Gawayne, he had reson to proffer hym lodgyng, mete, and
drynke, for that proffer com of his bloode, for he was nere kyn to hym
than he wyste off; but that sir Launcelot ded was of his grete jantylnesse
and curtesy" (295).

how this importance, both before and after Lancelot kills
Gareth, Malory adds speeches to stress their ties of mutual love
and respect.[27] However, Lancelot, like Gawain and Tristram,
suffers by comparison with Gareth: Gareth is outspoken for
hastity,[28] whereas Lancelot is adulterous.

Malory also made several modifications in the Gareth-Lance-
ot relationship. Lancelot's dubbing of Gareth, an episode
unique with Malory, is one of the most important. The five
allusions to the dubbing which are made late in *Le Morte
Darthur*[29] indicate that Malory intended the episode to be
instrumental in the unification of the entire book, making the
ast two "Tales" in a sense dependent upon the interpolated
"Tale of Gareth," and stressing Gareth's sense of fealty to
Lancelot. This change compares with the reversal of the Lance-
lot-Gareth relationship from what it was in the *Vulgate*; there
an apparently older Gaheriet stands guard over the young Lancelot before the latter is knighted. To effect this change, Malory
avoided numerous references to Gareth which are in the early
sections of the *Vulgate Cycle*, sections which lie behind the first
three "Tales" in his own version.[30] Thus he could present

[27] See 1088–89, 1112, 1162, 1199, and 1249; cf. 1114.
[28] A possible exception is the tryst which Gareth plans with Dame
Lyonesse, but which is hindered by Lynet. In his defense, however, it
should be recalled that the two lovers had previously exchanged some sort
of troth-plight (332). For further extenuation of Gareth's one taint, see
Margaret Adlum Gist, *Love and War in the Middle English Romances*
Philadelphia, 1947), especially pp. 27–29.
[29] Two such passages, apparently original with Malory, are in the "Great
Tournament" (1110) and in the scene when Aggravain and Mordred plot
against Lancelot (1162). See also 1113, 1189, and 1199.
[30] In at least one instance Malory omits a reference that has source
authority. Cf. *Works*, 79, with the source as found in *Merlin: Roman en
Prose du XIIIe Siècle*, eds. Gaston Paris and Jacob Ulrich, Société des
Anciens Textes Français (Paris, 1886), I, 273; this is the Huth *Merlin*. In
other instances Malory changes the name Gahariet (normally equivalent
to Gareth) to Gaheris: Gawain on his first quest has for his squire Gaheris
(102 ff.), though the Huth *Merlin* regularly names Gahariet (*Merlin*, II,
30–97). There is an extended passage concerning Gaheriet in the sources

Gareth as the young protégé of Lancelot in the "Tale of Gareth" and could maintain that relationship throughout the rest of the book.[31] Vida Dutton Scudder long ago pointed to another modification that fits the pattern just suggested when she said that perhaps the greatest loss from the prose *Lancelot* was Lancelot's friendship with Galahad, le Haut Prince: "But this figure could not have been introduced without weakening both Lancelot's single-hearted passion for Guenevere and his relation with Gareth. . . . Lancelot's genius for comradeship is sufficiently indicated by his devotion to Gareth, a devotion also essential to the catastrophe." [32]

Because of these modifications and because of the interpolation of the "Tale of Gareth," Malory was singularly successful in providing for that catastrophe a setting which is much more

---

for the "Tale of Lancelot," and each appearance of Gaheriet in the passage has been changed by Malory (cf. *Works*, 265 ff. and *Vulgate Version*, V, 205–10). Perhaps the most revealing change is that in which the name Gahariet does not become Gaheris; here even scribal error is virtually ruled out. The Old French passage, which can be found in *Works*, 1351, tells of six men who defeated Gawain, one of whom was "Gaherietz." Had Malory changed Gaherietz to Gaheris, he would have had the incongruity of a lesser knight defeating Gawain; furthermore, he did not want to mention Gareth so early in *Le Morte Darthur*. Consequently, Malory removed the names of Hector and Gaherietz and substituted those of Perceval and Pelleas.

[31] For the position of the "Tale of Gareth" in the chronology of the *Morte*, see further Charles Moorman, "Internal Chronology in Malory's *Morte Darthur*," *JEGP*, LX (1961), 242 and 245–46; and Wilfred L. Guerin, "The Functional Role of Gareth in Malory's *Morte Darthur*," unpublished M.A. thesis (Tulane University, 1953), pp. 92 ff. The three mentions of Gareth in the early sections of *Le Morte Darthur* do not weaken these arguments. Two (41 and 78) occur while Gareth is a young child, perhaps an infant. The third occurs in a description of Arthur's campaign against Lucius: Arthur "mevys over the mountaynes and doth many mervayles, and so goth in by Godarte that Gareth sonne wynnys" (242). But "Gareth" is probably a scribal error for "garett" (tower), the word found in the alliterative *Morte Arthure*: "Gosse in by Goddarde, the garett he wynnys . . ." (*Morte Arthure*, ed. Edmond Brock, EETS-OS, No. 8 [London, 1871], line 3104).

[32] Scudder, *Le Morte Darthur*, p. 377.

effectively ironic than the comparable French version. When the catastrophe itself comes, his improvements are consistent with those just mentioned. For example, although the *Vulgate* Gaheriet apparently knows of but does not warn Lancelot of the plot against him,[33] Gareth is free of any such duplicity. Also contrary to the *Vulgate*, Gareth is unarmed; by following the stanzaic *Morte Arthur* in this detail, Malory enhances both the drama and the pathos of Gareth's role. Finally, the *Vulgate* Gaheriet strikes the first blow and is struck at first not by Lancelot but by Ector. All of these modifications reflect the earlier characterization of Gareth in the "Tale of Gareth," where his friendship with Lancelot was first introduced and where Malory could say of the young man that "allwayes he was meke and mylde."

As we have seen, no source has been identified for the "Tale of Gareth." It has been my purpose to suggest that Malory created the "Tale," borrowing some characters and incidents from earlier romances, to serve specific functions within *Le Morte Darthur* as a whole. Following the accounts in the first three "Tales" of the rise of Arthur and of Lancelot, it presents a happy picture of the Round Table at the height of its effectiveness. This picture serves as background against which the coming evidences of human frailty and of inescapable catastrophe in the later "Tales" will be viewed. Further, the character of Gareth himself serves as a standard against which the behavior of Gawain and his other brothers is to be measured. Perhaps most important is Malory's clear presentation of Gareth at this point in his book as preparation for the later irony when Lancelot inadvertently kills him.

[33] *Vulgate Version*, VI, 272–73. Malory here is carefully working from both the French *Mort Artu* and the English stanzaic poem; see Chapter VIII of the present volume for evidence of Malory's using both sources.

CHAPTER V

"THE TALE OF TRISTRAM":
DEVELOPMENT BY ANALOGY

BY THOMAS C. RUMBLE

I

Because it seems so disproportionately long, so needlessly in-
terruptive of the central story, and so casually abandoned before
its well-known tragic end, Malory's "Tale of Sir Tristram" is
perhaps difficult to see as belonging integrally to the larger
structural and thematic plan of *Le Morte Darthur*. Many a
reader has been surfeited and more with the two books included, and relieved indeed to come at long last to Malory's
statement, "Here ys no rehersall of the thirde booke."

Scholarly opinion has been severer still. Malory's treatment
of the ·"Tristram" is regularly characterized in one way or
another as the further devitalization of an already devitalized
legend. Because he did not know the highly tragic conception
of the tale in the "indubitably finer early versions" of the poetic
tradition,[1] his own "mutilated and hybrid version"[2] is a "hotch-
potch of miscellaneous adventures,"[3] having its source, worse

[1] Vida D. Scudder, *Le Morte Darthur of Sir Thomas Malory* (New York,
1921), p. 233.
[2] *Ibid.*, p. 229.
[3] W. H. Schofield, *English Literature from the Norman Conquest to
Chaucer* (London, 1914), p. 211.

till, in some "poor reworked"[4] French prose rendering of the story—some "tardive et corrumpue"[5] version whose *matière* , like its introduction, "aussi ennuyeuse que longue et inutile."[6] Working from this worst of all possible sources, Malory is thought to have accomplished little more than a slavish "reduction," making additions and alterations both "timid in character and few in number."[7] And if the relatively "uninspired matter of his *Book of Sir Tristram*"[8] results from the fact that he was "at the mercy of his original [and] could not alter its fundamental character,"[9] critics have viewed with even more concern the destructive effect of the Tristram material upon the structure and design of *Le Morte Darthur* as a whole. In this respect E. K. Chambers felt that Malory had "bungled his structural problem," and "would have done better to have left the *Tristan* alone": "We expect a work of fiction to have a beginning, a middle, and an end; to progress, however deviously, . . . to an intelligible issue. The Morte d'Arthur does not satisfy this expectation."[10]

Two avenues lie open for possible explanation of all these seeming faults. The first has been explored thoroughly by Professor Vinaver, who holds that we are not intended to see *Le Morte Darthur* as a single and unified work, but as a "collection which grew up by means of successive additions of romances often unconnected with each other." One of the most important evidences of this, Vinaver feels, is "the fact that the whole of the

---

[4] Edwin H. Zeydel, *The "Tristan and Isolde" of Gottfried von Strassburg* (Princeton, N. J., 1948), p. 13.

[5] E. Vinaver, *Le Roman de Tristan et Iseut dans l'oeuvre de Thomas Malory* (Paris, 1925), p. 91.

[6] G. Paris, "Note sur les romans relatifs a Tristan," *Romania*, XV (1886), 601.

[7] *Works*, p. lxviii.

[8] *Ibid.*, p. lxxii.

[9] *Ibid.*, p. 1433.

[10] *Sir Thomas Malory*, English Association Pamphlet No. 51 (1922), pp. 4-5.

middle portion [the 'Gareth' and 'Tristram' sections] is unrelated to any of the themes which occur before or after." [11] This explanation, of course, does not so much solve Malory's "structural problem" as dissolve it; and if we pursue this approach, perhaps we had best concede from the start that, of all the tales included, the "Tristram" is the "least attractive" [12]—the one extracted most "at hazard" from its source and with least "art and combination." [13]

The second way open to us is more fruitful, I think. It requires simply a closer examination of the *kind* of structural problem that Malory faced and of his *intent* in its solution. We need not begin, as G. L. Kittredge urged for Chaucer, with the assumption that Malory "always knew what he was about." [14] Nor need we conclude that Malory fully achieved his intent. But we do need to proceed with some knowledge of the magnitude of the task that lay before him and with the realization that there is not a single section of *Le Morte Darthur* which shows any sign of having received the final revision that would have smoothed its joints and made its individual parts bear fully upon each other and upon the whole. Given the conditions that Malory was not, after all, a cleric or a professional writer, and that *Le Morte Darthur* was written most sporadically during the intermittent terms of his imprisonment, [15] we are probably no more than realistic in finding ourselves less disappointed in the architectural failures of the work than conscious of its successes.

[11] Vinaver's "separate tales" theory finds expression in nearly everything he has written concerning Malory since 1947. I am quoting here from his essay, "Sir Thomas Malory," *Arthurian Literature in the Middle Ages* (hereafter *ALMA*), ed. R. S. Loomis (Oxford, 1959), p. 544. His fullest statement of the theory is that set forth in the "Introduction" and "Commentary" of *Works*.

[12] E. K. Chambers, *Sir Thomas Malory*, p. 5.

[13] Sir Walter Scott (ed.), *Sir Tristrem* (Edinburgh, 1804), p. lxxx.

[14] *Chaucer and His Poetry* (Cambridge, Mass., 1956), p. 151.

[15] On these and other facts of Malory's life, see Edward Hicks, *Sir Thomas Malory, His Turbulent Career* (Cambridge, Mass., 1928).

This, at any rate, seems to me the more promising approach to Malory's "Tale of Sir Tristram" and to the structural function of that division within its larger framework. It is a long and rambling section, and revision would almost surely have reduced it considerably and made its relation to the rest of the work more evident and more emphatic. But its length and its great multitude of episodes and themes ought not to prevent entirely our separating essentials from incidentals and seeing as clearly as possible, at least, what seems to have been Malory's intent.

In the following pages, then, I wish to suggest that such criticisms as those that I have outlined here represent not only something of a misconstruction of Malory's purpose in *Le Morte Darthur*, but a considerable underestimation of his accomplishment as well. To a far greater degree than is generally recognized, I think, Malory did succeed in welding the really important themes of his "Tristram" and Arthurian stories. He may not have known at first hand the "indubitably finer early versions" of the French and German poems,[16] but probably none of these versions would have suited his purpose anyway. For in no version other than that of the "tardive et corrompue" prose romance could he have found the "Tristram" and Arthurian materials already so interfused. More importantly, in no other version were there already just the parallels and contrasts that he could cause to bear so implicitly, yet so clearly, on the principal matter of *Le Morte Darthur*: the birth and rise to power of King Arthur,

[16] This assumption is not really susceptible of proof. Vinaver argues the point, commenting that "the great tragic conception of the legend had been abandoned by the French prose-writer, and Malory had no means of knowing it" (*Works*, p. 1434); but Vinaver is also forced to remark that occasionally, and however "unknowingly," Malory "restores something of the original [poetic] version of the story" (*Works*, p. 1598). Similarly, in a review of Vinaver's *Tristan dans l'oeuvre de Malory*, L. E. Winfrey remarks that "it is interesting to find Malory, who knew only the corrupted prose versions [of the *Tristan*], returning in his way to the standpoint of the great verse romances of the twelfth century" (*MP*, XXVI [1928–29], 231–233).

the Lancelot-Guenevere-Arthur triangle, the tragic fall of the Round Table, and the "dolorous deth and departyng of them al."

II

If the exact source of Malory's "Tale of Sir Tristram" were extant and known, we could proceed fairly confidently to determine his intent in that section, charting precisely his additions, omissions, and alterations, and inferring with some degree of probability the motivation for these changes. Unfortunately this is far from the case. The most careful scholarship has failed to reveal Malory's exact source, and we now know not much more than was assumed from the start—that he probably worked from some now lost version of the French prose *Tristan* romance. This is to say little indeed when it is remembered that there are extant at least forty-eight manuscripts of the French prose *Tristan* [17] and medieval adaptations of that romance in nearly every major European language.[18]

[17] For a list of these MSS, and brief descriptions of each, see E. Vinaver, *Etudes sur le Tristan en prose* (Paris, 1925), pp. 37–58. Also, B. Woledge, *Bibliographie des Romans et Nouvelles en prose francaise antérieurs à 1500* (Paris, 1954), pp. 122–25; E. Löseth, *Le Roman en prose de Tristan, le roman de Palamède, et le compilation de Rusticien de Pise: analyse critique d'apres les manuscrits de Paris* (Paris, 1890), pp. xxii–xxiii; P. Paris, *Les manuscrits francois de la bibliothèque du roi* (Paris, 1836), Vols. I and II, passim; H. L. D. Ward, *Catalogue of Romances in the Department of MSS in the British Museum* (London, 1883), I, 356–64. In addition to the MSS listed and described in these works, other MSS and fragments are coming to light from time to time. Renée L. Curtis has noted "the existence of another, hitherto unknown, Tristan MS. at Brussels, No. 9086–9087 . . . the text [of which] is complete" ("An Unnoticed Family of 'Prose Tristan' Manuscripts," *MLR*, XLIV [1954], 428–33). For descriptions of recently discovered fragments, see J. Séguy, "Fragments mutilés du *Roman de Tristan* en prose," *BBSIA*, No. 5 (1953), pp. 85–95; and Miss F. Bogdanow, "Un nouveau fragment du roman de *Tristan* en prose," *Romania*, LXXX (1959), 516–22. Finally, between the years 1489 and

To judge from this large number of surviving manuscripts and adaptations, the French prose version of the *Tristan* story was in late medieval times even more popular than the *Lancelot*.[19] Yet in spite of the seeming wealth of these remains, the origin and development of this form of the story is anything but clear.[20] As with the early poetic tradition of the legend,[21] it is generally agreed that we must pose a hypothetical *"Ur*-version," from which, directly or indirectly, the remaining prose versions stem.[22] This hypothetical original is thought to date from about 1220–30,[23] and to derive most directly from the minstrel tradition of the Eilhart and Béroul poems—though the relatively late date of even the earliest of the extant prose manuscripts (about 1275) allows for a number of influences from the courtly tradition of the Thomas and Gottfried poems.[24]

1586 the French prose *Tristan* was printed no fewer than nine times, the printings having been based either upon MS. B. N. fr. 103 or upon a MS "qui ne diffère du 103 que par détails de style" (G. Paris, "Le Morte de Tristan et d'Iseut," *Romania*, XV [1886], 481, n. 2). Apparently these printed versions were not based successively upon one another, but upon different MSS—though this, of course, would not be true of the 1567, 1577, and 1586 reprints of Jean Maugin's "modernization." For descriptions of the printed versions, now very rare, see Vinaver, *Etudes*, pp. 58–62; and Löseth, *Roman de Tristan*, pp. xxi–xxiv.

[18] See Vinaver, "The Prose *Tristan*," ALMA, p. 346, n. 4; and W. Golther, *Tristan und Isolde* (Leipzig, 1907), pp. 127–35.

[19] J. D. Bruce, *The Evolution of Arthurian Romance*, (2 vols., Göttingen, 1923), I, 483.

[20] Vinaver's essay "The Prose *Tristan*," ALMA, pp. 339–47, and the previous studies referred to there.

[21] On this thorny subject, see the most recent and concise studies by Helaine Newstead, "The Origin and Growth of the Tristan Legend," ALMA, pp. 122–33; and F. Whitehead, "The Early Tristan Poems," ALMA, pp. 134–44. In both of these essays numerous and important previous studies are cited.

[22] Vinaver's *stamm, Etudes*, p. 34; Löseth's, *Roman en prose de Tristan*, p. xxiv.

[23] Bruce, *Evolution*, I, 487–88.

[24] Vinaver, "The Prose *Tristan*," ALMA, pp. 340–41; *Etudes*, pp. 8–20. Gertrude Schoepperle observed that the French prose *Tristan* may well preserve a tradition "if not older than that of the poems, at least independent of them" (*Tristan and Isolt: A Study of the Sources of the*

Between the earliest of the *Tristan* poems and the earliest of
the extant prose manuscripts, however, the Vulgate Cycle of
Arthurian romance had developed, and the most popular tale
of that cycle seems unquestionably to have been the prose *Lancelot*. Thus, complicating still further the growth of the prose
Tristan is the fact that although the prose *Lancelot* and *Tristan*
stories developed similarly, the *Lancelot* was clearly based originally upon motifs of the early *Tristan* poems [25] and reached the
fullest stage of its prose development earlier than did the *Tristan*.
In even the earliest of the remaining manuscripts, then, much
of the prose *Tristan* is not only derivative from two different
traditions of the still earlier poetic versions of the same story,
but influenced as well, paradoxically, by the already established
prose *Lancelot*. This last influence, as Bruce pointed out,

> means that the old Celtic story of lawless and irresistible pas-
> sion, with all the primitive elements, both of poetry and of
> barbarism, which had continued to cling to it even in the hands
> of the French metrical romancers, was now diluted with in-
> numerable episodes that reflected the occupations, tastes, and
> ideals of French lords and ladies in the first half of the thir-
> teenth century—endless descriptions of jousts and tournaments.

Romance, [2 vols., Frankfurt, 1913], II, 439). Jacob Kelemina also thought
that the prose romance represented a separate tradition, which, in turn,
derived from two very early poems (neither to be identified with the *Ur-
Tristan* or *Estoire*), and the accretions of early French prose writers
(*Geschichte der Tristansage nach den Dichtungen des Mittelalters* [Wein,
1923], pp. 1–29, 169–88). R. S. Loomis has questioned whether there ever
existed a written *Ur-Tristan* or *Estoire* (see August Closs, [ed.], *Tristan
und Isolt by Gottfried von Strassburg* [Oxford, 1947], p. xxxiii) and has
suggested that the legend probably developed in two different forms: "the
Bleheris tradition represented by Eilhart, Béroul, Thomas; [and] a Breton
tradition largely independent of Bleheris, represented by the Prose Tristan"
("Problems of the Tristan Legend," *Romania*, LIII [1927], 82–102).

[25] Bruce, *Evolution*, I, 484: "The Lancelot-Guenevere romance was, in
origin, merely a re-adaptation by Chrétien of the legend of Tristan and
Iseut." Also, W. T. H. Jackson, *The Literature of the Middle Ages* (New
York, 1960), p. 137: ". . . numerous incidents in the Lancelot story are
taken directly from a version of the Tristan legend or from intermediate
source material."

knight-errant adventures, love affairs conducted in the fashion of a highly organized society, with letters and poems (*lais*) addressed by the lover to his mistress—and so on.[26]

The relatively few scholars who have studied even a part of the numerous and widely scattered prose *Tristan* manuscripts are generally agreed that the remaining versions fall into two broad categories—the first often called the "vulgate" or "Luces de Gast" version;[27] the second variously referred to as the "common," the "cyclic," the "enlarged," or the "Hélie de Boron" *Tristan*.[28] The versions in the first of these categories are much the shorter, containing substantially only the basic plot material of the earlier poetic tradition, but augmenting that material with the kind of embellished episodic treatment which is so characteristic of nearly all of the French prose romances. The versions of the second category, on the other hand, include not only the *Tristan* story, but incorporate as well a version of the *Quest of the Holy Grail*,[29] and large segments of both the *Lancelot* and the *Mort Artu* romances.

[26] Bruce, *Evolution*, I, 484–85.

[27] H. O. Sommer classified the groups of MSS as "Vulgate" or "enlarged" (*Le Morte Darthur* [London, 1889–91], III, 279). Vinaver discusses and rejects Sommer's classification (*Etudes*, pp. 25–26). The form of the name de Gast varies widely among the MSS, some giving Gaut, Galt, Gant, Grant, Gail, etc., but Bruce was mistaken in believing that "the form, Gast, does not occur a single time in all the MSS of the Bibliothèque National and British Museum" (*Evolution*, I, 486, n. 8); according to Vinaver's *Etudes* (pp. 40, 45, 46, and 49), *Gast* is the form given in MSS. B. N, fr. 104, 12599, 6579, and B. M. Harley 4389.

[28] Bruce notes that this "enlarged" version is "longer and later" than the "earlier and better" Luces de Gast version, and that it is "sometimes called the 'Common version,' since it exists in much the largest number of MSS, and sometimes the 'cyclic version,' since MSS of this version regularly connect the romance with the Vulgate by a reference to the *Mort Artu* or even (in some MSS) by the incorporation of that romance and still further, by the incorporation of the greater part of the *Quest* branch" (*Evolution*, I, 484). The name "Helie de Boron" (and possibly "Luces de Gast") has long been thought fictitious (see G. Paris, *Romania*, XV [1886], 600–2; and *Merlin* [eds. Paris and J. Ulrich], *SATF*, I, xxvii–xxxvii).

[29] Vinaver, *Etudes*, p. 27: ". . . la première version donne un récit

On the whole, all of the existing prose *Tristan* manuscripts vary so markedly from each other in minor details that the task merely of cataloguing their divergences has proved a monumental one.[30] One manuscript, however,—B.N. fr. 103—differs from all the rest in returning to the older poetic tradition of the tale for its ending: here the lovers die in the court of the second Isoud (*Iseult as Blanches Mains*),[31] rather than in Cornwall and as a result of Mark's treacherous wounding of Tristan.[32] B.N. fr. 103 is a late manuscript—perhaps even slightly later than Malory's account of the story; and although its ending is unique among the remaining manuscripts, the same version is given by all of the printed editions—suggesting, perhaps, that by the late fifteenth and early sixteenth centuries this ending had become the more popular of the two.

We cannot know certainly which of the two endings was given in Malory's source manuscript—the "thirde booke" of which there is in *Le Morte Darthur*, of course, "no rehersall." From his bare summary of events, tucked away much later in the "Lancelot and Guenevere" division, we are probably quite safe in assuming that his source gave the ending of the usual prose manu-

---

abrégé de la *Quête du Saint-Graal*, tandis que la seconde l'accueille sans retouches."

[30] Löseth's *Le roman en prose de Tristan* . . . ; and *Le Tristan et le Palamède des manuscrits francaise du British Museum*, (Christiana, 1905).

[31] In MS. 103, as in the poems, Tristan lies dying of a poisoned wound. He has sent for the first Iseult (Iseult la Bloie), who can heal him if she will come; and the mariners are to return under a white sail if they bring Iseult, a black sail if not. Discovering these arrangements, the second Iseult becomes jealous and lies to Tristan concerning the color of the sail, whereupon, all hope seemingly lost, Tristan expires. Finding him already dead when she reaches him, the first Iseult swoons upon his breast and dies of sorrow embracing him.

[32] For the two endings, see J. Bedier, "La Mort de Tristan et Iseut d'après le MS. 103 . . . ," *Romania*, XV (1886), 496–510; and E. S. Murell, "The Death of Tristan from Douce MS. 189," *PMLA*, XLIII (1928), 343–83. The only other significant portion of the prose romance published is the first part of the Edinburgh MS. Adv. 19.1.3, *La Grant Ystoire de Monsignor Tristan "Li Bret,"* ed. Miss F. C. Johnson (Edinburgh, 1942).

scripts: "That traytoure kynge [Mark] slew the noble knyght sir Trystram as he sate harpynge afore hys lady, La Beall Isode, with a trenchaunte glayve . . . and La Beall Isode dyed sownyng uppon the crosse of sir Trystram, whereof was grete pité" (1149–50). But we are not at all safe, I think, in assuming that Malory knew *only* this ending, and that, in picturing Isoud's "sownyng uppon the crosse of sir Trystram," he *"unknowingly* restores something of the original version of the story." [33] The point is, to indulge for a moment in sheer speculation, that Malory could have known both endings, yet still have chosen to treat his material as he did. His problem, after all, was a structural one, a need to fuse a number of more or less heterogeneous and independent stories in such a way that all would be subordinate yet integral to the central story of the rise and fall of Arthur's kingdom. Keeping this structural need in mind, it seems to me no great difficulty to visualize what would have been the effects of the alternatives open to him. First of all, and very practically, had he "rehearsed" the latter part of his source manuscript, the "thirde booke," as he calls it, he would have had to follow a version of the *Quest of the Holy Grail* in which Tristan, not Lancelot, figured as the central adventurer. More importantly, regardless of which ending of the story his source gave and regardless of whether or not he knew both endings, it was very much to his purpose to avoid presenting so tragic and climactic an ending as that of the older poetic tradition, since such an episode would . unquestionably have tended to weaken the dramatic and tragic climax of *Le Morte Darthur* as a whole. In short, with many another, we may lament the general deterioration of the *Tristan* story in the French prose romances; the tragic situation was, as Bruce put it, "surely much finer in the old story." [34] And if the "Tale of Sir Tristram" were Malory's only

[33] Vinaver, *Works*, pp. 1597–98 (the italics are mine).
[34] *Evolution*, I, 490.

work, a self-contained romance, surely we might lament all th
more the further deterioration of the story in his hands. But it
place in the larger framework of *Le Morte Darthur* makes a]
the difference, I think; and even Malory's abandoning the well
known tragic climax of the tale requires a more reasonable ex
planation than his supposed naïve predilection for a happ
ending.[35]

The problem of Malory's "Tristram" source is an extremel
complex one. Lacking the exact manuscript that Malory worked
from, scholars have sought to deal with this problem by compar
ing his version of the story to that given in the most nearl
parallel of the remaining French prose manuscripts. Thus, a
early as 1891, H. O. Sommer noted the many similarities be
tween Malory's "Tristram" and several of the versions repre
sented by manuscripts in the British Museum and concluded
that he had probably worked from a single manuscript consisting

---

[35] Vinaver, *Works*, pp. lxxiv–lxxv: ". . . Malory whole-heartedly follow
his source; it is with genuine delight that he relates the blissful retiremen
of the lovers to Joyous Gard and leaves them there at the close of th
romance so that, in his favourite phrase, they may live 'cheerfully' eve
after. The happy ending is achieved here as in the *Tale of King Arthu:
and the Emperor Lucius* by the omission of the concluding part of th
original." This explanation seems to me even less satisfactory for "Arthu
and Lucius" than for the "Tristram." Arthur's Roman campaign usuall
ends with his being called back to England to deal with Mordred's usurpa
tion of his crown and queen, the battle between Arthur and Mordred i
Cornwall, their deaths, and the destruction of their armies and the Roun
Table (*Morte Arthure*, ed. E. Brock, EETS, pp. 102–28). But Malor
also knew the almost exactly similar circumstances of this ending from th
cyclic *Morte Artu* and from the English stanzaic poem, where Mordred'
defection takes place not during Arthur's absence in the Roman wars, bu
while Arthur is besieging Lancelot's castle at Benwick after discovering th
adulterous relationship between Lancelot and Guenevere. I think tha
Malory deliberately abandoned the ending of his source for "Arthur an
Lucius" in order to postpone those events until very near the end of hi
"hoole booke." The surest sign of this intention, it seems to me, is hi
substitution of Baudewyn for Mordred as the knight left as Arthur'
"dictour" for the duration of the Roman campaign (see *Works*, pp. 19
and 1369). For an historical-allegorical explanation of this substitution
see *Works*, pp. 1361-62.

of three parts—or, as Malory calls them, three "Freynshe bookes." [36] The first of these parts, according to Sommer, probably included approximately the matter of Books VIII and IX in Caxton's arrangement of *Le Morte Darthur*. The second part probably paralleled the whole of Malory's Book X and those episodes of Books XI and XII which deal with Tristram. The third part—had Malory chosen to use this extension of the French prose *Tristan* instead of reverting to the Vulgate Cycle for essentially the same material—probably rehearsed the *Quest of the Holy Grail* and centered that story around the adventures of Tristan, Perceval, and Galahad, as do all of the extant French prose manuscripts which include anything more than a mere summary of the Grail romance.

Sommer's identification of Malory's "Tristram" source was admittedly of the most general kind and was based upon very incomplete evidence—he had consulted only the British Museum manuscripts. More recently, Vinaver has re-examined the whole matter of Malory's originals and, referring to the "Tristram" and "Grail" sections of *Le Morte Darthur*, has claimed that "none of [Malory's] other compositions is as fully accounted for by its sources." [37] In his *Roman de Tristan dans Malory* [38] and in a considerable portion of the "Commentary" of his *Works of Sir Thomas Malory*,[39] Vinaver sets forth a detailed comparison of Malory's "Tristram" and a hypothetical composite source— a now lost French prose manuscript, "probably a single work which followed alternately each of the three versions [of MSS. B.N. fr. 103, 334, and 99]." [40]

Because of key similarities in the sequence of certain episodes, there is much to recommend Vinaver's identification of Mal-

[36] *Le Morte Darthur*, III, 288–99.
[37] *Works*, p. lxviii.
[38] See esp. pp. 155–220.
[39] Pp. 1432–1511.
[40] *Works*, p. 1437.

ory's "Tristram" and the parallel sections of these three manuscripts.[41] But if the primary purpose of a "source study" is to
discover where a later writer deviates from an earlier and to
pose the most logical explanations possible for those deviations,
the dangers of a detailed comparison such as Vinaver's should be
evident. The remaining French prose manuscripts, as I have
said, are so divergent that no one of them agrees in every detail
with any of the others; and while B.N. fr. 103, 334, and 99 may
each parallel Malory's "Tristram" in certain respects, it is nevertheless a hazardous critical approach to compare these manuscripts with Malory and to conclude on the basis of such a comparison that this or that detail of Malory's version was or was
not taken from his French source. Moreover, there are two
versions of the prose *Tristan*—the Spanish *Cuento de Tristan* [42]
and the Italian *Leggenda di Tristano* [43]—which have never been
used as part of the comparative evidence, and which, in fact,
parallel Malory in some respects more closely than any of the
French versions.[44] I do not wish to imply that Malory's source
was anything other than a "Freynshe booke," or even that the
three versions derive from a common French source.[45] But if

[41] See, however, the important reservations of E. Brugger, "Review of
Tristan dans l'oeuvre de Malory," *Zeitschrift für Französische Sprache und
Literatur*, LIII (1930), 131–69. E. Löseth had previously noted the marked
similarity between Malory's "Tristram" and the corresponding sections of
MSS. B. N. fr. 103 and 99 (*Le roman en prose de Tristan . . . d'apres
les manuscrits de Paris*, pp. xxii–xxiii).

[42] *El Cuento de Tristan de Leonis*, ed. G. T. Northup (Chicago, 1928).

[43] *La Leggenda di Tristano*, a cura di Luigi di Benedetto (Bari, 1942).

[44] In the interest of brevity I shall note here only a few of the similarities
between Malory's "Tristram" and the Spanish and Italian versions. I have
compared these versions in somewhat greater detail in an unpublished Ph.D.
dissertation, "The *Tristan* Legend and Its Place in Malory's *Morte Darthur*"
(Tulane University, 1955), and hope to deal with the subject more
thoroughly in a separate study.

[45] There has been much difference of opinion concerning the relationship
of the Spanish and Italian versions—whether they derive successively from
the same French source, one based upon the other, or independently. In
some respects (the sequence of events occurring late in the story, for ex-

we are to ascertain the most likely instances where Malory deviated from whatever version his source was, we are going to have to compare the details of his "Tristram" not only with all of the French prose manuscripts, but with the Spanish and Italian versions as well. In this way, if a given aspect of Malory's treatment is not to be found in *any* of the other versions, we may be at least a little surer than at present in ascribing that deviation to Malory's own invention.

It is a very attractive hypothesis, for example, to think that Malory deviated from his source in beginning his "Tristram" *in medias res*. On this point Vinaver has noted that "the French prose-writer devotes considerable space to the lives of Tristram's ancestors, and traces his pedigree to the first century of our era," [46] and that Malory "clearly aims at some degree of simplification within the [source] material which he retains." [47] If we could be sure that this lengthy prologue was not also omitted in Malory's source, I think we might go even further than Vinaver and say that Malory aimed at a substantially more artistic purpose than the mere "simplification" of his source material. For, among the many other events related in the French versions of this "longue et inutile" introduction, King Mark treacherously kills his brother Pernam in securing the

---

ample) they parallel each other, but correspond to no known French version. In other respects (the relationship of Mark and Meliadus, for example) the Italian version deviates markedly from the French, but is not paralleled by a similar deviation in the Spanish. In still other respects (the omission of Belinde's lament) the Spanish version deviates from the French where the Italian does not. For a thorough discussion of the complex relationships involved, see Northup's excellent commentary in the introduction to his edition of the *Cuento de Tristan* (pp. 1–78). Northup supports the view that the Spanish version derives from French through an Italian version (pp. 20–24).

[46] *Works*, p. 1444. This extremely detailed account of Tristram's ancestry —which G. Paris characterized as "aussi ennuyeuse que longue et inutile" ("Note sure les romans relatifs a Tristan," *Romania*, XV [1886], 601)— occupies in MS. B. N. fr. 103 nearly twenty-seven folios.

[47] *Works*, p. 1432.

crown of Cornwall for himself, and he is thus established even
before the actual beginning of the *Tristan* story as the cowardly
and false-hearted villain that he remains throughout. In Malory,
as I shall point out later, Mark's treachery grows out of the
internal incidents and conflicts of the story itself: he is not from
the very beginning the cruel and scheming antagonist that he
later becomes. Thus, if we knew Malory's exact source and
could show that he cut right to the heart of his story by omitting
its long and superfluous introduction, we might see his purpose
as being perfectly consistent with a larger plan for the treatment
of the character of King Mark. But however much we might
wish to attribute such a careful and artistic purpose to Malory's
own invention, the fact is that the *Leggenda* also begins *in
medias res*, and Malory's French source may well have begun in
exactly the same way:

There was a kynge that hyght Melyodas, and he was lorde of the contrey of Lyones. And this Melyodas was a lykly knyght as ony was that tyme lyvyng. And by fortune he wedded kynge Markis sister of Cornuayle, and she was called Elyzabeth, that was called bothe good and fayre.[48]	Lo re che Filice iera chiamato avea III figliuoli e IIII figliuole. L'uno de' figliuoli avea nome Meliadus e fue coronato del reame de Leonis. . . . Ma lo re Meliadus si iera prode e franco cavaliere, ed avea una sua donna, la quale avea nome reina Eliabel, la quale iera bella donna di suo corpo oltramodo.[49]

[48] *Ibid.*, p. 371.
[49] *Leggenda di Tristano*, pp. 1–2. I have omitted a very brief description
of King Felice's other two sons. So far as I know, the Italian version is
alone in giving Meliadus and Mark as brothers, rather than, as in other
versions, brothers-in-law. The first five folios of the *Cuento de Tristan* are
lacking; hence we cannot compare Malory's beginning with that of the
Spanish version. Northup comments, however, that the *Cuento* "must have
begun, as did the Spanish *Tristan de Leones* or the Italian *Tristano Ric-
cardiano*, with the birth of Tristram. The five lost folios would just account
for the matter found in Löseth, pp. 20–23: the death of Meliadus and the

In view of a good many evidences such as this from the Spanish and Italian versions, it seems clear that we need to be very cautious about what aspects of Malory's "Tristram" we attribute to his own originality.

By bringing more of the known prose versions of the *Tristan* into the comparison, then, I think we can become a little safer than in the past in identifying many of Malory's probable divergences from his source. But it will not be enough merely to catalogue these; far more important than his alterations are his reasons for those alterations, and wherever possible we must discover not only *what* Malory did with his sources, but *why*. To illustrate this point briefly, let me introduce but two of many possible examples—the well-known episodes of Tristram's voyage for healing after his battle with Morholt, and Tristram and Isoud's drinking of the love potion.

In most versions of the legend Tristram's voyage for the healing of the envenomed wound inflicted by Morholt takes the form of a "navigation d'aventure." In the poems the device used is the "rudderless boat" motif; in most of the prose versions the motif is simply that of the "hazardous journey." But Malory motivates Tristram's voyage for healing by causing Tristram to set out specifically for Ireland upon the advice of a "wytty lady"; and finding that this is not the motivation given in B.N. fr. 103, Vinaver comments merely that "by introducing this explanation of Tristram's journey to Ireland M[alory] has avoided any suggestion of the supernatural." [50] While Malory's motivation of Tristram's voyage is unlike that of the French prose romance, however, it is very closely paralleled by that of the

two attempts to poison Tristram" (*Cuento de Tristan*, p. 1). It should be noted here that the *Leggenda* later mentions Mark's having killed Pernam in securing the crown. If this detail was present in Malory's source, he may be due the credit for omitting it in accordance with his plan for the treatment of Mark's character, but this remains pure conjecture.

[50] *Works*, p. 1446.

Spanish *Cuento de Tristan,* and may have been, therefore, not Malory's invention, but a borrowing from his source. In the *Cuento* Tristram has languished for some time after his battle with Morholt, and all efforts to heal his wound have failed:

> E en esto vino una dueña a verlo, e dixole—Tristan, non vos dexedes perder, mas metedvos en aventura e buscat todo el mundo, e levaredes oro e plata, e por aventura fallaredes alguna dueña o donzella o cavallero que vos guaresça de la plaga.[51]

In the *Leggenda* [52] there is no lady connected with the motivation of Tristram's voyage; there, as in the French versions, the voyage is no more than a "hazardous journey," and Tristram does not undertake it specifically to seek a cure for his wound. Looking out upon the sea one day from the window of the "palaggio" to which he has been removed because of the stench of his wound, Tristram himself decides upon the "navigation d'aventure," calls King Mark to his bedside, and asks Mark to prepare a boat for him. In the French version of Adv. MS. 19.1.3 [53] "une dame" is introduced, but the episode is extremely brief and quite different from the versions of Malory and the *Cuento* on the one hand, and that of the *Leggenda* on the other. In this French version Tristram is visited by a lady who asks him why he does not seek help elsewhere, and he replies that he cannot ride because of his wound. Some time after the lady's visit Tristram looks despairingly out upon the sea one day, decides upon the voyage, and asks King Mark for a boat. Here again, however, so far from setting out with the specific hope of finding a cure for his wound, Tristram explains the motivation of his intended voyage as a search for death: he tells the king "qu'il vuelt mues morir sor meir que languir sor terre." Finally, the French version of B.N. fr. 103 gives a much expanded and

---

[51] Northup, *Cuento,* p. 89.
[52] Di Benedetto, pp. 28–29.
[53] Johnson, *Tristan "Li Bret,"* pp. 13–14.

still different account of the episode. As in Adv. 19.1.3, Tristram is visited by "une dame" who asks why he does not seek a cure for his wound "en autre terre," and he replies that he can neither ride nor "souffrir a estre porte en litiere." Again the lady goes away, and again it is Tristram himself who later thinks of the sea voyage—in this version, however, not through any wish for death, but specifically to seek healing: "pour savoir se Dieu me vouldroit mieulx envoier garison en autre terre qu'il ne fait en ceste cy." [54]

As Vinaver points out, since in Malory's version of this episode Tristram is advised by a "wytty lady" where to seek the cure for his envenomed wound, his voyage for healing ceases to be the "hazardous journey" that it is in the French versions. Yet in the *Cuento* Tristram's voyage is also motivated directly by the counsel of "una dueña." The one difference, of course, is that in Malory Tristram is advised *where* to seek his cure ("in the same contrey that the venym came fro"), whereas in the *Cuento* he is told simply to search "todo el mundo." Otherwise the two versions are close enough that, no matter what we say about Malory's having relieved the episode of "any suggestion of the supernatural," it is still entirely possible that the supernatural implications were already avoided in his source and that in this respect Malory followed his source closely.

There are some details of the motivation of Tristram's voyage for healing, however, in which Malory's version is not paralleled by any of the other versions remaining; and since these details fit so well the pattern of certain other alterations likely to have been Malory's, we can at least tentatively attribute them to his own invention. Of the versions now available for comparison, for example, only in Malory is King Mark a part of the audience to the lady's counsel that Tristram must seek his cure "in the same contrey that the venym came fro." In fact, only in Malory is

[54] MS. B. N. fr. 103, f. 36r, cols. a and b.

the king caused to seem truly concerned for Tristram; for the
"wytty lady" is in this version one of the "all maner of lechis
and surgeons" that "the kynge lette sende for," and when she
diagnoses Tristram's poisoned wound and prescribes his voyage
for healing, her advice is directly "seyde playnly unto the kynge."
Finally, only in Malory does King Mark immediately "lette
purvey for syr Trystrames a fayre vessell and well vytaled" without Tristram's asking. These are minor alterations, to be sure.
But since, as I shall point out, Malory also seems to have
altered his source material in other ways to effect a much more
consistent treatment of the character of King Mark than that
of the other versions, they are important. For this episode takes
place before the conflict between Tristram and King Mark for
the favor of Sir Seguarides' wife, which, in Malory, begins the
enmity between them. At the point of Tristram's battle with
Morholt and his subsequent voyage for healing, in other words,
the relationship between Tristram and King Mark is still "good
eme—fayre nevew." The systematic blackening of Mark's character has not yet begun, and Malory seems to have adjusted the
details of these earlier episodes accordingly.

Malory's treatment of the episode in which Tristram and
Isoud drink the love potion furnishes a similar example. One of
the major differences between the poetic and prose versions of
the *Tristan* story is the fact that in most of the prose romances
the importance of the love potion is almost totally diminished.
In the poems the lovers' conflicts are largely internal, centering
around the strife between love and duty on the one hand and
the demands of a mutual and an uncontrollable passion on the
other. In the prose versions the lovers are oppressed by forces
that are largely external. Their love is not so much an overpower-
ing emotion as it is a kind of willful and contrary reaction
against the frustrating intervention of King Mark—or more accurately, perhaps, against that of the Barons who are always at

Mark's ear, whispering of betrayal and inciting him to vengeance. And the whole difference, however complex its ramifications, lies in the prose writer's attitude toward the love potion. How, after the "love spot" and *geis* of the Old Irish *Aitheda,* was an extra-marital love such as Tristram and Isoud's to be motivated and sustained? For the courtly poets of the twelfth century the motif of a love potion served well enough. But for the thirteenth through the fifteenth centuries we must pose an audience other than courtly, at least in the older and stricter sense of the word; and the audience of the prose romances could scarcely be expected to accept a story so entirely controlled by such a supernatural motivation as a magic drink.[55] From the great host of prose romances on all subjects written during these centuries we can infer that the first interest of their audiences lay not in the psychologically intricate love dilemmas of the characters, but in the blacks and whites of heroes and villains and in their actions. That is one reason why there is in the prose *Tristan* romance only the sketchiest kind of development of the character of Isoud, and that is why the tragic love of Tristram and Isoud is central to the prose story not in its own right, but in the motivation that it furnishes for sustaining the conflict between Tristram and King Mark.

To be sure, the motifs of love and conflict are still mutually dependent in the prose *Tristan.* However much the one is subordinated to the other in its treatment, if Tristram's love for Isoud is to motivate his conflict with King Mark, that love must itself be motivated. But apparently the prose writer was not willing to allow so important a motivation to rest upon the

---

[55] By the time that Lancelot and Guenevere were firmly established as lovers, the "fatal framework" of their relationship was regularly explained in terms of Merlin's prophecy: "But Merlyon warned the kyng covertly that Gwenyver was nat holsom for hym to take to wyff. For he warned hym that Launcelot scholde love hir, and sche hym agayne" (*Works,* p. 97). Merlin, of course, had long been used as a device for prophecy, often replacing some older device of supernatural motivation.

magic power of a love potion, and especially if, as in most of
the poems, the effect of that potion diminished after three or
four years.[56] In the early prose manuscript Adv. 19.1.3,[57] the
scene in which the lovers drink the potion is unceremoniously
brief and insignificant in comparison with the intricate and
emphatic treatment it receives at the hands of the poets. It will
be remembered that Tristram has just won Isoud for King Mark.
Before they set sail for Cornwall, Isoud's mother prepares a
potion to be given Isoud and Mark on their wedding night and
entrusts it to the keeping of Brangwain and Gouvernal. On the
third day at sea, while playing chess, Tristram and Isoud become thirsty and unwittingly drink the "boivre amerous." A day
or so later ("un jor") they find themselves alone: "Tristans jut
a lui. Enci comencerent primierement lor amors." [58] And after
this summary treatment of the scene, neither the potion nor its
effect is mentioned again. Compared with this manuscript, B.N.
fr. 103 gives a much expanded version of the scene, recounting
not only Gouvernal's and Brangwain's consternation at having
given the lovers the wrong wine, but introducing the prose
writer's own reaction as well: "Ha, Dieu, quel boire! Or sont
entrez en la riote que jamais ne leur fauldra jour de leurs vies.
Car ilz ont beu leur destruction et leur mort. Cil boire leur
asemble bon et moult doulz, mais onquez doulce ne fu si
cher achetee comment ceste sera!" [59]

---

[56] On the duration of the efficacy of the love potion in the prose
romance, see Vinaver, "The Love Potion in the Primitive Tristan Romance," *Medieval Studies in Memory of Gertrude Schoepperle Loomis*,
ed. R. S. Loomis (1927), pp. 75–88. Vinaver contends that, as in the
Thomas poem, the effects of the potion are unlimited in duration in the
prose romance, but his contention is based on the version of B. N. fr. 103,
which is much influenced by the Thomas poem in other ways. Other MSS
do not make this point clear one way or the other.

[57] Vinaver dates this MS. in the 13th century (*Etudes*, p. 51).

[58] Johnson, *Tristan "Li Bret*," pp. 31–32. The brevity of the episode in
this MS. contrasts with over five hundred lines in the poem of Eilhart von
Oberge (2264–2798) and over twelve hundred in that of Gottfried von
Strassburg (11371–12573).

[59] MS. B. N. fr. 103, ff. 56va–57rb.

In Malory's "Tristram," in the Spanish *Cuento*, and in the Italian *Leggenda*, the account of the love potion episode is neither so abbreviated as in Adv. 19.1.3 nor so expanded as in B.N. fr. 103.[60] This fact may suggest simply that these three versions represent an intermediate stage of the development of the prose romance and derive from French manuscripts that are later than the thirteenth-century Adv. 19.1.3 and earlier than the fifteenth-century B.N. fr. 103.[61] But quantitative similarities and dissimilarities are by no means the only consideration here. For in the treatment of the love potion episode there are other differences between the versions of the French romances on the one hand and those of Malory and the Spanish and Italian writers on the other; and an examination of these differences may throw some further light on Malory's attitude toward his "Freynshe booke" and on his consequent treatment of that source material in *Le Morte Darthur*.

In the *Tristan* poems there existed one motif by means of which the French prose writer could motivate and sustain Tristram and Isoud's illicit love with a much surer sense of realism than the love potion affords. Thomas, of course, emphasizes the unlimited duration of the love potion in order to mitigate our reprobation of the lovers in their otherwise unsanctified relationship. In Eilhart and Béroul, on the other hand, where the effect of the love potion is limited, the character of King Mark is so degraded that he deserves little better than his role as cuckold. The French prose writer seems to have found this last motif exactly suited to his needs; and to make the conflict between Tristram and Mark still more explicit, he em-

---

[60] In Malory the episode occupies but three brief paragraphs (*Works*, 412); in the Spanish a little less; in the Italian a little more (Northup, *Cuento de Tristan*, pp. 111–12; Di Benedetto, *Leggenda di Tristano*, pp. 71–72).

[61] I have not been able to see all of the French MSS to verify this as thoroughly as I should like. To judge by those I have seen and by the careful descriptions of Vinaver's *Etudes* (pp. 37–58), however, as a general rule the early MSS are quite brief and the later ones much expanded.

phasized that motif in two further ways. First, he established the beginning of Tristram and Isoud's love for each other much earlier and much more naturally than it is established in the poems and largely abandoned the importance of the love potion as initiating their relationship. Secondly, he further blackened the character of Mark and his barons, making Mark a coward and his barons "felons." Both of these devices operate, as Bruce noted, "to lessen the opprobrium of the hero's adultery"; [62] and these are precisely the devices which Malory made still more emphatic in his attempt to rationalize the lovers' continuance in what must otherwise be seen for what it actually is—a purely illicit and guilt-ridden relationship.

The French prose romances—and especially the version of B.N. fr. 103—are highly serious in their treatment of the love potion episode. Even though the potion itself does not play as important a part in these versions as in the earlier poems, the prose writers nevertheless treated the scene in which the lovers drink that potion with some degree of dignity and some measure of faithfulness to the spirit of its treatment by the poets. Malory and the writers of the *Cuento* and *Leggenda*, on the other hand, show no such deference to tradition. Indeed the Spanish writer very nearly makes a mockery of the scene: having drunk this "vino enamorado," and having briefly repaired to their quarters to consummate the "loco amor" which results, the lovers return to the deck of the ship to finish the game of chess they had begun. And the Italian writer is not above concluding his version of the scene with a poor bit of punning on the word *giuoco*: having drunk the "beveraggio amoroso," the lovers leave off playing their "giuoco di scacci" and go below-deck to begin playing "quello giuoco.... que in tutta loro vita lo giucarono volontieri."

Malory's treatment of this scene, like that of the Spanish and

[62] *Evolution*, I, 490.

Italian writers, deliberately minimizes the importance of the love potion as a motivating factor in the subsequent adulterous relationship between Tristram and Isoud. Moreover, in the alteration of one detail of that scene, Malory emphatically places the responsibility for that adulterous relationship squarely upon the lovers themselves; and in so doing, he presents an interpretation of the character of Isoud which is not only different from that of the French prose romances, but which permits us to see Isoud as a considerably more attractive figure than we have customarily thought her to be.

But although Malory's treatment of the love potion episode is by no means so irreverent as that of the Spanish and Italian writers, he does treat the scene lightly. Tristram and Isoud jokingly banter about the "draught of good wyne" which Tristram suggests their servants have "kepte for hemselff," and "than they lowghe and made good chere and eyther dranke to other frely." Yet even this seems a part of Malory's larger plan. For, whatever her redeeming features, the Isoud of the French romances has been rather generally condemned for her treatment of her faithful maid, Brangwain, following the episode of the love potion. In every version of the story but Malory's, Brangwain is made at least partially responsible for the mistake of giving Tristram and Isoud the potion which was intended for Isoud and Mark. And as the result of her responsibility for Isoud's loss of "le nom de pucellage," in every version but Malory's Brangwain is obliged to play the role of the substituted bride on Mark and Isoud's wedding night. Finally, in every version but Malory's, Isoud comes to fear Brangwain's knowledge; and to insure her own peace of mind, she treacherously plots to have Brangwain murdered by two woodsmen. The murder does not come off, of course, and apparently Isoud is later genuinely repentant of her treatment of Brangwain; yet from this point to the end of the story there is an unpleasant shadow

cast over her character, and we never quite forgive at least her
initial "mal intention."

The character of Isoud is not especially important to Malory's
"Tristram," but he does appear to have felt it a dubious procedure to motivate the central conflict of the story—that between Tristram and King Mark—by so unattractive a figure as
Isoud becomes in the French romances after her attempt on
Brangwain's life. Whatever his reason, Malory deliberately
altered what was almost surely the version of his source in order
to avoid any suggestion of treachery in Isoud's character. He
included the attempted murder of Brangwain, to be sure; but he
entirely vindicated Isoud by causing that attempt to be insti-
gated by two of her jealous servants—"two ladyes that . . .
ordayned for hate and envye for to distroy dame Brangwayne
that was mayden and lady unto La Beale Isode." In fact, after
Brangwain is "bounde honnde and foote to a tre" for three days,
rescued by Palomides, and taken to a nunnery to recover, Malory
tells us that "whan Isode the quene myssed hir mayden, wete
you well she was ryght hevy as evir any quene myght be, for of
all erthely women she loved hir beste and moste" (419). Moreover, in Malory's version Brangwain is not made to suffer the
indignity of the substituted bride plot, and Isoud's character is
thus relieved of the stigma attached to her part in that scheme.
The important point is that Malory's considerable deviations
from his source in these two episodes permit us to regard Isoud
in a much more favorable light than we ever see her in the
French romances; and these deviations are in turn made possible
by his very slight alteration of the love potion scene.

Vinaver's only comment on Malory's treatment of his source
in the love potion episode is that the "flakette of gold" from
which the lovers drink is in the French manuscript "a silver
cup." [63] Quite aside from the fact that this comment is in-

[63] *Works*, p. 1452.

accurate,[64] it is also insufficient—particularly in that it omits the one really important difference between Malory and his probable source and the significance of that difference. For, while all other versions make either Brangwain or Gouvernal (or more often both) responsible for the mistake of giving Tristram and Isoud the love potion, Malory causes Tristram to find that drink by accident; and Tristram's joking remark about the "good draught" that their servants had "kepte for hemselff" seems clearly a touch of realism designed to emphasize the fact that neither of the servants is in any way responsible for giving the lovers the drink which, nominally, at least, motivates "leur destruction et leur mort" in the French romances. Thus the way is cleared for Malory to absolve Isoud of the opprobrium which becomes connected with her later treatment of Brangwain in the other versions.

A really close comparison of Malory's "Tristram" and all of the other versions remaining will disclose quite a number of the kinds of differences that I have tried to illustrate here. Moreover, such a comparison reveals what seems to me a fairly complex and consciously worked out pattern of interrelationships among these differences and suggests that while Malory followed the general outline of his source quite closely, he nevertheless made a good many alterations of details; and it is often just these alterations which seem designed to affect not only the "Tristram" itself but its relation to the whole of *Le Morte Darthur*.

In the following pages I shall have occasion to refer often to Malory's *probable* alterations of his source material. Where the "Tristram" source is concerned, lacking the exact manuscript from which he worked and wishing to proceed on the basis

[64] In the French, Brangwain pours the "boire amoureaux" from one of the "vaisseaulx d'*argent*," but the lovers drink, as in Malory, from a "couppe d'*or*" (MS. B. N. fr. 103, f. 56v, col. a).

badest possible comparison, I have made use not only
~maining French versions but of the most nearly anal-
panish and Italian versions as well. Even so, I must em-
~ the tentativeness of the comparison. The difficulties in-
~ in discovering the exact nature of Malory's treatment of
his sources are scarcely fewer now than over forty years ago,
when E. K. Chambers commented: "It is an intricate subject,
for which all the evidence is not yet available, while some of
what is available has not always been wisely used." [65]

III

Malory's "Tale of Sir Tristram" occupies nearly one third of
Le Morte Darthur. Essentially, the problem of his treatment of
that "Tale" is whether its inclusion serves any functional purpose
in relation to the larger story of his "hoole book" of Arthur and
his knights. Surely we beg the question in saying merely that
Malory attempted a redaction of all of the Arthurian material
that he could lay hands upon. And surely we oversimplify in
saying, as Miss Scudder does, that the larger purpose of *Le
Morte Darthur* is "to present the three controlling interests of
the Middle Ages—love, religion, war—in . . . the story of the
rise and fall of chivalry, with its three loyalties, to the overlord,
to the lady, and to God"; and that the typical exponent of
loyalty to the lady is "Tristram, the eternal lover." [66]

One thing is clear enough. The "Tristram" story is not wholly
necessary to the high theme of the noble rise and tragic fall of
the Round Table. However influenced the French *Tristan* romances were by Arthurian materials, the French cyclic Arthuriad

---

[65] *Sir Thomas Malory*, English Association Pamphlet No. 51 (1922),
p. 1.
[66] *Le Morte Darthur: A Study of the Book and Its Sources*, pp. 185–86.

had done quite well without a *Tristan*. From a consideration of structure alone, all that is needed to portray the establishment and disintegration of Arthur's noble realm is a *Merlin*, a *Quest of the Holy Grail*, and a *Lancelot*, with these romances centering, as they do in the French cyclic versions, around the figure of Arthur. As A. B. Taylor puts it, "the combination of a prose 'Merlin' and a prose 'Lancelot' yields an almost complete account of Arthur's life from birth to death, while the prose romances of the Holy Grail weld the principal knights of his court together into one unified company animated by one common aim." [67]

But Malory did include the "Tristram," and apparently not merely with the intent of swelling the proportions of his "hoole book" to a size one third greater than it would otherwise have been. For, to Malory far more than to his French predecessors, I think, the Arthurian story was a tragedy. More important, it was to him a moral tragedy. Naturally he was bound to some extent by the traditions of his source material; yet to portray the real tragedy of the fall of Arthur's realm, he had to make clearer than ever before the *causes* of that tragedy. It is just this sense of causality that is missing in the French cyclic Arthuriad —no matter in what combination we put together a *Merlin*, a *Quest*, and a *Lancelot*. And it is just this sense of causality that is underscored, though implicitly rather than explicitly, by the addition of the "Tristram" material. In the French Arthurian story the causes underlying the fall of the Round Table are indistinct. Compared to Malory's version, only dimly do we ever see there why the major characters should end as completely defeated in their worldly aspirations as they do—Guenevere in a nunnery, Lancelot in a monastery, and Arthur slain by the hand of his incestuously begotten son and nephew. But compare these people with Isoud, Tristram, and King Mark, and many

[67] *Introduction to Medieval Romance* (London, 1930), p. 72.

things come clear. Murder, it seems, will out; and so, apparently
will intrigue, adultery, incest, and all of the other promiscuitie
that have come to infect the whole dissolute Arthurian worl
before its testing in the search for the Holy Grail. The ver
symbol of this degeneracy is the Lancelot-Guenevere-Arthur tri
angle, of course. No one realizes this more fully than Guenever
herself, and nowhere is it given more explicit expression than in
her words, when, after her final retreat to the nunnery at Almes
bury, she is visited by Lancelot:

> "Thorow thys same man and me hath all thys warre be
> wrought, and the deth of the moste nobelest knyghtes of the
> worlde; for thorow oure love that we have loved togydir ys my
> moste noble lorde slayne. Therefore, sir Launcelot, . . . I
> commaunde the, on Goddis behalff, that thou forsake my com-
> pany. And to thy kyngedom loke thou turne agayne, and kepe
> well thy realme frome warre and wrake, for as well as I have
> loved the heretofore, myne harte woll nat serve now to se the;
> for thorow the and me ys the floure of kyngis and knyghtes
> destroyed." (1252)

But lest the adulterous love between Lancelot and Guenever
be thought an anomaly—a single flaw in an otherwise perfect
world—Malory introduced the parallel motif of the Tristram
Isoud-Mark triangle; and he seems deliberately to have put off
letting us know the disastrous consequences of that affair until
the very point at which we see the whole Round Table society
begin to weaken and crumble under the weight of its own
excesses. Moreover, as if the Cornwallian triangle were not
enough, we find in the "Tristram" section of the story the extremely unattractive and incongruous affair between Sir Lamo
rak and Queen Margawse, the iniquitous wife of King Lot of
Orkeney—the same woman, incidentally, concerning whom
Merlin earlier admonished Arthur: "Ye have done a thynge late
that God is displesed with you, for ye have lyene by youre syster

and on hir ye have gotyn a childe that shall destroy you and all
the knyghtes of youre realme" (44).

The "Tristram" section, then, seems designed to complement
Malory's Arthurian story and to throw into a sharper relief than
would otherwise have been possible not only the tragic fall of
an almost perfect world but the reasons for that fall. Yet to
state the end is not to state the means. We want to know not
only what Malory did, and why, but *how*; and this last question
is probably best answered in terms of his treatment of such
matters as characterization, chronology, structure, and theme.

Little has been written on the subject of Malory's characterization. His people are perhaps too entirely what they seem to
demand minute analysis. Moreover, those critics who have commented at all on the matter have unfortunately been inclined
to compare Malory's characters with their prototypes in the
older poetic versions of the legend, where the poet "draws out
his details with a lingering sweetness, and penetrates each successive emotion." [68] Howard Maynadier's comment is typical:
"With all their external reality, Malory's characters are only
partially alive, for Malory had but little psychological interest
in them and but little invention. Accepting his people as he
found them, he did not develop them further." [69] It may well
be that Malory's characters "are only partially alive"—particularly from the point of view of the modern reader. But whatever their shortcomings in this respect, Maynadier is only partly
right. Throughout *Le Morte Darthur* it is primarily action that
counts; people are seen for what they are in terms of what they
do, and their actions are allowed to stand silently symbolic of
the causes which are constantly at work bringing about the ruin
of a world that seems so fair. Yet that Malory accepted his

[68] Scudder, *Le Morte Darthur*, p. 231. Miss Scudder here compares
Malory's "Tristram" with Gottfried's poem; she could scarcely have chosen
two versions so completely in contrast to each other.

[69] *The Arthur of the English Poets* (New York, 1907), p. 233.

people as he found them, without developing them further, is not quite the case. For, in spite of his lack of psychological interest, and especially in the "Tristram" division, he nevertheless did there some rather remarkable things to make the characters of his source material fit into the all-important action of his own larger story.

I have already touched upon the character of Isoud. Of the three main characters in the "Tristram" section, she is least important. In the older French romances, both in poetry and in prose, she is far from an attractive heroine. In the prose version of Malory's probable source, for example, she pits Tristram and Palomides against each other in a tournament, determined to take the winner as her paramour. Later, as I have said, she forestalls Mark's discovery of her loss of "le nom de pucellage" by letting Brangwain play the part of the substituted bride, while she herself goes to Tristram's chamber to spend her wedding night. Finally, again, there is her perfidious plot to have Brangwain killed. Malory changed all this, and apparently not through any mere desire to ameliorate her character. For her role in *Le Morte Darthur* there was no need to transform her character completely, but she did have to be made sufficiently attractive to motivate logically the central conflict between Tristram and King Mark, especially if the efficacy of the love potion were to be as drastically minimized as it is. As for consistency of characterization, it will be remembered that before the fatal Tristram-Isoud-Mark triangle is established, Tristram had already encountered one rather ruthless lady in the episode of his rivalry with Mark for the favor of Sir Seguarides' wife. He had won that lady, but he had also fared badly at her hands and had resolved even then: "I shall beware what maner of lady I shall love or truste." Thus, unless the love potion were much more potent than Malory makes it out, Tristram would hardly have been attracted by the Isoud of the French romances; and far from having treated her character with "but little invention," Malory seems instead to have rectified the inconsistencies of his French predecessors.

In the characterization of Tristram, Malory had occasion to make but few alterations of his probable source. From his point of view, Tristram must be subordinated always to Lancelot, and the "Tristram" section of the story must be seen always against its larger and more important Arthurian background; but to a great extent these matters were already accomplished in the French prose tradition that he was following, and he needed only to emphasize them still further. As Miss Scudder notes, the most obvious indication of the emphasis which Malory wished to place upon the Arthurian connections of the "Tristram" section is the fact that "he throws nearly all he cares to tell about the lovers into the eighth book, and proceeds in the ninth and interminable tenth to wander off into Arthur-land at large." [70]

The most significant difference between Malory's characterization of Tristram and that of the French prose versions is that Malory establishes the love between Tristram and Isoud much earlier and much more naturally than do the French romances. To Malory, the voyage for healing had little meaning except insofar as it brought Tristram and Isoud together for the first time. The healing itself is given the briefest possible treatment in order that we may get on to what matters most:

> Than the kynge [Anguish] for grete favour made Tramtryste to be put in his doughtyrs awarde and kepyng, because she was a noble surgeon. And whan she had serched hym she founde in the bottom of his wounde that therein was poyson, and so she healed hym in a whyle.
>
> And therefore sir Tramstryste kyste grete love to La Beale Isode, for she was at that tyme the fayrest lady and maydyn

[70] *Le Morte Darthur*, p. 229.

of the worlde. And there Tramtryste lerned hir to harpe and she
began to have a grete fantasy unto hym. (385)

Once this "grete love" and "grete fantasy" is established, we
pass immediately to the "grete envy betwyxte Tramtryste and
sir Palomydes," for Palomides also "drew unto La Beale Isode
and profirde hir many gyfftys, for he loved hir passyngly welle."
In the French romances Isoud is somewhat materialistic: asked
by Brangwain which of these two knights she will have, she
replies that she will choose the one who proves of most prowess
in the coming tournament.[71] In Malory, however, once the lovers
have declared themselves, Palomides' attentions are clearly un-
welcome to Isoud. She begs Tristram to enter the tournament;
and when he does so and defeats Palomides, he charges Palomides, "upon payne of youre lyff, that ye forsake my lady, La Beale
Isode, and in no maner of wyse that ye draw no more to hir"
(388).

Shortly after the tournament Isoud's mother discovers that
"Tramtryste" is really "Trystrames," the slayer of her brother,
Morholt. In the older poems, of course, it is Isoud herself who
makes this discovery, and she runs upon Tristram with his own
sword in an attempt to avenge the death of her uncle. In the
prose romances in which Isoud is at all connected with the scene
of Tristram's discovery,[72] her reaction is a completely passive
one. Malory, however, has already established the love between
Tristram and Isoud; and, compared to the older versions, Isoud's
reaction is somewhat startling. After the queen has discovered
Tristram's true identity,

[71] See Adv. 19.1.3 (Johnson, *Tristan "Li Bret,"* pp. 17–18); B. N. fr.
103, f. 39r, cols. a and b.
[72] Isoud takes no part in the discovery scene in Adv. 19.1.3, nor in the
Cuento or *Leggenda.* She is present in B. N. fr. 103, but the circumstances
are not at all as in Malory (see Vinaver's comment, *Works,* 1447–48).

"Alas!" than seyde she unto hir doughter La Beale Isode, "this is the same traytoure knyght that slewe my brother, thyne eme."

Whan Isode herde her sey so she was passynge sore abayss-shed, for passynge well she loved Tramtryste and full well she knew the crewelnesse of hir modir the quene. (389)

Following this discovery, Tristram is banished from the Irish court; but before his departure, there is the tender scene of the lovers' parting—a scene which, like the other indications of the early love between the two, was almost surely Malory's own invention:

"A, jantyll knyght!" seyde La Beale Isode, "full wo I am of thy departynge, for I saw never man that ever I ought so good wyll to," and therewithall she wepte hertyly.

"Madam," seyde sir Trystramys, "ye shall undirstonde that my name ys sir Trystrames de Lyones, gotyn of a kynge and borne of a quene. And I promyse you faythfully, I shall be all the dayes of my lyff youre knyght."

"Gramercy," seyde La Beale Isode, "and I promyse you there agaynste I shall nat be maryed this seven yerys but by your assente, and whom that ye woll I shall be maryed to hym and he woll have me, if ye woll consente thereto." (392)

From this point on in Malory's version of the story there is little doubt about the lovers' feelings toward each other; the motivation of the love potion is clearly superfluous.

Upon Tristram's return to Cornwall there follows the unpleasant episode of his rivalry with King Mark for the favor of "an erlys wyff that hyght sir Segwarydes." Malory seems to have had but little heart for this adventure; possibly he would have omitted it entirely had he been able. Unfortunately, however, it was probably the one episode in his source which would serve as the turning point for the "good eme—fayre nevew" relationship between Tristram and Mark, the one episode by means of which could be established between uncle and nephew the enmity that plays so great a part in excusing Tristram and Isoud's continuing adulterous relationship. The version of this episode which Malory probably found in his source, however, would have been totally inconsistent with the characterization of Tristram that he had thus far presented. Accordingly, to judge by the remaining prose versions, he altered the episode considerably. In the French romances Tristram becomes enamored of Sir Seguarides' wife immediately after returning from Ireland. This causes no wonder in those versions, of course, for there Tristram and Isoud have scarcely seen each other, much less fallen in love. But Malory seems to have felt that he must allow at least a decent interval between the tender scene of the lovers' parting and the scene in which Tristram and Sir Seguarides' wife "wente to bedde with grete joy and pleasaunce." To provide that interval, and thus to minimize as much as possible Tristram's obvious inconstancy, Malory added the following to the version of his probable source:

> And whan he saw hys tyme [Tristram] rode unto his fadir, kynge Melyodas, and there he had all the chere that the kynge and the quene coude make hym. And than largely kynge Melyodas and his quene departed of their londys and goodys to sir Trystrames. Than by the lysence of his fadir he returned ayen unto the courte of kynge Marke.
>
> And there he lyved longe in grete joy longe tyme, untyll at the laste there befell a jolesy and an unkyndenesse betwyxte king Marke and sir Trystrames, for they loved bothe one lady, and she was an erlys wyff that hyght sir Segwarydes. (393) [73]

[73] Is this incident of Tristram's visit "unto his fadir" the reason Malory has kept Meliadus alive so long? In the poems Meliadus dies shortly after Tristram's birth; in the prose versions he dies when Tristram is about seven years old, just after Tristram's new and jealous step-mother has attempted to poison Tristram in order to provide for the succession of her own anticipated offspring by Meliadus.

Finally, Tristram is required to return to Ireland, this time to bring Isoud back to Cornwall to be married to King Mark. Mark "charges" Tristam with this adventure (we shall discover his motives below); and Tristram, the "trewyst" and "moste wor-shyppful" knight of the world save only Sir Lancelot, "wolde nat refuse the messayge for no daunger nother perell that myght falle" (403). Thus is established the motivation of conflicting loyalties. When Tristram returns to King Anguish's court, "the joy that La Beale Isode made of sir Trystrames there myght no tunge telle, for of all men erthely she loved hym moste" (411); and Tristram is apparently much tempted by King Anguish's proposal: "if that ye lyste to wedde [Isoud] yourselff, that is me levest." But Tristram is on a "messayge" for his king; he replies simply, "and I dud so, I were shamed for ever in this worlde, and false to my promyse." Tristram's loyalty in this instance to the code by which he lives, together with Malory's steady degradation of King Mark's character, seems clearly designed to excuse, or at least to rationalize, his later adulterous relationship with Queen Isoud.

Malory's most successful deviations from the French prose tradition of the story have to do with his re-characterization of King Mark. As I have said, the blackening of Mark's character had already largely been accomplished for him. Bruce pointed out in this respect that

> the [French prose] author's object . . . in this degradation was to lessen the opprobrium of his hero's adultery, but the tragic situation was, surely, much finer in the old story, where even the nephew committing the wrong could not dispute the essentially noble and generous character of the king and could plead no excuse for dishonoring him, save the force of a passion which was as irresistible as Fate.[74]

[74] *Evolution*, I, 490.

The passion "irresistible as Fate" is, of course, that which is brought about by the love potion; but that the tragic situation was "much finer in the old story" is open to some difference of opinion. For if, as in Thomas's poem, the love potion is made the single and all-important explanation of the lovers' conduct, the motivation for the entire story becomes completely external, and what results is, in a sense, more nearly sheer pathos than tragedy. Eilhart and Béroul must have felt something of this, since in their poems the effect of the love potion is made to last only three or four years; thereafter Tristram and Isoud continue their adultery largely as a matter of free will. The French prose writer also seems to have disliked the essential passivity of Tristram and Isoud's positions if their relationship is motivated solely by the external fact of the love potion. Accordingly, he attempted to minimize that traditional motivation and to substitute for it the wholesale blackening of the character of the wronged husband. Unfortunately, he overshot his mark, and the resulting characterization is often completely inconsistent, and quite as much externally motivated as had been the characterizations of Tristram and Isoud in the poems.

As we have seen, the initial factor in the French prose writer's degradation of King Mark lies outside the Tristram story itself. In the French prose romance, before Tristram's part of the story gets under way, Mark's treachery is fully established by the incident of his cowardly murder of his brother, Pernam, at "la fontaine au lyon." We cannot be sure whether Malory deliberately omitted this incident or whether it (and the rest of the introduction of the prose romance) was already omitted in the manuscript of his source.[75] If the omission was Malory's,

---

[75] The incident is briefly summarized in Adv. 19.1.3 (Johnson, p. 5); in B. N. fr. 103 (f. 28v, cols. a and b); and in the *Leggenda* (Di Benedetto, p. 2). It is not given in the *Cuento* at all, but might have been included in the matter of the missing first five folios. B. N. fr. 103 represents the enmity between Tristram and Mark as beginning "ce jour meisme que Tristan fust ney."

however, it is in keeping with his other attempts to treat the character of Mark consistently and to furnish the motivation for his degradation in events that take place within the Tristram story proper. All of the prose versions, for example, contain an episode in which, through the prophecy of a "nain," King Mark is warned of Tristram's future prowess and of the fact that he will bring about Mark's death and the ruin of his realm.[76] Because of this warning Mark attempts to have Tristram slain while the latter is still a child; and the attempt results in some versions in the murder of Meliadus, Tristram's father. At this very early point in the French romance, at any rate, "le roy Mark ne doubtoit homme au monde autant comme il faisoit Tristan." [77] Yet later, when Tristram comes to Mark's court, arranges to do battle with Morholt, and then makes known his identity, Mark welcomes him with open arms: " 'Nepeue Tristan, flour dessus tous damoiseaulx, por quoy t'estu si longuement cele envers moy? Se je t'eusse congneu, je ne t'eusse pas pour riens octroye la battaille.' "[78] Malory omitted the episode of the dwarf's prophecy not only because of the inconsistency that it produced but, again, because it did not provide the central conflict of his story with a motivation which grew out of the internal events of that story. In other words, in contrast to the version of the prose romances, in *Le Morte Darthur* we are permitted to see the degradation of Mark's character develop: his treachery is not a foregone conclusion.

Awkward though it was to Malory for other reasons, the episode of Mark's conflict with Tristram over that "lyght lady," Sir Seguarides' wife, provided the first incident in his story by

[76] Adv. 19.1.3 (Johnson, pp. 7–8); in the *Leggenda* (Di Benedetto, p. 12) and B. N. fr. 103 (f. 30r, cols. a and b) the episode of the prophecy is not given, but is understood to have taken place since it anticipates Meliadus' death and an attempt upon Tristram's life. If the episode was included or implied in the *Cuento*, as is likely, it would have been part of the five lost folios.

[77] B. N. fr. 103, f. 30r, col. b.

[78] *Ibid.*, f. 34v, col. b.

means of which he might logically begin to develop the darker side of Mark's character. To see just how important this episode is in establishing the enmity between Mark and Tristram, we shall have to go back to the beginning of Malory's story and note the earlier relationship between the two. Having heard of King Mark's need for a champion to do battle with Morholt and thus deliver Cornwall from the necessity of paying tribute to Ireland, Tristram comes to Mark's court to offer his service. When it develops that Morholt "woll nat fyght with no knyght but he be of blood royall," and Mark asks about Tristram's lineage, Tristram replies:

> "I am commyn of fadir syde and modir syde of as noble bloode as [Morholt] is; for, sir, now shall ye know that I am kynge of Melyodas sonne, borne of your owne sister dame Elyzabeth that dyed in the foreste in the byrth of me."
> "A, Jesu!" seyde kynge Marke, "ye ar welcom, fayre nevew, to me." (379)

After the battle with Morholt has been arranged and Tristram has revealed his relationship to Mark, both the king and his barons "wepte to se and undirstonde so yonge a knyght to jouparté hymself for theire ryght." Tristram defeats Morholt, but at the end of their battle he is so "sore wounded and sore forbledde, that he myghte nat within a lytyll whyle stonde." Gouvernal comes to the island where the battle has taken place and brings Tristram back,

> and whan [Tristram] was commyn unto the londe kynge Marke toke hym in his armys, and he and sir Dynas the Senescyall lad sir Tristrames into the castell of Tyntagyll; and than was he cerched in the beste maner and leyde in his bed. And whan kynge Marke saw his woundys he wepte hertely, and so dud all his lordys. "So God me helpe," seyde kynge Marke, "I wolde nat for all my londys that my nevew dyed." (383)

Tristram's "invenymed" wound does not heal; he lies in bed "a moneth and more, and ever he was lyke to dey of the stroke that sir Marhalte smote hym fyrste wyth the spere": "Than was kynge Marke and all hys barownes passynge hevy, for they demed none other but that sir Trystrames sholde nat recover. Than the kynge lette sende for all maner of lechis and surgeons, bothe unto men and women . . ." (384). The voyage for healing follows, as we have seen; and when Tristram is discovered to be Morholt's slayer, he explains his actions to King Anguish: "Wete you well . . . I dud the batayle for the love of myne uncle kynge Marke and for the love of the contrey of Cornwayle . . ." (391). Finally, when Tristram is banished from Ireland by King Anguish, he "toke the see, and with good wynde he aryved up at Tyntagyll in Cornwayle. And whan kynge Marke was hole in hys prosperité there cam tydynges that sir Trystrames was aryved, and hole of his woundis. Thereof was kynge Marke passynge glad, and so were all the barownes" (393).

Up to this point in Malory's version of the story, then, there is no hint of the treachery and cowardice that become so distinctly a part of King Mark's character later on. As Malory seems to have seen it, the problem was to cause those characteristics to evolve naturally from some incident within the story itself; and the "jolesy and unkyndenesse" that "befelle betwyxte kyng Marke and sir Trystrames" over the wife of Seguarides was the one incident in Malory's probable source which would suit his purpose. In the *Tristan* poems Mark's hostility to Tristram is inspired primarily by his barons, who are jealous of him and fearful that he will inherit the kingdom of Cornwall after Mark's death. In the prose versions Mark's hostility is made more emphatically his own; yet the jealousy of Andret (Mark's other nephew) and several other barons still plays an important part in motivating that hostility, and Mark's character is in some ways ambiguous, if not actually inconsistent, because of the prose writer's compromise. We have already seen several instances in which, in Malory's version of the story, King Mark "and all hys barownes" are "passynge hevy" when Tristram is wounded, or "passynge glad" when he is healed. Concerning these passages, Vinaver comments that Malory "seems to *ignore* the fact that in F[rench] the barons are hostile to Tristan." [79] But Malory seems not so much to have "ignored" the hostility of the barons in his source as to have altered his source deliberately in order to center the hostility against Tristram completely in the character of King Mark, and thus to develop his principal conflict in terms of one villain and one hero.

Malory's attempt to focus the hostility against Tristram in Mark alone is to be seen in still another apparent alteration of his source in the episode of the tryst with Seguarides' wife. The lady sends a "dwarff" to Tristram to bid him, "as he loved hir, that he wolde be with hir the nexte nyght folowynge." After the message is delivered, Mark intercepts the dwarf and makes him "by force to tell hym all why and wherefore that he cam on message to sir Trystrames." [80] Learning of the "steavyn" that "was sette betwyxte Segwarydes wyff and sir Trystrames," Mark determines to ambush Tristram, kill him, and take his place in the rendezvous that has been arranged. In the prose versions Tristram goes to this "steavyn" in the company of his two squires, Perrin and Matael; [81] thus not only is the ensuing battle very one-sided in Tristram's favor, but to Mark is attributed a great deal of courage in carrying out his attack against these unexpected odds. Malory, however, reverses these odds: "So kynge Marke armed and made hym redy and toke two knyghtes of his counceyle with hym. And so he rode byfore for to abyde by the wayes for to wayte uppon sir Trystrames." In

---

[79] *Works*, pp. 1446, 1448, 1450 (the italics are mine).

[80] The entire episode is given in *Works*, pp. 393–95.

[81] These are the brothers of Brangwain in the French prose versions.

the description of the battle that follows, Malory forgets himself momentarily in seeming to give the two knights to Tristram, thus betraying the version of his source and giving us at the same time a clear indication of his own intent: "And as sir Trystrames cam rydynge uppon his way with his speare in his hande, kynge Marke cam hurlynge *uppon hym and hys two knyghtes* suddeynly. . . ." During the remainder of the fight, of course, the two knights are consistently Mark's; after Tristram has "russhed [Mark] to the erthe and brused hym, . . . he ran to the one knyght and effte to the tothir, and smote hem to the colde erthe, that they lay stylle."

Although Tristram is wounded in this encounter, he goes on to his rendezvous with Sir Seguarides' wife; and, as we have seen, the two "soupede lyghtly and wente to bedde with grete joy and pleasaunce." But the importance of the whole episode lies in what it leads to; for as a result of their rivalry over Seguarides' wife, "as longe as kynge Marke lyved he loved never aftir sir Trystramys. So aftir that, thoughe there were fayre speche, love there was none" (396). And while in the prose romances Tristram is later sent to Ireland at the instigation of Mark's jealous barons, Malory clearly motivates that "message" in terms of Mark's recently acquired hatred of Tristram:

> So whan this was done kynge Marke caste all the wayes that he myght to dystroy sir Trystrames, and than imagened in hymselff to sende sir Trystramys into Irelonde for La Beale Isode. For sir Trystrames had so preysed her for hir beauté and goodnesse that kynge Marke seyde he wolde wedde hir; whereuppon he prayde sir Trystramys to take his way into Irelonde for hym on message. And all this was done to the entente to sle sir Trystramys. (403)

Malory may have had "but little psychological interest" in his characters, as Maynadier suggests; but he nevertheless managed to present those characters at once more dramatically and more ısistently than they had been presented in the usual version ɔf the French prose romances. For in Malory's version of the story the love between Tristram and Isoud and the conflict between Tristram and Mark motivate, and are motivated by, each other. Moreover, far from having had "but little invention," Malory did the one thing necessary to improve upon his source: he avoided making these central motifs of love and conflict depend upon purely external factors, and he thus presented a clear, organic relationship between the incidents and characters of his story.

IV

I have already pointed out that one of the most consistent aspects of Malory's handling of his "Tristram" source seems designed to emphasize Tristram's subordination to Lancelot— "the trewyst knyghte that ever was on lyve." As a result, almost from its very beginning we see the "Tristram" division develop in relation to the larger structural and thematic framework of the Arthurian story. Conversely, there is evidence to suggest that Malory treated his sources for the earlier sections of *Le Morte Darthur* in such a way as to prepare for the inclusion of the "Tristram." Before turning to structural and thematic relationships, however, we need briefly to clarify the chronological place of the "Tristram" within the larger story.

Professor Lumiansky has called attention to the "carefully planned internal time-scheme for Malory's whole book" and the necessity for regarding some divisions of the work as "retrospective narrative." [82] In the modern novelist's vocabulary the device which Malory used would probably be called a "flash-

[82] R. M. Lumiansky, "The Question of Unity in Malory's *Morte Darthur*," TSE, V (1955), 35–39.

back"; and in several of the links between early sections of *Le Morte Darthur* Malory clearly anticipates his use of this device by leaving obvious time-gaps to be filled by later parts of the work. Enough has been written on the subject to show that the most significant of these time-gaps is that between the first and second divisions—the "Tale of King Arthur" and the "Tale of King Arthur and the Emperor Lucius." [83] The first of these divisions ends shortly after Lancelot's birth; at the beginning of the second, both Lancelot and Tristram are grown and established as knights. As is the case with so many of the other scenes that take place "off stage" in *Le Morte Darthur*, we do not see Lancelot's coming to court. But since the *Tristram* and *Lancelot* stories are so closely parallel in the chronology of their other events, Lancelot probably comes to court not long before Tristram, who is not presented to King Arthur until two-thirds of the way into the "Tristram" section—well over half way through *Le Morte Darthur*. Between these first two divisions, then, some twenty years or more must be presumed to have elapsed—an interval which, by means of a "flashback," is filled by many of the events of the "Tristram" section that Malory introduced later in the work.[84]

Once we recognize that in several of the divisions following the "Tale of King Arthur and the Emperor Lucius" Malory was making use of this relatively simple "flashback" device, it is possible to dispel immediately one common and persistent misconception in the interpretation of *Le Morte Darthur*. It has

[83] Lumiansky, "The Question of Unity," p. 37; R. H. Wilson, "How Many Books Did Malory Write?" *University of Texas Studies in English*, XXX (1951), 11–12; Charles Moorman, "Internal Chronology in Malory's *Morte Darthur*," *JEGP*, LX (1961), 240–49. On the *explicit* ending Malory's first section, see my note, "The First *Explicit* in Malory's *Morte Darthur*," *MLN*, LXXI (1956), 564–66.

[84] Lumiansky points out that the section immediately preceding the "Tristram"—the "Tale of Gareth"—is to be seen as taking place during a similar time interval, "right after Tale II and before the 'Tale of Lancelot' " ("Question of Unity," p. 36).

frequently been remarked that the work contains a number of remarkable incongruities which render some of its parts totally inconsistent with others. Vinaver comments, for example, that

> some of [Malory's] characters appear as fully fledged knights before they are born, while others reappear after their deaths. Tristram is an example of the former anomaly: he is a prominent character in Caxton's Book VII, although his birth is not related until Book VIII. Breunis Saunz Pity, on the other hand, is killed in Book VII and returns to life in the subsequent books.[85]

If we realize, however, that much of Caxton's Book VIII takes place in point of time *before* the events of Book VII, we have no occasion at all to regard such matters as these as inconsistencies. Moreover, if we realize that Malory has not followed a strictly forward-moving chronological pattern, we have even less occasion to resort to the hypothesis that *Le Morte Darthur* was composed as a series of separate romances.

Once we are aware, then, that much of the early "Tristram" division makes "a clear if unannounced loop" [86] back to the time interval between Tales I and II, we begin to see how carefully Malory went about planning to include that story. In the early parts of *Le Morte Darthur* a number of the characters and events of the "Tristram" division are anticipated, and these anticipations frequently required Malory's alteration of his sources. In the Balin episode, for example, King Mark comes upon the scene in which Merlin is burying Lanceor and Columbe, and Merlin writes upon the tomb the names "Launcelot du Lake and Trystrams," saying to Mark: "Here shall be . . . in this same place the grettist bateyle betwyxte two knyghtes that ever was or ever shall be, and the trewyst lovers; and yette none of hem shall slee other." And when King Mark asks Mer-

[85] *Works*, p. xxii.
[86] R. H. Wilson, "How Many Books?" p. 12.

in's name, the latter replies with an obvious foreshadowing of later events: " 'At thys tyme,' seyde Merlion, 'I woll nat telle ou. But at that tyme sir Trystrams ys takyn with his soveraigne ady, than shall ye here and know my name; and at that tyme ye hall here tydynges that shall nat please you' " (72).[87] Later, ust after the joust between Gawain and Morholt, Malory leliberately altered his source to elevate Tristram from fifth to econd place among the knights who will become of sufficient prowess to best Gawain in jousting.[88] Finally, toward the end of the episode concerning the adventures of Gawain, Ywain, and Morholt, Malory further altered his source: (1) to introduce "the erle Fergus that aftir was sir Trystrams knyght"; (2) to make Morholt a knight of the Round Table (as he is in the later "Tristram" division, but not in any of the French romances); [89] and (3) to inform us that "sir Trystrams many dayes aftir fought with sir Marhaute in an ilande. And there they dud a grete batayle, but the laste sir Trystrams slew hym. So sir Trystrams was so wounded that unnethe he myght recover, and lay at a nunrye half a yere" (179).[90]

[87] In the French version of this prophecy, Merlin refers simply to the time that Tristram will be taken "avoec s'amie" (see the Huth *Merlin*, eds. Paris and Ulrich, I, 230–31). Vinaver comments on Malory's alteration that "whereas in M[alory] the allusion to Isode is obvious, in F[rench] it is clearly not intended to be understood by Mark" (*Works*, p. 1304). Since he views the tales as separate romances, Vinaver naturally avoids the conclusion that Malory's alteration may be specifically designed to anticipate a later event.

[88] In Malory (*Works*, p. 162) the order of these knights is: "sir Launcelot de Lake, sir Trystrams, sir Bors de Gaynes, sir Percivale, sir Pelleas, [and] sir Marhaus"; in the Huth *Merlin* (II, 240) the order is given: "Li uns en fu Lancelos del lac; li autres ot non Hestor des Mares; li tiers ot non Booirs li essilliés; li quars ot non Gahariés; li quins ot non Tristans li amoureus, li niés le roi March; li sisimes fu chis Morhous dont je parole en cest conte chi."

[89] Vinaver, *Works*, p. 1357.

[90] As Vinaver notes (*ibid.*), the source for the late incidents of the Gawain, Ywain, and Morholt adventure is unknown, but the "characters, including Marhalte himself, belong to the Prose Romance of Tristan."

An analysis of Malory's treatment of his sources in the earl
divisions of *Le Morte Darthur* helps to clarify not only th
chronological place of the "Tristram" story but its structur
and thematic relationships as well. I have already noted E. I
Chambers' feeling that Malory "rather bungled his structur
problem" because *Le Morte Darthur* does not satisfy our e:
pectation that a work of fiction should have a beginning,
middle, and an end and should progress, however deviously, t
an "intelligible issue." But, like Vinaver, Chambers was trouble
by such apparent incongruities as the fact that "knights wh
have been killed in one book live to fight and be killed again i
another"; [91] and once we see the extent of the chronologica
overlapping among the various sections of the story, we may nc
only dismiss most of such objections as these but show tha
with the inclusion of the "Tristram" section Malory brough
the work to a considerably more "intelligible issue" than Chan
bers thought. For in *Le Morte Darthur* the "Tristram" provide
precisely the "middle" that the French Arthurian cycle lacke
We need only read the Huth *Merlin* to realize how abrup
would be the passing from that romance directly to the *Ques*
of the Holy Grail, and how little prepared we would then b
for the tragic conclusion following the *Quest* in one of the cycli
Lancelot or *Mort Artu* romances. Or—to make even more ob
vious the structural importance of the "Tristram" in Malory'
work—we need only read some of the more recent so-calle
"abridged" editions of *Le Morte Darthur*, in which the chie

Despite a good deal of such evidence as this, Vinaver seems to believe tha
Malory had not even read the Tristram story at the time of composin
these early sections, much less planned to incorporate that material late
in his work. For further discussion of Malory's early anticipations of late
characters and incidents, see R. H. Wilson, "Malory's Early Knowledge o
Arthurian Romance," *University of Texas Studies in English*, XXI)
(1950), 33–50; and "How Many Books?" pp. 8–11.
[91] *Sir Thomas Malory*, pp. 4–5.

bridgement seems to be an almost total suppression of the middle—the "Tristram" section.[92]

To Malory, as I have said, the Arthurian story represented a tragedy. At the end of *Le Morte Darthur* it is not the death of Lancelot that really counts, nor even that of King Arthur. What matters most is that an entire and almost perfect system of human endeavor, begun with highest aspirations, has degenerated and collapsed. Nearly five centuries have passed since the work was completed; yet if we probe just beneath the surface of the seemingly interminable adventures of these "arraunt nyghtes of kynge Arthurs courte, and all justynge, huntynge, and all maner of knyghtly gamis," we still see the theme which Malory appears to have intended—the noble rise, the testing, and the tragic fall of one of the most potentially perfect institutions in the history of Western thought. Consider the ideals to which that institution is dedicated near the beginning of *Le Morte Darthur* (and this passage is almost certainly Malory's addition to his source):

> Than the kynge stablysshed all the knyghtes and gaff them rychesse and londys; and charged them never to do outerage nothir morthir, and allwayes to fle treson, and to gyff mercy unto hym that askith mercy, uppon payne of forfiture of their worship and lordship of kynge Arthure for evirmore; and allwayes to do ladyes, damesels, and jantilwomen and wydowes socour: strengthe hem in hir ryghtes, and never to enforce them uppon payne of dethe. Also that no man take no batayles in a wrongfull quarell for no love ne for no worldis goodis. So unto thys were all knyghtis sworne of the Table Rounde both

[92] See, for example, the abridged edition of C. R. Sanders and C. E. Ward (*Le Morte Darthur* [New York, 1940]). In the "Foreword" of this edition the editors announce that they have "sought to preserve all of Malory's story except the incidents which threaten to destroy its unity." The "Tristram" section, they maintain, "badly needed pruning," and they have therefore "reduced it severely."

olde and yonge. And every yere so were they sworne at the hygh feste of Pentecoste. (119–20)

Ideals, of course, have a habit of being at variance with realities. The discrepancy between the two and the recognition of that discrepancy have from earliest times furnished at least an implicit and underlying motif in the portrayal of human tragedy. In *Le Morte Darthur* there is need for time and space to show the development of that discrepancy; and, structurally the "Tristram" division satisfies this need, bridging as it does the high expectations with which the Round Table is established in the early books, and the essential inadequacies of that institution which become so apparent in the later divisions and which lead so inevitably to the tragic denouement—"the dolorous deth and departyng out of thys world" of "Kynge Arthur and all hys noble knyghtes of the Table Rounde."

The opening books of *Le Morte Darthur* are books of prophecy. The prose is terse, the atmosphere charged with anticipation. Here is established an edifice of almost superhuman ideals; "herein," as Caxton said, "may be seen noble chyvalrye, curtosye, humanyté, frendlynesse, hardynesse, love frendshyp, vertue." But almost as though it were a matter of tragic necessity, in the very ground upon which this edifice is built there are also sown the seeds of its destruction; for herein we see, as Caxton further said, the persistent flaws of "cowardyse, murdre, hate, and synne." Superhuman ideals, we learn, are still to be in conflict with human capacities—or, more precisely, with human limitations.

King Arthur's court is barely established, its high dedication barely formulated, when "thyder com unto hym [his syster on the modirs syde], kynge Lottis wyff of Orkeney." Queen Margawse is "a passynge fayre lady, wherefore the kynge caste grete love unto hir and desired to ly by her. And so they were agreed and he begate uppon hir sir Mordred," the nephew-son who is

ter to play so important a part in bringing about the destruc-
on of Arthur's realm. Prophetically, that same night, after
rthur's begetting of Mordred, "the kynge dremed a mervaylous
reme whereof he was sore adrad": "hym thought there was
)m into hys londe gryffens and serpentes; and hym thought
ey brente and slowghe all the people in the londe; and than he
nought he fought with them and they dud hym grete harme
nd wounded hym full sore . . ." (41). Nor is King Arthur "sore
drad" needlessly. The "gryffens and serpentes" of his dream
re obviously prefigurative symbols of the lusts and envies which
re to contribute so mightily to Mordred's later part in the col-
ipse of this whole society. Merlin understands this situation,
nd in a passage which will bear repeating, he makes perfectly
lear what shall be the consequence of Arthur's relationship with
is sister:

> "Ye have done a thynge late that God ys displesed with you,
> for ye have lyene by youre syster and on hir ye have gotyn a
> childe that shall destroy you and all the knyghtes of youre
> realme. . . . Hit ys Goddis wylle that youre body sholde be
> punyssed for your fowle dedis." (44)

hortly after this speech, in even more pointed terms, Merlin
varns King Arthur: " 'Thou goste to thy dethe warde, and God
)e nat thy frende' " (49).

With the incident of Arthur's incestuous begetting of Mordred, Malory set in motion a chain of events which, almost
otally unconnected in his French sources, provide a dominant
ind carefully planned underplot for the entire *Le Morte Dar-*
hur. Every succeeding division of the book, however remote
rom Arthur's court, however apart from the principal action of
the story, is to be seen against the background of this chain of
events; and the *leitmotif* that these events comprise serves not
only as a linking device for an otherwise heterogeneous series

of episodes but also as a constant reminder of the tragic co
clusion toward which the principal action of the story is co
stantly moving—slowly, perhaps, but as inexorably as fate
self. Four weeks after May Day, the day upon which Merl
had prophesied that Mordred should be born,

> kynge Arthure lette sende for all the children that were borne
> in May-day, begotyn of lordis and borne of ladyes . . . and
> all were putte in a shyppe to the se; and som were four wekis
> olde and som lesse. And so by fortune the shyppe drove unto
> a castelle, and was all to-ryven and destroyed the moste party,
> save that Mordred was cast up. . . . (55–56)

But it is not merely "by fortune" that Mordred alone of all th
children born on May Day is cast up—or at least not by fortur
in the usual sense, "by accident." For the "fortune" tha
motivates this and the succeeding events of Malory's trag
underplot is something like the Boethian concept of Fortur
as an agent of controlling Providence, or like the Greek a*
ankaios*—the force of a compelling necessity which, as in a
tragedy, seems designed to obstruct the best efforts of eve
the gods to circumvent the predetermined *telos* toward whic
the entire action of the story is so inexorably impelled.

Once he had set it in motion, Malory connected this trag
underplot of *Le Morte Darthur* with two other matters, bot
of which, given their relation to the initial fact of Arthur's in
cestuous begetting of Mordred, are to contribute more sign
ficantly than in any version of the story before Malory's to th
ultimate fall of the Round Table. The first of these matters ha
to do with the later quest of the Holy Grail. Because he is n
longer "a clene knyght withoute vylony," King Arthur is unabl
to achieve the sword of the "damoisel . . . which was sent
frome the grete Lady Lyle of Avilon." Balin achieves that sword
however; and there follow the well-known incidents of th

Dolorous Stroke," his own death and that of his brother
Balan), and finally Merlin's prophecy concerning the quest
: the Grail. In disposing of one of Balin's two swords, Merlin
hophesies: "There shall never man handyll thys swerde but the
este knyght of the worlde, and that shall be sir Launcelot othir
lis Galahad, hys sonne. And Launcelot with hys swerde shall
e the man in the worlde that he lovith beste: that shall be sir
;awayne" (91). Merlin "lette make by hys suttelyté" that
alin's other sword

> was put into a marbil stone stondynge upryght as grete as a
> mylstone, and hoved allwayes above the watir, and dud many
> yeres. And so by adventure hit swamme downe by the streme
> unto the cité of Camelot, that ys in Englysh called Wyn-
> chester, and that same day Galahad the Haute Prynce com with
> kynge Arthure, and so Galaad . . . encheved the swerde that
> was in the marble stone hovynge uppon the watir. And on
> Whytsonday he enchevyd the swerde, as hit ys rehersed in
> THE BOOK OF THE SANKGREALL. (92) [93]

The second of the two matters with which Malory connected
he incestuous begetting of Mordred is even more important,
oncerning as it does the feud between the houses of King
'ellinore and King Lot. King Arthur's abortive attempt to
lestroy Mordred by destroying all of the children "begotyn of
ordis and borne of ladyes" on May Day results in a considerable
lisaffection among his nobles: "many lordys and barownes of
hys realme were displeased for hir children were so loste" (56).

[93] It is worthy of note how often in Malory's work such anticipations
s these are placed at the end of an episode in which he has digressed from
is main story—as though he clearly had an eye on the general plan for
is "hoole book" and wished to keep that plan before his reader at every
pportunity. Wilson also calls attention to many of the anticipations that
am citing here ("a good many details which appear to be original with
Malory"), but with the reservation that these "need not imply that when
Malory wrote them he intended to tell the anticipated story" ("How Many
Books?" p. 9).

Most displeased of all the nobles is the now alienated King Lot "that of late tyme before he had bene a knyght of kynge Arthur and wedded the syster of hym" (77). Having withdrawn from King Arthur's court, in the Balin episode Lot joins forces with King Rion and King Nero to make war upon Arthur. Malory faced a double problem with respect to his treatment of the motivation of these early events. In his French source [94] he found that King Lot's withdrawal from Arthur's court and his subsequent attack upon Arthur's forces were acts of vengeance occasioned by the fact that Arthur had presumably drowned Mordred; the adulterous relationship between Arthur and Lot's wife was of little importance. Malory evidently wished to establish exactly in reverse the significance that his source attached to these two incidents. Accordingly, he minimized Arthur's blame in the drowning of the children, altering his source to add that for this despotic act "many putte the wyght on Merlion more than of Arthure" (56). Thus in *Le Morte Darthur* King Lot is little enough concerned with the fate of Arthur's bastard son (as well we might expect under the circumstances); instead he withdraws from court and attacks Arthur's forces in retaliation for having been made a cuckold. In this new motivation Malory established more firmly than ever the fact that the initial cause of his tragic underplot consists specifically in Arthur's incestuous begetting of Mordred: "And for because that kynge Arthure lay by hys wyff and gate on her sir Mordred, therefore kynge Lott helde ever agaynste Arthure" (77).

King Lot is slain in his battle against Arthur, and his death leads to a family feud the effects of which, more surely even than the effects of the Grail quest, are directly responsible for the fall of the Round Table. King Pellinore, we learn, "bare the wyte of the dethe of kynge Lott," and Malory interrupts his story to

[94] The episode is interwoven with other parts of the story in the Huth *Merlin*, I, 202–61.

iticipate one of the consequences of Lot's death: "Sir Gawayne
venged the deth of hys fadir the ten yere aftir he was made
iyght, and slew kynge Pellynor hys owne hondis" (77–78).
rom this point on in the story we are reminded again and again
f the strife which was brought about initially by Arthur's in-
:stuous cuckolding of King Lot, and of the dissension and
ltimate disaster to which that strife will lead. Near the end of
ie Balin episode, for example, Balin and "an ermyte" bury
alin's companion, Peryne de Mount Belyard, who has just been
illed by the invisible knight, Garlon: "And there the ermyte
id Balyne buryed the knyght undir a ryche stone and a tombe
oyall. And on the morne they founde letters of golde wretyn
ow that sir Gawayne shall revenge his fadirs deth kynge Lot
n kynge Pellynore" (81). Later, in the Torre and Pellinore
oisode, Pellinore brings his son, Torre, to court, and Torre and
;awain are made knights. King Arthur then establishes Pel-
nore as a knight of the Round Table, "and thereat had sir
;awayne grete envy and tolde Gaherys hys brothir, 'Yondir
nyght ys putte to grete worship, whych grevith me sore, for
e slewe oure fadir kynge Lott. Therefore I woll sle hym,' seyde
;awayne, 'with a swerde that was sette me that ys passynge
encheaunte' " (102).

We do not see Gawain's slaying of King Pellinore. This is
nother of the many incidents which take place "off-stage" in
e *Morte Darthur* and are merely reported by other characters
iter in the story. But in order to continue the chain of events
•hich had begun with King Arthur's begetting of Mordred, and
o make that chain of events bear directly upon the later
•estruction of the Round Table, Malory effected in the Balin
pisode the most ingenious alteration possible in the treatment
f his early source material: he replaced one of Pellinore's sons,
ir Agloval, with Sir Lamorak.[95] In this seemingly insignificant

[95] *Ibid.*, I, 261.

deviation from his source Malory clearly anticipated the stru[c]-
tural and thematic relation of the "Tristram" section to th[e]
whole of *Le Morte Darthur*; for, as we shall see, late in th[e]
"Tristram" the feud between the houses of Pellinore and L[ot]
is brought to a climax with the treacherous slaying of S[ir]
Lamorak by Gawain and his brothers. Note how carefully Ma[l]-
ory worked to prepare for that event. Shortly after the openin[g]
books of *Le Morte Darthur* we lose sight of King Pellinore, an[d]
not until well into the "flashback" of the "Tristram" division [do]
we learn that he has been slain by Gawain and his brothers. B[ut]
as early as the "Tale of Gareth" Malory began to establish S[ir]
Lamorak as the third-most knight of prowess in King Arthu[r's]
realm. Just before Gareth's battle against the Red Knight, f[or]
example, Sir Persant tells Gareth:

> "All the worlde seythe that betwyxte three knyghtes is de-
> parted clerely knyghthode, that is sir Launcelot du Lake, sir
> Trystrams de Lyones and sir Lamerok de Galys. Thes bere
> now the renowne, yet there be many other noble knyghtis
> . . . but there be none that bere the name but thes three
> abovyn seyde. Therefore God spede you well," seyde sir
> Persaunte, "for and ye may macche that Rede Knyght ye shall
> be called the fourth of the worlde." (316)

From this point until well into the "Tristram" section Malo[ry]
went out of his way to heighten the prowess and reputation [of]
Sir Lamorak, deliberately building up to the reaction that wi[ll]
follow his treacherous slaying at the hands of Gawain and h[is]
brothers. More and more often we are reminded, sometim[es]
almost parenthetically, that Sir Lamorak is "the clennys[t]
myghted man and the beste-wynded of hys ayge that was o[n]
lyve but if it were Sir Trystram othir sir Launcelot." Eve[n]
Palomides, who in Malory's probable "Tristram" source is a f[ar]
better knight than Lamorak, is made to remark: "Alas . . . [I]
may never wyn worship where sir Trystram ys, for ever whe[re]

ys and I be, there gete I no worshyp. And yf he be away, for
e moste party I have the gre, onles that sir Launcelot be
ere, othir ellis sir Lamerok" (529). And when, as in the
ench prose romance, Sir Lamorak receives a fall at the hands
Palomides, Malory hastens to insert an explanation: "Here
en may undirstonde that bene men of worshyp that man was
ver fourmed that all tymes myght attayne, but somtyme he
s put to the worse by malefortune and at som tyme the
yker knyght put the byggar knyght to a rebuke" (484).

As I have said, it is in the "Tristram" section of Le Morte
rthur that the feud between the houses of Pellinore and Lot
ches a climax. The "Tristram" begins leisurely enough. For
time we are removed almost completely from the scene of
e principal action; we have, after all, a different story in hand.
t well before the middle of the "Tristram" division Malory
ought his two stories together and increased the tempo of the
ents which comprise his tragic underplot. Sir Lamorak's
vorshyp" becomes more and more spoken of, and the envy
d treachery of Gawain and his brothers become more and
ore apparent. In a tournament held at King Arthur's court
r Lamorak wins the "gre," having bested, among other knights,
r Gawain:

> Than the kynge was gladde and so was all the felyshyp of the
> Rounde Table except sir Gawayne and his bretherne. And
> whan they wyste that hit was sir Lameroke they had grete
> despyte of hym, and were wondirly wrothe wyth hym that he
> had put hym to such a dishonoure that day. Than he called
> to hym prevaly in counceyle all his bretherne, and to them
> seyde thus:
> "Fayre bretherne, here may ye se: whom that we hate
> kynge Arthure lovyth, and whom that we love he hatyth. And
> wyte you well, my fayre bretherne, that this sir Lameroke woll
> nevyr love us, because we slew his fadir, kynge Pellynor, for we
> demed that he slew oure fadir, kynge Lotte of Orkenay; and for

the deth of kynge Pellynor sir Lameroke ded us a shame to oure
modir. Therefore I woll be revenged." (608)

Events move swiftly from this point. As is implied by Gawaii
speech to his brothers, Sir Lamorak has for some time be
"asoted uppon" Queen Margawse. Now Gawain and his brothe
set a trap "with entente to slee sir Lamerok"; worse yet, they u
their own mother as bait for that trap. There follows one
the most unpleasant incidents in the whole of *Le Mor
Darthur*. According to the brothers' plan, when Lamorak "wen
unto the queny bed, and she made of hym passynge grete j
and he of her agayne," he was to have been taken naked ar
slain. But Gawain chose the wrong brother to do this job; f
when the time comes, instead of slaying Sir Lamorak, in a seizu
of revulsion Gaheris "suddaynly . . . gate his modir by tl
heyre and strake of her hede." Reproached by Lamorak, Gahei
explains his "fowle and evyll" deed:

> "Thou haste put my bretherne and me to a shame; and thy
> fadir slew oure fadir, and thou to ly by oure modir is to muche
> shame for us to suffir. And as for thy fadir, kynge Pellynor, my
> brothir sir Gawayne and I slew hym . . . and now is my modir
> quytte of the for she shall never shame her chyldryn." (611–12)

Reaction sets in immediately; we are told that "for this mat
was the kynge passynge wrothe and many other knyghtes
Gaheris is banished from the court, and Sir Lancelot predic
that still more serious consequences will follow:

> "Sir," he tells the king, "here is a grete myscheff fallyn by
> fellony and by forecaste treason, that your syster is thus sham-
> fully islayne. . . . And I dare say also that ye shall lose that
> good knyght sir Lamerok . . . for sir Gawayne and his
> bretherne woll sle hym by one meane other by another." (613)

Lancelot is all too right in his prediction, but the consequenc
are to be even more serious than he believes. For the strife b

een the houses of Lot and Pellinore comes to infect the whole
King Arthur's court and to split that court into the opposing
tions which will shortly bring it to disaster. Clearly here in
e "Tristram" division the stage is being set for the final
gedy.

Sir Lamorak continues to be "moche preysed" at court, and
is inspires more than ever the ill feeling of Gawain and his
others—not only against Lamorak himself but against all
ose who "drewe unto hym" as well. At the end of the third
y of the tournament at Surluse, for example,

> whan Launcelot knew sir Lamerok he made muche of hym;
> for of all erthely men he loved hym beste excepte sir Trystram.
>   Than quene Gwenyver comended hym, and so did all good
> knyghtes, and made muche of hym, excepte sir Gawaynes
> brethirne. (660)

ncelot, of course, has sided with Sir Lamorak in this conten-
on between the families of Pellinore and Lot; and in so doing
s incurred, almost as much as Lamorak himself, the "grete
vye and despyte" of Gawain and his brothers. And their envy
directed not only against Lamorak and Lancelot; it touches
en that "grete bourder and passynge good knyght," Sir Dina-
n—"for they hated hym oute of mesure bycause of sir
merok." As though to emphasize here the disastrous effects
at this family feud is to have upon the Round Table, Malory
ded to his probable "Tristram" source an anticipation of the
ter slaying of Sir Dinadin by Gawain's brothers: "And aftir,
. the queste of the Sankgreal, cowardly and felonsly they slew
r Dynadan, whyche was a grete dammage . . ." (615).

Late in the "Tristram" division the conflict between the
milies of Lot and Pellinore reaches a climax. Just as Lancelot
ad predicted, King Arthur does "lose that good knyght sir
amerok." Again we find that the action has taken place "off-

stage," presumably shortly after the tournament at Surluse.
Palomides reports the incident to Tristram:

> "And that day that sir Lamorak was slayne he ded the moste
> dedis of armys that ever I saw knyght do in my lyeff, and whan
> he was gyvyn the gre be my lorde kynge Arthure, sir Gawayne
> and his three bretherne, sir Aggravayne, sir Gaherys, and sir
> Mordred, sette uppon sir Lamorak in a pryvy place, and there
> they slew his horse, and so they faught with hym on foote
> more than three owrys bothe byfore hym and behynde hym,
> and so sir Mordred gaff hym his dethis wounde byhynde hym
> at his bakke, and all to-hewe hym: for one of his squyers tolde
> me that sawe hit." (699)

Following the death of Sir Lamorak, scarcely an episode occurs
which is not connected in one way or another to the previous
events of this feud between the houses of Pellinore and L
Time after time other knights lament the loss of Lamorak, "the
good knyght that sir Gawayne and his brethirn slew by treson,"
more and more often we are reminded of "the dethe of kyng
Pellynore that was shamefully slayne by the hondys of sir
Gawayne and his brothir sir Gaherys." [96] The names of Gawa
and his brothers almost literally become bywords for "morthe
and treson." But most important of all, late in the "Tristram"
division, the "grete envye and despyte" in which Gawain an
his brothers had once held Lamorak now passes to Lancelot
and we begin to see clear foreshadowings of the "warre and
wrake" which is to bring about the dissolution and destructi
of the Round Table.

The remaining episodes of this tragedy are familiar. We pa

---

[96] *Works*, pp. 716, 810, 829, 1049, 1059, 1088, 1112, 1149, 1170, 118
and 1198. Wilson also refers to a number of the passages listed here, an
remarks that Malory's "inserted references to events in the *Tristan* (pa
ticularly the deaths of Lamorak, Tristram, and Isode), and in [his] versi
of the *Suite*, further heighten the impression that the two closing tales a
the earlier ones come out of the same world" ("How Many Books,
p. 10).

m the turbulence and intrigue of the "Tristram" division
the mystical "advysiouns" and metaphysical explications of
₂ "Quest of the Holy Grail"; and for a time, since Arthur's
ights are intent upon a common and other-worldly objective,
ne measure of harmony prevails. But gradually it becomes ap-
rent that the real testing of the Round Table has already
ken place in the "Tristram" division of the story, and that,
th the exception of "two white bulls and one spotted," the
ly Grail is not to be achieved by such "erthely Knyghtes"
Arthur's. By twos and threes they drift back to court and
ume their old ways. In spite of the oath which he had taken
ring the Grail quest to abstain from the "quenys felyshyp,"
ncelot now returns to the adulterous embrace of Guenevere.
ordred and Agravain, feeling once again their "grete despyte"
Lancelot, forcefully bring the adulterous relationship to King
thur's knowledge; and, unable any longer to overlook his
een's unfaithfulness, Arthur reluctantly grants them permis-
n to trap the lovers in Guenevere's chamber. At first Gawain
ll not be included in this plot against Lancelot; "wyte you
ll," he tells Mordred and Agravain, "and there aryse warre
d wrake betwyxte sir Launcelot and us . . . there woll many
nges and grete lordis holde with sir Launcelot" (1162). Even
ng Arthur cautions Mordred and Agravain: " 'Beware,' seyde
nge Arthure, 'for I warne you, ye shall fynde hym wyght.' "
ιt caution is of little avail; the trap will be set:

> "Lat us deale!" seyde sir Aggravayne and sir Mordred.
> So on the morne kynge Arthure rode an-hyntynge and sente
> worde to the quene that he wolde be oute all that nyght. Than
> sir Aggravayne and sir Mordred gate to them twelve knyghtes
> and hyd hemselff in a chambir in the castell of Carlyle. (1164)

Sir Bors has some notion of what is going on—or at least
me apprehension. When the tryst is set between the lovers,
₂ tries to dissuade Lancelot from keeping that tryst:

"Sir," seyde sir Bors, "ye shall nat go thys nyght be my counceyle . . . for I drede me ever of sir Aggravayne that waytith uppon you dayly to do you shame and us all. And never gaff my harte ayenste no goynge that ever ye wente to the quene so much as now, for I mystruste that the kynge ys oute thys nyght frome the quene bycause peradventure he hath layne som wacche for you and the quene. Therefore I drede me sore of som treson." (1164)

But Lancelot will not be dissuaded; and that night, as "t[l] quene and sir Launcelot were togydirs," they are surprised [l] "thes fourtene knyghtes all armed at all poyntes, as they shul[c] fyght in a batayle." In the struggle that ensues, Lancelot ki[l] Sir Agravain and all of the rest of the knights except S[ ] Mordred; but the queen is taken, and the following day she [is] condemned to be burned. Then, in rescuing Guenevere fro[m] the fire, Lancelot inadvertently kills two of Gawain's oth[e] brothers, Gaheris and Gareth. With this unfortunate eve[n] even Gawain is finally drawn into the conflict. Lancelot escap[e] with Guenevere, and Gawain and King Arthur combine the[ ] forces to besiege the lovers at Joyous Gard. News of the disse[n] sion having reached Rome, Lancelot is permitted through [a] papal decree to restore Guenevere to Arthur and to withdra[w] to his own country. Gawain and Arthur follow Lancelot, how ever; and Arthur makes the fatal mistake of leaving his kingdo[m] in charge of Mordred, who promptly attempts to usurp bot[h] Arthur's crown and queen. When the news of Mordred's r[e] bellion reaches France, Arthur and Gawain return to Englan[d] and in the battle which takes place upon their landing, Gawai[n] is killed. Before he dies, Gawain writes to Lancelot, beggin[g] him to forget old differences and to join King Arthur in puttin[g] down Mordred's revolt. But Lancelot comes too late; befor[e] he arrives the armies of Mordred and Arthur stand poised o[n] the plains of Salisbury, ready for the catastrophic battle whic[h] Merlin had prophesied in the early pages of the book.

Malory's tragic underplot for *Le Morte Darthur* began with
Arthur's incestuous begetting of Mordred and with a prophetic
dream of "gryffens and serpentes." Now, on the eve of the
Battle of Salisbury, "uppon Trynyté Sunday at nyght," Arthur
has another prophetic dream, its imagery closely paralleling that
of the first:

> And in hys dreme hym semed that he saw uppon a chafflet a
> chayre, and the chayre was faste to a whele, and thereuppon
> sate kynge Arthure in the rychest clothe of golde that myght be
> made. And the kynge thought there was undir hym, farre from
> hym, an hydeous depe blak watir, and therein was all maner of
> serpentis and wormes and wylde bestis fowle and orryble. And
> suddeynly the kynge thought that the whyle turned up-so-
> downe, and he felle amonge the serpentis, and every beste toke
> hym by a lymme. (1233)

The following day Arthur and Mordred almost effect a truce;
but while they parley in the middle of the battlefield, significantly an adder appears underfoot. A sword is drawn, and then
"there was but russhynge and rydynge, foynynge and strykynge,
and many a grym worde . . . and many a dedely stroke. . . .
And thus they fought all the longe day, and never stynted tylle
the noble knyghtes were layde to the colde erthe" (1235-36).

The Wheel of Fortune has come full circle; the god Ananke
has been served. Little remains to be told except of the repentance of Guenevere and Lancelot, and of their "departynge
oute of thys worlde." But all is not entirely lost; the one distinctive merit of true tragedy is that it distinguishes sharply
between catastrophe and sheer calamity—and, applied to *Le
Morte Darthur*, that distinction is perhaps nowhere better expressed than in the words of Mrs. Nellie Aurner:

> As in all great tragedy involving the destruction of noble hopes,
> the impression remaining is one of exaltation rather than de-
> pression. Life has been widened and deepened by the heroic

effort to achieve that which transcends mortal power. The ideal which has been set just beyond the ability of human attainment has projected the sphere of ambition into other-world realms, and has sublimated human love and the loyalty of brotherhood into spiritual relations.[97]

V

The later parts of Malory's "Tale of Sir Tristram"—thos parts which "wander off into Arthur-land at large" [98]—serve i effect as a bridge between the matter of the "Tales" precedin and following the "Tristram." The motif of the civil strif that results from Arthur's incestuous begetting of Mordre develops from episodes in earlier divisions of the work an prepares for the testing of the Round Table that takes place i the "Grail" division, and for the tragic disintegration of th whole institution of chivalry in the end. Even in the considera ble attention paid to Palomides, and in the motif of his eventua conversion to Christianity, we move gradually from the worldl concerns of the later parts of the "Tristram" to the othe worldly concerns of the "Grail" story.

But the early parts of the "Tristram"—those parts into whicl Malory "throws nearly all he cares to tell about the lovers" [99]— also have significant structural and thematic relationships to th "hoole booke" of *Le Morte Darthur*. Through the similaritie and contrasts presented there between the courts of King Mar and King Arthur, we see more clearly than would otherwis have been possible not only the essential inadequacies of thi chivalric society but the way in which those inadequacies brin about the fall of Arthur's realm.

[97] *Malory: An Introduction to the Morte Darthur* (New York, 1938) pp. xxviii–xxix.
[98] Scudder, *Le Morte Darthur*, p. 229.
[99] *Ibid.*

In the different French romances which comprise the development of the *Tristan* legend, the conception of the central love story varies, as A. B. Taylor puts it, "from conventional courtly love to frank libertinism." [100] In Malory's version of the story, however, the love between Tristram and Isoud is neither of these things—neither because both. Their love, like that of Lancelot and Guenevere, is the love between a knight and his "sovereign lady"; yet, like that of Lancelot and Guenevere, it is also a great deal more. For in *Le Morte Darthur*, far more emphatically than in any previous form of the Arthurian story, all things have a point of reference in the moral issues at stake; and the horn of chastity is as surely a test of the ladies of this chivalric world as is the quest of the Holy Grail for the men. That both of these tests are so inadequately "enchyved" seems from Malory's point of view symptomatic of one of the chief flaws underlying the tragic fall of the Round Table. However much the character of King Mark is blackened in the "Tristram," and however much that procedure tends to diminish our reprobation of the relationship between Tristram and Isoud, we are somehow never allowed to forget that that relationship is, after all, an adulterous one, and that, like the relationship between Lancelot and Guenevere, it is thus symbolic of the moral degeneration to which the potentially perfect world of Arthur's realm is so inevitably being brought.

I have already commented on the parallel development of the Tristram and Lancelot stories in their earlier forms, and the fact that many of their characters and plot elements had been closely imitated from each other. In one sense the profusion of similarities between the two stories creates in *Le Morte Darthur* a kind of redundancy of incident and episode, and it is probably just this redundancy that has caused some editors to abridge the "Tristram" so drastically and so unhesitatingly.

[100] *Introduction to Medieval Romance*, p. 95.

Yet in another and more important sense these similarities of incident and episode reinforce each other, and it is precisely their cumulative force that emphasizes the one overwhelming contrast between the stories. For, toward the middle of the "Tristram," when the Tristram and Isoud narrative is finally brought abreast and linked with that of Lancelot and Guenevere, there is established a kind of pattern for the latter story by means of which the perfidy of the Lancelot-Guenevere-Arthur triangle is made to seem not necessarily unique, but for that very reason all the more disastrous in the tragic consequence to which it leads. There is, after all, a very great difference in the importance of the two courts involved, and, hence, in the importance of the devastation to which they are brought. Sir Lamorak puts the matter most pointedly when, after Tristram rebukes him for having caused the horn of chastity to be sent to King Mark's court instead of King Arthur's, he replies: " 'Well,' seyde he, 'and hit were to do agayne, so wolde I do, for I had lever stryff and debate felle in kyng Markys courte rether than in kynge Arthurs courte, for the honour of bothe courtes be nat lyke' " (443).[101] This, of course, is litotes with a vengeance. Lamorak has so understated the contrast between the two courts that their one similarity is all the more emphatic. The "*honour* of bothe courtes" may "nat be lyke," but by this point in the story we have had every occasion to observe that the *morality* is essentially the same. The degradation of King Mark's character, it is true, tends to diminish our reprobation of the adulterous relationship between Tristram and Isoud; and

---

[101] So far as I can find this passage is original with Malory. In all of the prose versions of the *Tristan* it is Lamorak, of course, who causes Morgan le Fee's horn of chastity to be sent to Mark's court instead of Arthur's. The proof it gives of Isoud's infidelity leads in all versions to Tristram's banishment and his subsequent marriage to the second Isoud. But only in Malory's version, when Tristram and Lamorak meet again on the isle of Nabon le Noyre, does Lamorak give this explanation as his reason for having diverted the horn of chastity to King Mark's court.

something of our tolerance, I suspect, carries over to our attitude toward the same relationship between Lancelot and Guenevere. But the contrast and the comparison implicit in Lamorak's remark illustrate clearly what seems to me one of Malory's most original interpretations of his older and more heterogeneous sources for *Le Morte Darthur*: the tragic fall of King Arthur's noble realm is not the result of the actions of individuals taken separately, no matter how high their station; rather, it is the result of the excesses of this whole chivalric system of social and sexual relationships, and in the end Lancelot, Guenevere, Arthur, Gawain, and Mordred are thus to be seen merely as figures in a tragedy the whole of which is infinitely greater than the sum of its parts.

CHAPTER VI

"THE TALE OF THE SANKGREALL":
HUMAN FRAILTY

BY CHARLES MOORMAN

Concerning Malory's handling of the French Vulgate Cycle *La Queste del Saint Graal*, Professor Vinaver says,

> Malory's *Tale of the Sankgreall* is the least original of his works. Apart from omissions and minor alterations, it is to all intents and purposes a translation of the French. . . . His attitude [toward the source] may be described without much risk of over-simplification as that of a man to whom the quest of the Grail was primarily an *Arthurian* adventure and who regarded the intrusion of the Grail upon Arthur's kingdom not as a means of contrasting earthly and divine chivalry and condemning the former, but as an opportunity offered to the knights of the Round Table to achieve still greater glory in *this* world.[1]

And earlier Vinaver had called Tale VI "a confused and almost pointless story, a beautiful parade of symbols and bright visions . . . deprived of its spiritual foundation, of its doctrine, and of its direct object."[2] Accordingly, Vinaver attempted throughout his introduction and notes to this "sixth romance," to show in detail how Malory "secularizes" the Grail. In spite

[1] *Works*, pp. 1521–22.
[2] *Malory* (London, 1929), p. 84.

of these claims, I think it possible to show that Malory's changes
are far from mere "omissions and minor alterations" and that
Malory's handling of his source material is both purposeful and
highly original.

Since Vinaver's statements about Malory's "Grail" are based
upon his assumption that Malory "regarded each of his works
as an independent 'tale' or 'book' and did not think it necessary
to make them consistent with one another," [3] Tale VI becomes
in his opinion an autonomous piece having little or no connection with any other division of the work. This assumption almost completely precludes the possibility that Malory deliberately changed the "direct object" of the French text for purposes of his own. Yet even a cursory glance at the preceding
section, the "Tale of Tristram," not to mention the innumerable
prophecies of Merlin in Tale I, would seem to refute this contention. Ector and Perceval are cured of their wounds and
Lancelot of his madness by the Grail; Lancelot begets Galahad
on Elaine; the prophecy is made that Galahad will succeed in
the Grail quest and that Lancelot will not; Bors sees the Grail.
Surely all these events in the "Tristram" are preparation for
the coming "Tale." More significantly, Malory leaves his
"Tristram" material before the final tragedy of the lovers, presumably because the following adventure in his source is
Tristram's Grail quest. Also, Malory connects the "Tristram"
and the "Grail" by having the christening of Palomides, the
last event in the "Tristram," and the seating of Galahad, the
first event in the "Grail," happen on the same day. In the same
way, the seventh division, the "Tale of Lancelot and Guenevere," opens with a statement of Arthur's joy at the return of
the Grail knights.

It is almost certain, therefore, that Malory took great pains
to connect the Grail adventure with the rest of his story, and

[3] *Works*, p. xxxii.

it does not seem overly conjectural to assume that Malory fitted the Grail action into his thematic scheme as well as into his narrative pattern.[4] If so, surely no change which Malory makes from his source can be considered unimportant. My general purpose in this chapter, then, is to examine three large groups of source alterations in Malory's "Tale of the Sankgreall"—the changes in religious material, the changes in characterization, and the changes which relate to the unifying of the Grail quest with the rest of *Le Morte Darthur*—in order to demonstrate that Malory consciously attempted in his "Tale of the Sankgreall" to present the Grail quest as an integral part of his own particular version of Arthurian history.

As Vinaver points out, in this division Malory adheres closely to the plan of his French source. Malory follows exactly the tapestry-like interweaving of the adventures of the Grail knights —Perceval, Lancelot, Gawain, Bors, and Galahad—in the French book; he neither adds nor eliminates any of the major episodes of the quest. Yet certainly the "Grail" changes under Malory's hand. The Vulgate *Queste* is primarily a theological treatise on salvation, in which innumerable hermits expound visions and symbols. The nature of the source made Malory's problem twofold: he needed (1) to reduce, without injury, the religious fabric and tone of the whole, and (2) to adapt the material before him to his history of Arthur's court and to the theme which he had been expounding from the beginning of his book.

The Grail quest in Malory's source was—except for the experiences of Galahad, Perceval, and Bors—a failure resulting from man's inability to exchange temporal, courtly values for a religious principle which transcended them. This division of

[4] P. E. Tucker ("The Place of the 'Quest of the Holy Grail' in the 'Morte Darthur,'" MLR, XLVIII [1953], 319) states that he believes the Grail quest to be a turning point in Malory's conception of Lancelot's character and hence in the thematic movement of *Le Morte Darthur*.

values is the principal theme of the Vulgate *Queste*, reinforced at every stage by the allegorical qualities of the French book. The failure of most of the French Grail knights symbolizes the failure of mankind generally; it is not the failure of a particular court. Malory, it seems to me, having envisioned from the beginning an Arthurian cycle of growth, decay, and fall, saw in the Grail a symbol not of mankind's general failure, but of the ultimate failure of Arthur's would-be ideal secular civilization, a failure which he projected in the Lancelot-Guenevere relationship, in the prophecies of Merlin, and in the feud between the houses of Lot and Pellinore, and which was to culminate in the dissension and struggle of the last two "Tales." Malory's changes do not then stem from his not understanding the religious tone of the French *Queste*; he always preserves the core of the French book's doctrinal statements, no matter how great his deletions. All the changes which Malory makes are necessary to his plan for the whole Arthurian cycle, and it is difficult to see how he could have treated this material in any other fashion and yet have made it function within his preconceived plan.

Malory's greatest changes in the purely religious sections of his French source occur in the hermits' explanation of the knights' visions. The basic pattern is this: one of the knights falls asleep, dreams, and—puzzled by his vision—goes to a hermit for illumination. Such hermits' explanations are the natural vehicles for the French writer's theological commentaries, and these long digressions fill a great part of the French book. Malory's method of dealing with these divisions shows quite clearly his intent in the "Grail." He pares away from the hermits' comments the purely religious commentary which is alien to his purpose, yet he is always careful to keep, usually in summation, the religious core of the argument presented. Thus, it would seem to be a mistake to assume that Malory completely "secularizes" the Grail. Malory is transforming his material

according to his own pattern, while retaining the essential re
ligious feeling and atmosphere of the source.[5] For example, ii
the Perceval section, Malory reduces the hermit's explanatioi
of the mystical lion and serpent episode, which fills two largo
pages in H. Oskar Sommer's edition of the French *Queste*,[6] to
a bare two paragraphs; yet he trims his material so carefully
that the main points of the exposition and symbolism are re
tained:

> She which rode uppon the lyon, hit betokenyth the new law of
> Holy Chirche, that is to undirstonde fayth, good hope, belyeve
> and baptyme; for she semed yonger [than] that othir hit ys
> grete reson, for she was borne in the Resurreccion and the Pas-
> sion of oure Lorde Jesu Cryste. And for grete love she cam
> to the to warne the of thy grete batayle that shall befalle the.
> . . . And she that rode on the serpente . . . betokenyth a
> fynde. And why she blamed the that thou slewyst hir servaunte,
> hit betokenyth nothynge < aboute > the serpente ye slewe;
> that betokenyth the devyll that thou rodist on to the roche. And
> whan thou madist a sygne of the crosse, there thou slewyst hym
> and put away hys power. And whan she asked the amendis and
> to becom hir man, than thou saydist nay, that was to make the
> beleve on her and leve thy baptym. (915)

By such changes in the religious materials of his source,
Malory is not attempting to "secularize" the Grail. Had this
been his purpose, he could very easily have omitted the hermits

---

[5] For instances of Malory's reductions of the elaborate theological com-
mentaries of the hermits see *Works*, pp. 882, 892, 898, 927, 945, and 990.
Treatment of Malory's presentation of the Grail legend can be found in
R. S. Loomis, *The Grail: From Celtic Myth to Christian Symbol* (New
York, 1962).

[6] *The Vulgate Version of the Arthurian Romances: Volume VI, Les Adventures Ou La Queste del Saint Graal*, Carnegie Institute of Washington:
Publ. No. 74, VI (1913), 72–73. The best modern edition of Malory's
source for the "Grail" is that by Albert Pauphilet for the *Classiques
francais du moyen âge* in 1923. Page references in this chapter to the
French text are to this edition.

altogether, thereby increasing the pace of the narrative and shifting the reader's attention completely to the physical adventures of the knights. But this was not his wish. The dreams of the knights retain their essential religious significance, but they do not retain their original function as occasions for homiletics.[7] The religious significance is essential to Malory's use of the Grail within *Le Morte Darthur*; but the extended homilies are not.

Malory's alteration of the religious material in his French source to fit his concept of a unified Arthurian story can be observed also in his treatment of the sins of the Round Table and of the Grail knights. In fitting his material to his theme Malory nearly always makes specific and relevant the rather general sins mentioned in the Vulgate *Queste*. For example, in a crucial passage (1025) in which Galahad calms the boiling well in the "perelous foreyste," the French source says that Galahad could calm the fire since "en lui n'avoit onques eu eschaufement de luxure" (262). As Vinaver states, the well is a symbol of "man's sinful nature" (1568). But Malory adds a phrase in which he says that the well was a "sygne of lechory that was that tyme muche used." Since in Malory's scheme the Arthurian world is undermined from the beginning by "lechory" (Uther and Igraine, Arthur and Morgause) and since one of the contributing factors to the downfall of the court at "that tyme" is the Lancelot-Guenevere relationship, the shift in meaning from the general ("man's sinful nature") to the specific ("lechory") bears importance and relevance to Malory's whole Arthurian story which did not exist in the French text. Again, Malory has a hermit tell Gawain that he should long ago have given himself over to "knyghtly dedys and vertuous lyvyng"

---

[7] That Malory's task was not to "secularize" the Grail may be demonstrated by the fact that in three places (888, 891, 997) he cuts away needless battle detail. Plainly, Malory wishes to omit all unnecessary material, be it religious or secular.

(891). Malory's French source states that Gawain should have served our Lord and Saint Eglise (54). In Malory's book Gawain's sins are against the ideal knightly code; to blame Gawain for not being a saint would have been in this context contradictory. Malory consistently makes the generalized textbook sins of his French source into the actual sins of the Round Table; in such fashion he uses this sort of religious material for his own purposes.[8]

Malory also frequently transforms the hazy symbols of the French *Queste* into tangible, concrete parts of a real quest. Perhaps the most effective single change in this direction lies in the presentation of the Grail itself as it appears in one major scene (893). Lancelot, having fallen asleep at the Chapel Perilous, awakens to find a sick knight praying there for aid. The table holding the Grail is mysteriously brought to the knight, and according to Malory, "he towched the holy vessell and kyst hit" (894). Vinaver states that this action is wholly out of keeping with the mysticism of the source and that it would be "unthinkable in the French *Queste*" (1539), since there the sick knight kisses only the silver table on which the Grail is brought (59). Yet, is it not strange that only three lines earlier, Malory has added to the French source a phrase in the sick knight's prayer—"Fayre swete Lorde whych ys here within the holy vessell"—which, despite the equivocation that "here within" may be taken in the "figurative sense," insists on the fact of the transubstantiation? The point is, I think, that Malory, in making the Grail itself more tangible and concrete than does his source, does not diminish in the least its mystical

---

[8] I note one possible exception to this general statement: in the Gawain section a hermit condemns the court "for their synne and their wyckednesse" (946). The French source reads "par lor luxure et par lor orgueil" (156). It may be, however, that Malory felt his general rendering to be a stronger indictment of the court than was the statement found in the source, especially in the substitution of "wyckednesse" for "orgueil."

qualities. Malory is also quite capable of adding supernatural elements where he feels them necessary. Twice (998, 1003) he assigns to a mystical voice commands given to Galahad by other characters in the French text; presumably Malory's purpose is to lend these commands supernatural authority.

Malory's modifications of the characters of the Grail knights also reveal his purpose and originality in adapting the French Grail materials to his unified Arthurian history. For the most part, Malory had no serious problems in handling the traditional Grail knights; he had very few preconceived ideas of Perceval and Galahad, and Bors' conduct in the Grail quest could be adapted without difficulty to his conception of Bors' role in the whole of *Le Morte Darthur*.[9] But Lancelot is Malory's hero, and from the beginning Malory had elevated him to the primacy of all the knights. Quite naturally, then, Malory will turn his main attention to the figure of Lancelot in developing his version of the Grail quest. To say this, however, is not to say that Malory takes it upon himself to "protect Launcelot" (1523) from the sort of treatment he received in the French book. Malory cannot protect Lancelot, since he is fully aware that to do so would be to defend the whole complex of adultery and strife that he had been preparing all along to indict. What Malory does, therefore, is to continue to use Lancelot as he had used him in the earlier "Tales," as the perfect earthly knight, the best exemplar of Round Table civilization. Seen in these terms, the Grail quest takes on a new significance within *Le Morte Darthur*. The quest would seem, in the light of these changes which Malory makes from his source, to represent to him the greatest of the court's adventures and the final test of the Round Table. If the Grail is to be attained, it must therefore be won by the finest knight the Round Table has to offer—Lancelot. In Lancelot's failure lies

[9] Cf. R. M. Lumiansky, "Malory's Steadfast Bors," *TSE*, VIII (1958), 5–20.

the failure of the whole system, since Lancelot, though the perfect embodiment of the system, himself represents the sins which are to lead to the destruction of this society. Throughout the "Grail" Malory begins to underline the failure of Lancelot, and through his failure to prepare for the coming catastrophe.

Malory would thus seem to regard Lancelot as a tragic hero, as the man whose greatest strength, his devotion to the chivalric code, is at the same time his greatest weakness and his downfall.[10] A lesser knight, Bors, can, as we shall see, substitute the celestial standard for the courtly and so achieve the Grail, but Lancelot cannot so shift values. He is himself the personification of the secular chivalric way of life; to abandon it would be to abandon his own identity.

As a tragic hero, he possesses a tragic flaw. Malory settles on instability as the chief sin of Lancelot, just as perhaps lechery, used in a very inclusive sense, is made the main sin of the Round Table.[11] It is obvious that the two are closely linked;

[10] Tucker (p. 393), in discussing Lancelot's pride, states that Malory "magnifies Launcelot's sense of his own prowess until it becomes a fault in his knighthood."

[11] Tucker, in discussing Lancelot's character, also regards Lancelot's instability as his chief sin. Tucker, however, views Lancelot as wavering between two sorts of chivalry—"good" (that directed by the chivalric code and represented by the Grail) and "bad" (that directed by his love for Guenevere). On the other hand, I would prefer to see Lancelot wavering not between two degrees of chivalry, but between his own avowed conception of chivalry as a secular ideal (and this would include his love for Guenevere) and a religious ideal which itself transcends chivalry. Tucker also contends that Malory "was already uneasy over the connexion of love and chivalry when he came to the quest" and that because "he found Launcelot condemned as the knight-lover, but being certain that knighthood was a noble ideal, he began to distinguish between good chivalry and bad." This thesis, however, seems to me to ignore a distinction important to the interpretation of *Le Morte Darthur*, that Malory did not condemn love as a part of the knightly code (see Malory's own "Tale of Gareth"), but instead condemned the adultery which was an integral part of the system of courtly love as he found it reflected in his French source (cf. my "Courtly Love in Malory," *ELH*, XXVII [1960], 163–76).

aken together, they include the theme of Malory's book. There are two Round Tables—the ideal, which Merlin made in 'tokenyng of rowndnes of the worlde, for men sholde by the Rounde Table undirstonde the rowndenes signyfyed by ryght" (906), and the real, founded upon lechery, shot through with civil strife, and ending with adultery. The tragic instability of the members of the fellowship makes them fluctuate between the two Round Tables and permits the lechery that brings on the collapse of the court. The Grail quest had existed from the beginning ("Whan Merlyon had ordayned the Rounde Table he seyde, 'By them whych sholde be felowys of the Rounde Table the trouth of the Sankgreall sholde be well knowyn'" [906]); but so had the seeds of downfall in the birth of Arthur and the conception of Mordred, whom Merlin himself could not destroy. The two strands, instability and lechery, meet in Lancelot and in meeting define the nature of the tragedy:

> Than, as the booke seyth, sir Launcelot began to resorte unto quene Gwenivere agayne and forgate the promyse and the perfeccion that he made in the queste; for, as the booke seyth, *had nat sir Launcelot bene in his prevy thoughtes and in hys myndis so sette inwardly to the quene as he was in semynge outewarde to God, there had no knyght passed hym in the queste of the Sankgreall.* But ever his thoughtis prevyly were on the quene, and so they loved togydirs more hotter than they ded toforehonde, and had many such prevy draughtis togydir that many in the courte spake of hit . . . (1045).[12]

[12] The italics represent Malory's addition. For other instances of the changes which Malory makes from his source in order to emphasize Lancelot's instability, see 948 (a hermit's statement that Lancelot "ys nat stable"); 897 (Lancelot's own statement that he has always done battle "were hit ryght other - wronge"); 1011 (the famous passage in which Lancelot, "somewhat wery of the [holy] shippe," goes "to play hym by the watirs side"); and 1204 (Lancelot's statement that in him "was nat all the stabilite of thys realme"). Other passages cited by Tucker occur on pp. 931–35. Vinaver condemns nearly all of these additions—e.g., his comments on the first (1551) and third (lxxvii) of those mentioned above—

In Tale VI Malory has accordingly changed a great many of the French passages concerning Lancelot in order to demonstrate in action Lancelot's instability. Very early in the Grail quest (863) a "lady on a whyght palferey" comes to court seeking Lancelot. She tells him that he is no longer the best knight of the world, for Galahad has now come. Malory then adds to Lancelot's modest reply in the source that he knows he "was never none of the beste"; the answering statement by the maiden: " 'Yes,' seyde the damesell, 'that were ye, and ar yet, of ony synfull man of the worlde.' " For Malory, even the best of the fellowship of the Round Table cannot accomplish the spiritual quest. Lancelot himself realizes his lack. He says:

> My synne and my wyckednes hath brought me unto grete dishonoure! For whan I sought worldly adventures for worldely desyres I ever encheved them and had the bettir in every place, and never was I discomfite in no quarell, were hit ryght were hit wronge. And now I take uppon me the adventures to seke of holy thynges, now I se and undirstonde that myne olde synne hyndryth me and shamyth me, that I had no power to stirre nother speke whan the holy bloode appered before me (896).

In Malory's source, says Vinaver, "Lancelot, instead of referring to his successes in *worldly adventures*, stresses his 'deadly sin' " (1540). Yet it seems to me apparent that Malory, far from excusing Lancelot by referring to his achievements, actually uses this comparison between chivalric success and religious failure to condemn the perfect secular hero. Such changes as these serve an important purpose: by keeping Lancelot's worldly exploits before us, Malory can keep the contrast of appearance (the ideal Round Table) and reality (Lancelot and Guenevere) uppermost in the reader's mind. In other words, Malory does

---

on the grounds that they are "out of keeping with the spirit and letter of the French" (1551).

not in the least ignore Lancelot's sin; he deepens it by having the hermits hold up before Lancelot a picture of his potential greatness, a greatness which, were it not for sin, might have saved the Round Table civilization.

Malory also underscores Lancelot's inability to remain firm in the faith by adding a passage in which a hermit admonishes Lancelot that he "loke that [his] harte and [his] mowth accorde" (897). The hermit's point—that Lancelot, although he understands the difference between heavenly virtue and knightly virtue, cannot act upon that realization—is shown clearly in Lancelot's behavior in the quest. For example, immediately after Lancelot has heard the speech of an "olde man" from heaven telling him that he has "used wronge warris with vayneglory for the pleasure of the worlde" (928), he meets the sick knight of the Chapel Perilous who took his horse and armor after the Grail had healed him. Does Lancelot remember his instruction about using "wronge warris and vayneglory for the pleasure of the worlde"? "So whan Sir Launcelot saw hym he salewede hym nat fayre, but cryed on hyght, 'Knyght, kepe the, for thou deddist me grete unkyndnes.' And than they put afore them their spearis, and sir Launcelot com so fyersely that he smote hym and hys horse downe to the erthe, that he had nyghe brokyn hys neck" (929). The French source of this passage makes clear that the sick knight challenges Lancelot (132), but Malory's syntax seems to me to indicate that he saw in this episode a fine instance of Lancelot's inability to avoid fighting, and consequently had Lancelot make the challenge. After his painful experience at the Chapel Perilous, Malory's Lancelot is "somwhat . . . comforted" in the rising of the sun (896); in the French book, he feels even more ashamed of his actions (62). Again, Malory has Galahad, at the end of the quest, bid Bors remind Lancelot to "remembir of this worlde unstable" (1035), and, to reinforce the point, Malory adds a final passage in which Bors delivers this message (1036). The purpose of this final passage is, of course, to end the Grail quest with a severely chastened Lancelot and not to make Lancelot the Grail hero.

Thus, Malory accomplishes what he must with Lancelot; he makes him the protagonist of the quest without making him the Grail knight. That knight is, of course, Galahad, and an analysis of Galahad's character in *Le Morte Darthur* reveals another aspect of Malory's purpose and theme. Needless to say, the success of Galahad in the Grail quest does not in any way affect the fate of the Round Table; as I have said, Lancelot's failure assures us of the coming catastrophe. Therefore, Malory must treat Galahad, not as a regular knight of the Round Table, but as a heavenly knight, sent to Arthur to accomplish only this one mission, and, by example, to reveal the inadequacies of the other knights and of the secular civilization which they represent.[13] For this reason, Malory regularly elevates and dehumanizes Galahad in his adaptation of the French book. It is true that Galahad of the source is little more than a symbol; yet Malory is careful to reduce even further his physical reality as a member of the company. The most obvious change is one which links Galahad with the Trinity. In an important addition (854) Malory describes Galahad as being "semely and demure as a dove." This is our first introduction to Galahad, and since the time is that of the vigil of Pentecost, we may be fairly sure that Malory is attempting to suggest a link between Galahad and the Holy Ghost. Malory also makes an effort to divorce Galahad from the actual life of the court by deleting the rather detailed French account of both Galahad's instruction in chivalry by Lancelot and the vigil which Galahad makes before becoming a knight (2–3). Thus Malory uses

[13] Charles Williams, in the elaborate reconstruction of the Arthurian cycle contained in *Taliessin through Logres, The Region of the Summer Stars,* and the fragmentary *Figure of Arthur,* makes much the same point concerning the function of Bors and Galahad.

Galahad only as a supernatural object lesson in heavenly chivalry, as a knight whose deeds do not in any way affect the fate of the Round Table.

Malory met with a somewhat similar problem in dealing with the figure of Perceval. It would appear from the French book's treatment of Perceval that he is little more than an extra and slightly soiled Galahad. As the original Grail knight, he had to appear in the story, but he has no function there except to serve as an excuse for introducing a few more hermits. Malory, it would seem, can find no real dramatic or thematic function for Perceval; and as a result, instead of attempting to adapt his presence to the theme of *Le Morte Darthur*, he merely reduces Perceval's role. It is in the treatment of Perceval, therefore, that Malory makes his most extensive cuts, presumably to speed up the narrative as much as possible.

Bors would seem to represent a third level in Malory's technique of characterization. He is the minor knight who, lacking both Lancelot's greatness and Lancelot's sin, is able to achieve the Grail by following the path leading from temporal values to spiritual values, the path which Lancelot is unable to follow. Bors is characterized by his first remarks as a man who thinks entirely in terms of the everyday chivalric secular virtues: " 'Sir,' seyde he, 'I am a knyght that fayne wolde be counceyled, that ys entirde into the queste of the Sankgreall. For he shall have much erthly worship that may bryng hit to an ende' " (955). That Malory deliberately intends to characterize Bors as interested only in "erthly worship" is clear; the French source states that Bors feels that the Grail quest is a search "ou cil avra tant honor, qui a fin la porra mener, que cuer d'ome mortel nel porroit penser" (162). Vinaver here objects to Malory's secularized rendering (1551), but the point is that Bors, not Malory, is the speaker and that Malory is here establishing the beginnings of Bors' character development. This point may be further

demonstrated by the fact that in the French source a hermit
at this stage in the action presents a long speech explaining the
values of baptism, after which he and Bors debate at length
the effects of baptism (162–65). Malory omits this material,
not because he does not understand the doctrines involved,
but because he cannot have Bors, as he conceives him, indulg-
ing at this time in a theological discussion.

Shortly after the interview with the hermit, Bors meets a
damsel who laments the fact that she must find a champion to
fight against Prydam le Noyre in order to save her lands (957).
In the French text, the lady must give Bors a full explanation
of her situation before he is willing to agree to become her pro-
tector (169). Malory, however, has Bors follow the normal
chivalric pattern by volunteering his services immediately (957),
though he knows nothing of the justice of her claim. Soon after
this, we see some reflection of Bors' worldly reputation. A lady
approaches Bors and asks him to protect her: "Than she con-
joured hym, by the faythe that he ought unto Hym 'in whose
servys thou arte entred, for kynge Arthures sake, which I
suppose made the knyght, that thou helpe me and suffir me nat
to be shamed of this knyght'" (961). It is not that the lady
conjures Bors "for kynge Arthures sake," which is directly contrary to the French (1552). The passage makes considerably
more sense if interpreted to mean that she conjures him by
God "in whose servyse" he is entered, and that he has entered
this service for earthly glory and for Arthur's sake, not from
holiness or even from a desire, like Gawain's, merely to see the
Grail clearly. Bors again reveals his habit of thinking in worldly
terms when he is confronted by a beautiful woman (later we
find that she is a devil); Malory says that she seemed to Bors
"the fayryst lady that ever he saw, and more rycher beseyne than
ever was quene Guenyver or ony other astate" (964). The
comparison to Guenevere is Malory's addition, and while such

comparisons to Guenevere are standard in medieval literature, it would here seem to demonstrate Bors' habit of thinking in terms of Round Table adventure.

Bors' conversion can be said to come at about this point in the narrative, and, having established his early character, Malory follows his source very carefully from this point on. The lady swears that unless Bors shares her bed she will commit suicide. Bors, true to his vows to a hermit, refuses; when the lady and her gentlewomen jump from the battlements, he crosses himself and sees the tower and the ladies disappear. Thereafter, Bors devotes himself to the service of God. He soon denies the courtly system entirely (969–74) by refusing to resist the onslaughts of his brother Lionel, even though Lionel has killed a hermit and has sorely wounded Bors and Collegrevaunce. He even turns his back upon knightly loyalty in this scene by refusing to protect Collegrevaunce against Lionel's attacks. The point here would seem to be that Bors has chosen to remain steadfast in his service to God, and that in doing so he has found that he must repudiate the chivalric code.

Bors' constancy to God is just the quality which Lancelot lacks, and Malory makes an effort to present the two knights in parallel fashion in order to demonstrate their differences. Early in the section devoted to Bors, the hermit who admonishes Bors to eat nothing save bread and water "founde hym in so mervales a lyffe and so stable that he felte he was never correpte in fleysshly lustes but in one tyme that he begat Elyan le Blanke" (956). The word "stable" (Malory's only addition to the passage) seems deliberately chosen in order to place Bors in contrast to the unstable Lancelot. Throughout his adventure, in the source as well as in Malory, Bors eats only bread and water, though he is tempted with "many deyntees" (956); he refuses the "grete gyfftes" of a lady (960); he will not leave his quest to sojourn with the father of the rescued maid (962); he resists

the sexual attractions of the fair witch; and, finally, he turn
his back upon the whole code of chivalric honor. In short, h
is stable, true to the spiritual ideal of the quest, and, throug
his single-minded attention to duty, able to do what Lancelo
for all his nobility, cannot do. Bors' refusal to yield to th
temptations placed before him is, in Malory's view, doub
commendable, since from the beginning he lacked real statu
as a knight; unlike Lancelot, Bors was "tendir-herted" (th
phrase is Malory's addition) and consequently was especiall
tempted by the fiend (968).[14]

The final Grail knight to be considered here is Gawair
Again, in this characterization, Malory is preparing for th
final scenes of *Le Morte Darthur*; Gawain's coming lack e
reason is here prophesied. The Gawain of the French source
indistinguishable from the other knights except by the fact tha
he resigns the quest early, having himself originated it. Br
Malory has very skillfully changed the nondescript Gawain e
the source into an almost totally unsympathetic character, th
traditional "light" Gawain, and thus has prepared for his late
enmity toward Lancelot. For example, in the French *Queste*
Gawain welcomes Lancelot home after the journey in which h
knighted Galahad (4); Malory omits this material. In th
French source, Gawain refuses to attempt to draw the swor
from the stone because, as he says, he is far inferior to Lancelo
who has already refused to draw (6); Malory, at this point
omits Gawain's explanation and allows his curt refusal to b
understood merely as stubbornness. The French Gawain, upo
perceiving Arthur's sadness at the departure of the Gra
knights, repents his having initiated the quest (18); Malor
omits this point. Again, Malory omits a remark in the Frenc

---

[14] Lumiansky's "Malory's Steadfast Bors" demonstrates that Bors' con
duct in the Grail quest is consistent with the development of his cha
acter in *Le Morte Darthur*.

Queste (197) to the effect that many were grieved and angered by Gawain's wound. Thus, at every opportunity Malory degrades the character of Gawain. During Gawain's own Grail adventure, Malory has few changes to make; here the hermits thoroughly degrade Gawain.

Having seen Malory's changes in the religious materials and in the characterizations which he found in his source, we may now examine Malory's general purpose in adapting the French *Queste del Saint Graal*. His first consideration would seem to have been to make connections between this "Tale" and the other segments of *Le Morte Darthur* and to tighten, by means of foreshadowing devices, the chain of events within the Grail quest itself. For example, Malory's Galahad, unlike the Galahad of the French source, comes to Arthur's court wearing an empty scabbard (859), and it is obvious that Malory is here foreshadowing Galahad's pulling the sword from the stone. Again, the abbot of a monastery, in talking to Bors, remarks that Lionel is "a murtherer and doth contrary to the Order off Knyghthode" (968). The corresponding French passage accuses him of having "nule vertu de Nostre Seignor" (186). The point of the abbot's statement becomes clear a little later when Lionel kills a hermit who attempts to separate the quarreling brothers. The hermit's remark is thus a simple foreshadowing device. Malory also adds within the context of the Grail quest an allusion to Lancelot's dying a hermit (948). Besides bolstering our opinion of Malory as a conscious and skilled craftsman, these examples should help to make clear that Malory did know as he wrote what was still to come in his source.

The single most important linking of the Grail adventure with the whole of *Le Morte Darthur* is Malory's identification of the sword which Galahad pulls out of the stone with the sword of Balin le Sauvage. Galahad says: "Now have I the swerde that somtyme was the good knyghtes Balyns le Saveaige, and he was a passynge good knyght of hys hondys; and wit thys swerde he slew hys brothir Balan, and that was grete pit for he was a good knyght. And eythir slew othir thorow dolerous stroke that Balyn gaff unto kynge Pelles, the whych nat yett hole, nor naught shall be tyll that I hele hym" (863 In spite of the two versions which Malory gives of the "dolerou stroke," [15] it seems clear that he intends to link thematicall the incident of Balin's wounding of King Pelles with the ac venture of the Grail knight, Galahad. By connecting Balin an Galahad, Malory has perhaps knowingly established anothe symbol for the fall of the Round Table. There are two effect of the "dolerous stroke": (1) it makes necessary the Gra quest in order that the Grail knight cure the Fisher King an redeem the Waste Land, and (2) it brings about the confusio and consequent slaying of the two brothers, Balin and Balar at each other's hands. I would conjecture that, to Malory, th: slaying of brother by brother is a major symbol for the civ strife of the Round Table. The masking and consequent cor fusion of knightly opponents can be observed on almost ever page of *Le Morte Darthur*. Thus very often the sworn brother of the Round Table fight bitterly against one another in ig norance. Many of the major conflicts of the book are cause by brother contending against brother, culminating in the fina conflicts between Gawain and Gareth, between Lancelot an Gareth, between Arthur and his son Mordred.

It is possible that Malory has so altered his source in orde to allow Galahad to pull from the stone a symbol, perhap even one of the causes, of the internal dissension which bring on the destruction of the Round Table. Even within the confine of the "Grail," Malory takes care to underline at every oppor

[15] Later (990) we learn that King Pelles received the stroke for darin to touch the forbidden sword. This inconsistency, however, like the con fusion of the Fisher King and King Pelles, comes to Malory from hi source.

tunity this motif of brother fighting against brother. Gawain kills Ivain, and Malory adds to Ivain's final speech the line "And now forgyff the God, for hit shall be ever rehersed that the tone sworne brother hath slayne the other" (945). Again, in the battle between Bors and Lionel, Malory reinforces the fact of their relationship by having Bors' heart counsel him not to fight Lionel "inasmuch as sir Lyonnell was hys elder brothir, wherefore he oughte to bere hym reverence" (970). A voice from heaven prevents Bors from attacking Lionel, and Malory adds a dialogue between the two brothers in which Bors says upon leaving the scene, "For Goddis love, fayre swete brothir, forgyffe me my trespasse," to which Lionel answers, "God forgyff you, and I do gladly" (974). Malory's intention, I think, is to show that Bors' reluctance to join symbolically in the civil strife of the Round Table by fighting his brother makes him in large part worthy to come at last to the Grail.

A final indication that Malory intends the "Grail" to point toward the fall of the Round Table may be seen in the behavior of the King. Arthur is conscious at the beginning of the quest that the end is near: " 'Now,' seyde the kynge, 'I am sure at this quest of the Sankegreall shall all ye of the Rownde Table departe, and nevyr shall I se you agayne hole togydirs, therefore ones shall I se you togydir in the medow, all hole togydirs! Therefore I wol se you all hole togydir in the medow of Camelot, to juste and to turney, that aftir youre dethe men may speke of hit that such good knyghtes were here, such a day, hole togydirs' " (864). The French passage from which this speech is taken is matter of fact; it has none of the poignancy and grief which the passages assumes in Malory through the King's fourfold repetition of "hole togydirs." The high point of the Round Table is at this celebration of Pentecost. Under the light from the Grail, the incivility and internal dispute are forgotten for the moment; "than began every knyght to beholde other, and

→ *eyther saw other, by their semynge, fayrer than ever they were before*" (865).[16] Surely this change—like those Malory effects in religious material, in characterization, and in devices which link the "Grail" with the book as a whole—is not a "minor alteration"; rather it is integral to Malory's original purpose of assimilating the "Tale of the Sankgreall" into the whole of *Le Morte Darthur*.

[16] The italics represent Malory's addition.

CHAPTER VII

"THE TALE OF
LANCELOT AND GUENEVERE":
SUSPENSE

BY R. M. LUMIANSKY

Although a number of able scholars have devoted minute attention to Malory's actual borrowing from sources for the "Tale of Lancelot and Guenevere," relatively scant comment is available concerning the related question of the literary purpose and general effect behind this actual borrowing.[1] Thus we are now fairly certain of just where Malory found particular materials for this division, and of just what within it seems original on his part; but there is ample room for a detailed discussion of why Malory used these particular source materials, rejected or altered their contexts in the sources in many instances, and often added seemingly original matter to them. The evidence gained from a careful examination of Malory's text and of his sources points to his intention of having this seventh division serve a very specific function as suspense within *Le Morte Darthur* as a whole. The originality in the following analysis will hinge around two points: (1) the claim that Malory means us to understand at the end of the "Grail" that Arthur is aware of the Lancelot-Guenevere adultery and has forgiven the lovers;

---

[1] Vida D. Scudder has discussed this related question; see *Le Morte Darthur of Sir Thomas Malory* (New York, 1921), pp. 311–34.

and (2) the suggestion that a single pattern for suspense recur in the narrative situation presented by each of the five sul divisions of the seventh 'Tale.' Also offered here are (1) a new analysis of Malory's structural technique in the "Poisone Apple" and the "Fair Maid of Astolat," and (2) new explana tions for the presence in this division of the "Great Tourna ment," the "Knight of the Cart," and the "Healing of Si Urry."

Within the "Tale of Lancelot and Guenevere" the sourc relationships for the five subdivisions are as follows: [2]

Caxton, Book XVIII
1. "The Poisoned Apple"—Based on the Old French *Mort Ar tu* and the Middle English *Le Morte Arthur.*
2. "The Fair Maid of Astolat"—Based on the Old French *Mort Artu* and the Middle English *Le Morte Arthur.*
3. "The Great Tournament"—No known source.

Caxton, Book XIX
4. "The Knight of the Cart"—Based on the Old French Prose *Lancelot.*
5. "The Healing of Sir Urry"—No known source.

[2] See *Works*, pp. 1573–99; E. T. Donaldson, "Malory and the Stanzaic *Le Morte Arthur*," *SP*, XLVII (1950), 460–72; R. H. Wilson, "The Prose *Lancelot* in Malory," *University of Texas Studies in English*, XXXII (1953), 1–13; and the earlier items cited in these references. In "A Source for the 'Healing of Sir Urry'" (*MLR*, L [1955], 490–92), P. E. Tucker suggested that Malory got the idea for this subdivision from a part of the Aggravain section of the Prose *Lancelot* (Sommer, V, 224–28, 231, 254,

The seventh division is mainly concerned with the relationship between Lancelot and Guenevere: their attitudes toward
each other, Arthur's attitude toward them, and public opinion
of them within the Round Table group. In this respect, the
seventh division continues and fits in with an important developing theme running through the earlier divisions of *Le
Morte Darthur* and projecting forward into the eighth division.[3]
In the "Tale of Arthur" the King sees, loves, and decides to
marry Guenevere; Merlin warns Arthur that Lancelot and
Guenevere will love each other, but Arthur weds her anyway
(39, 97–98). In the "Tale of King Arthur and the Emperor
Lucius" we have an indication of Lancelot's love for Guenevere:
he is "passynge wroth" because Tristram is allowed to join Isoud
in Cornwall instead of going to fight the Romans, whereas
Lancelot must leave Guenevere and go to the wars with Arthur
(195); but we have here no suggestion of affection on Guenevere's part specifically for Lancelot. In the "Tale of Lancelot"
Malory's choice and arrangement of source material seem especially dictated by his desire to show in that division the current state of the Lancelot-Guenevere relationship; the five indications of their relationship within the division—four of which
are original with Malory—make clear that at this time Lancelot
loves Guenevere but she, though holding him in highest regard,
has still given him no assurance that she will grant him her
love. Thus the third division serves to show Lancelot and
Guenevere, in their own minds and in the minds of society
at large, drawing more closely together in preparation for the

---

268–69, 275). In the Old French text, we find a quest for the best knight
to remove an arrow from a wounded knight. All Arthur's other knights
fail, but Lancelot accomplishes the task. Certainly several similarities exist,
but the differences are so great that, in my opinion, Tucker exaggerates
when he calls this bit of the *Lancelot* the "source" for the "Healing of
Sir Urry."

[3] Donaldson discusses this matter briefly on pp. 469–70 of "Malory and
the Stanzaic *Le Morte Arthur*."

adultery; but we have here no hint of suspicion on Arthur's part.[4]

The "Tale of Gareth" contains no reference to the Lancelot-Guenevere relationship. There are, however, in the "Tale of Tristram" sixteen passages of varying length which concern the attitudes of Lancelot and Guenevere toward each other, Arthur's attitude toward them, and the recognition of the adulterous affair by society at large.[5] The total effect of these passages is to show the commencement of the adultery and its development to a degree that awareness of it has spread widely; but there is no indication as yet that Arthur is suspicious. When Morgan le Fay, in an effort to win Lancelot for herself, sends Tristram to the tournament at the castle of the Harde Roche with a shield on which she has put three figures symbolizing Arthur, Lancelot, and Guenevere, the Queen immediately recognizes this clear reference to her adulterous relationship with Lancelot; but Arthur is simply puzzled by the figures and suspects nothing (554–60). Later, when Mark writes directly to Arthur concerning the Lancelot-Guenevere adultery, the King refuses to believe him (616–18); and, still later in this division, we see clearly that Arthur suspects nothing, for he believes that Lancelot went out of his mind because of Elaine, while many others know that Guenevere was the cause (832–33). One other aspect of the Lancelot-Guenevere relationship in the "Tale of Tristram" should be noticed here briefly. Most of the way through this very large division complete harmony characterizes the relationship between Lancelot and Guenevere; but as the fifth division nears its conclusion, we find the first of a number of instances in *Le Morte Darthur* of the lovers' being at odds

[4] "The Relationship of Lancelot and Guenevere in Malory's 'Tale of Lancelot,'" *MLN*, LXVIII (1953), 86–91.

[5] These passages occur in *Works*, pp. 425, 430, 436, 459–60, 485, 486–87, 554–60, 566, 616–17, 653–70, 681, 792–809, 827, 831–33, 839, 845.

because of Guenevere's jealousy and quick temper. In consequence of Lancelot's unwitting connection with Elaine, the
Queen angrily forbids him to remain in the court or ever again
to come before her; as a result, he is insane for two years
(802–8). In time, however, Guenevere deeply laments her action (809), and when Lancelot returns to the court the Queen
makes him great cheer and the adultery continues (831–32).
In the light of these important developments, it would seem
that one main intention Malory must have had for the "Tale
of Tristram" was to move the Lancelot-Guenevere relationship
much farther along than it had earlier appeared in *Le Morte
Darthur*.

Then, the "Tale of the Sankgreall" immediately takes up this
progressive treatment of the relationship by showing Guenevere's reluctance to have Lancelot leave her (853, 872); and
throughout this division we of course find heavy emphasis upon
the adultery and its limiting effect upon Lancelot in his quest
of the Grail.[6] A chief development by the end of this division
is that Lancelot, having fully realized the implications and effects of his guilt, promises to give up the adulterous relationship
with Guenevere. And a most important point is that by the end
of the Grail quest Arthur, as well as everybody else connected
with the Round Table, has had opportunity to become fully
aware of the adulterous relationship which existed between
Lancelot and Guenevere before the "Grail," and which was
made clear to the reader in the "Tale of Tristram."

At the beginning of the "Grail," Arthur was in no way suspicious of Lancelot as his wife's lover (856, 867) but two passages—original with Malory—show that at the end of the
"Grail" the King acquired full knowledge of the earlier adultery:

---

[6] The pertinent passages occur in *Ibid.*, pp. 853, 856, 862, 863, 864–65,
867–68, 872, 894, 896, 897, 898–99, 927, 928, 930, 932, 933–34, 941,
1014, 1015, 1017, 1036.

And there sir Launcelot tolde the kynge of hys aventures that befelle hym syne he departed. And also he tolde hym of the aventures of sir Galahad, sir Percivale, and sir Bors whych that he knew by the lettir of the ded mayden, and also as sir Galahad had tolde hym. (1020)

And whan they had etyn, the kynge made grete clerkes to com before hym, for cause they shulde cronycle of the hyghe adventures of the good knyghtes. So whan sir Bors had tolde hym of the hyghe aventures of the Sankgreall, such as had befalle hym and his three felowes, which were sir Launcelot, Percivale and sir Galahad and hymselff, than sir Launcelot tolde the adventures of the Sangreall that he had sene. And all thys was made in grete bookes and put up in almeryes at Salysbury. (1036)

It is difficult to see how Lancelot, in recounting fully his Grail adventures, could conceal the adultery and its limiting effects.[7] Surely, when Lancelot told of his interview with the first hermit (896–99), the King would have understood that the Queen whom Lancelot had loved for years was Guenevere, and that the hermit's specifying of Lancelot's old sin as lechery referred to his adulterous relationship with Guenevere.

Malory must therefore have wanted us to realize, as we begin the seventh large division, that Arthur has thus learned of the earlier adultery between Lancelot and Guenevere, that he has been willing to forgive the lovers in order to save the Round Table, and that he is now placing his hope for the future stabil-

---

[7] Vinaver (*Ibid.*, p. 1524) strangely implies that Malory is confused in this matter of Lancelot's recounting the Grail adventures to Arthur; in his view Lancelot could not have had sufficient knowledge to place on record "the adventures of the Sangreall that he had sene." However, the text makes clear, first, that Bors—who did have knowledge of all that happened during the Quest—also reported to the King; and, second, that the clause "that he had sene" is meant to modify "adventures," not "Sangreall." Lancelot was of course in a position to report those adventures which he himself had experienced ("sene"), as well as those he had learned about from the "lettir of the ded mayden" and from Galahad.

ity of his marriage and his kingdom in Lancelot's changed ways as a result of his experiences and promise during the "Grail." Considerable support for this analysis of the situation at the end of the "Grail" is to be found by considering (1) the reaction of the court at large, (2) Aggravain's behavior, and (3) Arthur's later words and actions.

As we have seen, the "Grail" ends with a full recital of events to the King. Since this recital "was made in grete bookes and put up in almeryes at Salysbury" (1036), the court at large presumably knows that Arthur had learned of the earlier adultery but had forgiven Lancelot and accepted his promise that the relationship would not begin again. Consequently, "than was there grete joy in the courte" (1045), joy springing from the general hope that the Round Table has been punished sufficiently for the earlier adultery by the losses during the "Grail," and can now continue unhampered in happiness and nobility. But Malory immediately points out that this hope is short-lived, for when the adultery begins again he tells us that "many in the courte spake of it" (1045). And a few lines later, Lancelot warns Guenevere "that there be many men spekith of oure love in thys courte" (1046). Such attention here to the reaction of the court at large is hard to account for unless we understand that Arthur's forgiving the lovers and putting his faith in Lancelot's promise are general knowledge. Certainly, in the "Tale of Tristram," when the earlier adulterous relationship was in progress, there was not this concern with public opinion. There Arthur would not believe Morgan le Fay's symbols or Mark's letter (554–60, 616–18); but now the King has knowledge of the former relationship, and the matter is much more delicate.

It is Aggravain who in the "Tale of the Death of Arthur" will inform the King of the recommenced adultery, and his behavior throughout is made more readily understandable by the analysis set forth above of the situation at the end of the "Grail." Examination of all the passages in *Le Morte Darthur* concerning Aggravain shows that Malory paid close attention to the progressive development of this knight for his climactic role.[8] Early in the book Aggravain is simply mentioned as one of the sons of Morgause. At the end of the "Tale of Gareth" he marries a very rich lady named Lawrell. Then come a number of instances in which he is overcome by various knights; in fact, he never defeats another knight in the whole book, a situation hardly conducive to his being a happy man. We next find two instances of his behaving in cowardly and treacherous fashion —the murders of Dinadan and Lamorak—and about two-thirds of the way through the "Tale of Tristram" we are told of Aggravain's hatred of Lancelot, of which the latter is aware. But we hear no more of Aggravain for over three hundred pages. It should be noted that despite his hatred for Lancelot, and despite his having dealt treacherously with Lamorak, Aggravain has so far given no indication of an intention to report the adulterous relationship of Lancelot and Guenevere, now widely known to the court at large, to Arthur. But, right after the "Grail," when the King has forgiven the lovers and accepted Lancelot's promise, Aggravain is introduced again: Malory emphasizes this knight's attention to the recommenced adultery and his characteristic of talking a great deal, which cause Lancelot to fear that Aggravain will tell the King of the recommenced adultery. That, of course, is exactly what happens later. The point to be observed here is that in the "Tale of Tristram" Aggravain did not report the adultery to Arthur because he knew the King would not believe him any more readily than he believed Mark; but after the King's forgiving the lovers and putting his faith in Lancelot's promise, Aggravain knows that he is now in a position to convince Arthur, if he can produce evidence. No

[8] For references to these passages, see *ibid.*, p. 1661.

ther explanation seems to account for Malory's handling of
Aggravain throughout *Le Morte Darthur*.

Perhaps the clearest support for my reading of the situation
t the end of the "Grail" is to be found in Arthur's actions and
words in the "Tale of the Death of Arthur" when Mordred tells
him of the events which resulted from the trap Aggravain laid
or Lancelot. Contrary to Gawain's wishes, Aggravain will tell
Arthur that "sir Launcelot holdith youre quene, and hath done
onge, and we be youre syster sunnes, and we may suffir hit no
enger" (1163). The King is loath to believe this accusation
without proof, though we are told that he has "a demyng" of
he adultery, presumably as a result of events which occurred in
he seventh division. Then Aggravain proposes the trap: the
King shall announce his intention to hunt the next day and to
e away from the court the next night; Lancelot will stay at
ome and will visit the Queen; Aggravain and other knights
will lie in wait and capture Lancelot in this compromising sit-
ation. Arthur agrees, and events unfold as Aggravain has
predicted, except that he and all the waiting knights save
Mordred are killed. Mordred, wounded, runs to the King and
eports the situation. Arthur then sadly speaks as follows:

> "And alas . . . me sore repentith that ever sir Launcelot
> sholde be ayenste me, for now I am sure the noble felyshyp
> of the Rounde Table ys brokyn for ever, for wyth hym woll
> many a noble knyght holde. And now hyt ys fallen so . . .
> that I may nat with my worshyp but my quene muste suffir
> dethe," and was sore amoved. (1174)

Note the two occurrences of "now" in this speech. The point
s that in the former instance, after learning of the earlier
adultery through the full report of the "Grail," Arthur could
with honor forgive the lovers and hope to save the Round Table
because of Lancelot's promise. But now, in this instance, he can
ee no honorable way to forgive Lancelot and Guenevere and

save the fellowship; thus the King is deeply saddened. Unle..
we assume this contrast, the force of the "now's" is lost.

Gawain remonstrates at length, begging Arthur to forgiv
Lancelot, but to no avail (1174–77). The arrangements fe
punishing the Queen proceed; Lancelot rescues her, but ki..
Gaheris and Gareth in the process. When he receives th
news, the King faints with grief; upon recovering, he says:

> And much more I am soryar for my good knyghtes losse than
> for the losse of my fayre quene; for quenys I myght have inow,
> but such a felyship of good knyghtes shall never be togydirs in
> no company. And now I dare sey . . . there was never
> Crystyn kynge that ever hylde such a felyshyp togydyrs. And
> alas, that ever sir Launcelot and I shulde be at debate! A,
> Aggravayne, Aggravayne! . . . Jesu forgyff hit thy soule, for
> thyne evyll wyll that thou haddist and sir Mordred, thy brothir,
> unto sir Launcelot hath caused all this sorow. (1184)

These words make very clear that Arthur's concern has alwa.
been far less for the behavior of his Queen than for the welfa..
of the Round Table. And it is perhaps not overly fanciful to s..
in his proud statement that no other king ever held togeth..
such a fellowship, a reminiscence of the personal sacrifice h..
earlier had to make by forgiving the lovers in an attempt t
preserve the Round Table.

It would seem fair, then, to state that at the end of th
"Grail" and at the beginning of the "Tale of Lancelot an.
Guenevere," Malory intends us to understand that Arthur, ha..
ing learned of the earlier adultery through Lancelot's accoun.
of his experiences during the "Grail," decided to forgive th
lovers and to place his hope for the future of his fellowship i
Lancelot's promise to refrain from further adulterous relatio..
ship with the Queen. Accordingly, the whole fate of the Roun.
Table at this point in *Le Morte Darthur* is governed by the on.
question of whether or not Lancelot can keep his word. Let u

now see how Malory handles this question in the "Tale of Lancelot and Guenevere." For a time Lancelot holds to his promise,
and "than there was grete joy in the courte" (1045), but Malory
does not for long keep from the reader the full answer to this
chief question. On the first page of the "Tale of Lancelot and
Guenevere," we find the following passage:

> Than, as the booke seyth, sir Launcelot began to resorte unto
> quene Gwenivere agayne and forgate the promyse and the
> perfeccion that he made in the quest; for, as the booke seyth,
> had nat sir Launcelot bene in his prevy thoughtes and in hys
> myndis so sette inwardly to the quene as he was in semynge
> outewarde to God, there had no knyght passed hym in the
> queste of the Sankgreall. But ever his thoughtis prevyly were
> on the quene, and so they loved togydirs more hotter than
> they ded toforehonde, and had many such prevy draughtis
> tygydir that many in the courte spake of hit, and in especiall
> sir Aggravayne, sir Gawaynes brothir, for he was ever opynne-
> mowthed. (1045)

This passage removes from the reader's mind—though not
from King Arthur's—any possibility of suspense in connection
with Lancelot's promise during the "Grail." Malory, however,
did provide the reader with suspense and dramatic interest for
the seventh division of his book. He so presented the materials
from his sources, and he so augmented these borrowings with
original matter, as to place before the reader two large and related questions throughout the seventh division. First, we are
shown further instances of lack of harmony between Lancelot
and Guenevere, and we wonder whether these difficulties will
lead to a permanent separation which will put an end to the
adultery and perhaps save the Round Table. Second, we see
Arthur pulled two ways: on the one hand, he very much wants
to believe that Lancelot will keep his promise; but, on the other
hand, he cannot ignore the increasing reasons for suspicion that

the adultery has recommenced. The reader therefore constantly wonders at what point the King will finally become fully aware of the recommenced adultery. Malory's handling of these two questions throughout the seventh division, as we shall see below, involves the repetition through the five subdivisions of a single pattern which makes for suspense: beneath the surface of events matters are far from ideal, but superficially all ends well in each of the five instances. In this way the seventh division functions as suspense in *Le Morte Darthur* as a whole: in the ascent toward the resolution in the eighth division of the Lancelot-Guenevere relationship whereby each separately comes to a pious end in a religious establishment; and in the descent toward the complete ruin which the Round Table will experience in the eighth division when this superficial stability is shattered by Arthur's having incontrovertible proof that the adultery is again in progress. We shall now see, through an examination of the content and sources of each of the five subdivisions, exactly how Malory presented this suspense in the "Tale of Lancelot and Guenevere."

First, we should consider the large alteration Malory made in the order of presentation for the "Poisoned Apple" and the "Fair Maid of Astolat." Vinaver has indicated how in the Old French *Mort Artu* the two episodes are interwoven in a complicated tapestry-like scheme, involving frequent alternation of parts of each episode plus interspersed bits of other stories.[9] Letting (a) equal the "Poisoned Apple," (b) the "Fair Maid of Astolat," and other letters parts of other stories, he finds the following progression: $a^1b^1a^2b^2x$ b^2y b^2z b^2m b^2n b^2p $a^3a^6a^4b^3a^5$. Since Vinaver does not think that Malory also made use of the Middle English stanzaic *Le Morte Arthur* in preparing the seventh division, he sees Malory's technique here chiefly as the unraveling of the interwoven narrative threads of the *Mort Artu* in

[9] *Ibid.*, pp. 1572–78.

order to present the two episodes as complete units in the order
(a) and (b). But Wilson and Donaldson have clearly shown
that Malory did use the Middle English poem, itself based on
the *Mort Artu*, as well as the Old French prose text in preparing
this division.[10] A reconsideration of Malory's structural technique here is therefore in order, and we must view *Le Morte
Arthur* as an intermediate step between the complicated interweaving of *Mort Artu* and the simple unified progression of *Le
Morte Darthur*. The very important fact is that the Middle
English poet did about nine-tenths of the unraveling of the
Old French tapestry-like technique himself: he reduced the
progression to $b^1a^1b^2a^2$.[11] This situation makes Vinaver's complicated argument almost completely irrelevant, and we see that
Malory's work here, insofar as structural presentation is concerned, involved only two matters: (1) taking the remaining
small step to unify b^1 with b^2 and a^1 with a^2, and (2) reversing
the order of episodes to get the progression (a) and (b). A reason for his making these two changes is not far to seek.

In the whole of the "Poisoned Apple" Arthur believes that
Lancelot is holding to his promise made during the "Grail";
thus, throughout this subdivision the King has no suspicion that
the adultery has recommenced. When the rest of the court
knows that Lancelot and Guenevere now "loved togydirs more
hotter than they ded toforehonde," Arthur remains ignorant
(1045). The King is unable to understand why the Queen cannot keep Lancelot near her, and he wishes that Lancelot were

---

[10] See the articles cited in note 2 above. For the purposes of my argument, it does not matter who is right here. Everyone agrees that Malory
used *Le Morte Arthur* as well as *Mort Artu* for later sections of *Le Morte
Darthur*; surely we can therefore assume that Malory was already familiar
with the Middle English poem when he was preparing the two episodes
now under consideration.

[11] J. D. Bruce (ed.), *Le Morte Arthur* (London, 1903). The passages
concerned are as follows: The "Fair Maid of Astolat"—b^1 (137–839); b^2
(952–1317); The "Poisoned Apple"—a^1 (840–951); a^2 (1318–1671).

present to save her from the stake (1051). When Lancelot has defeated Mador and saved the Queen, Arthur is most courteous to him and promises to reward him; then "there was made grete joy, and many merthys there was made in that courte" (1058–59). On the other hand, in the "Fair Maid of Astolat" the King at first has reason to suspect that the adultery has started again, because both the Queen and Lancelot do not accompany him to the tournament at Winchester (1065); later, however, when he penetrates Lancelot's disguise (1066), his suspicions are allayed. Since Malory in the "Tale of Lancelot and Guenevere" as a whole will present Arthur as having increasing reason for suspicion, as we approach the complete revelation to him of the recommenced adultery in the "Tale of the Death of Arthur," the obvious requirements of climactic arrangement for this matter led Malory to unify each of the two subdivisions and to put the "Poisoned Apple," with no evidence of Arthur's suspicion, before the "Fair Maid of Astolat," in which his suspicion, though rapidly stilled, is nonetheless present.

Let us now return to the main issue in this discussion: Malory's use of the five subdivisions of the "Tale of Lancelot and Guenevere" to provide suspense in the progress of *Le Morte Darthur* as a whole, suspense derived from the two related questions stated earlier—the increasing lack of harmony between Lancelot and Guenevere, and the degree of Arthur's awareness of the recommenced adultery. As we just saw, in the "Poisoned Apple," there is no indication of the King's being at all suspicious; however, the growing lack of harmony between the two lovers—which, as we noticed earlier, was introduced in the "Tale of Tristram"—forms the central theme in this subdivision. Right after we are told that the adultery has recommenced (1045), we learn that Lancelot "had many resortis of ladyes and damesels which dayly resorted unto hym that besoughte hym to be their champion." He accepts these requests in order to please Christ and also to allay suspicion by avoiding the Queen: "Wherefor the Quene waxed wrothe with sir Lancelot." She accuses him of slackening love for her; he maintains that religion, caution, and regard for her reputation explain his actions; she is not convinced and expels him for the second time from the court and her presence. Though very sad, Lancelot this time does not faint or become insane; rather, he seeks advice from his kinsmen, and Bors sends him to Sir Brascias, a nearby hermit. As he departs, Lancelot charges Bors, "in that ye can, gete me the love of my lady quene Gwenyvere." Here, then, at the beginning of the subdivision we see a separation of the lovers resulting from Guenevere's unreasonable anger. After Lancelot's departure, the Queen makes every effort to seem undisturbed, and, in a parallel to his earlier accepting the requests of many ladies, she arranges a banquet for twenty-four knights. Thus, in a way wholly original and directly connected with the lack of harmony between Lancelot and Guenevere, Malory sets the stage for the episode of the poisoned fruit.[12] As this subdivision progresses, Patryse dies of the poisoned apple, Mador accuses the Queen of treason, and Bors agrees to defend her "onles that there com by adventures a better knyght than I am to do batayle for her" (1053). When Bors tells Lancelot of this arrangement, the latter is happy at the opportunity to relieve Bors and win the Queen's good graces again. And that is exactly what happens: when Lancelot has overcome Mador, the Queen and he "made grete joy" of each other (1059). For the first subdivision, therefore, we see a pattern specifically designed to furnish suspense: in the beginning the two lovers are at odds and it looks as if they may be permanently separated, but as events unroll Lancelot saves the Queen and they are reunited in their

---

[12] These matters are absent from the *Mort Artu* (see *Works*, p. 1583) and from *Le Morte Arthur*.

adulterous relationship. On the surface all now seems well in
Arthur's court, but actually the adultery is leading it to its
doom.

This pattern of suspense is present, as we saw earlier, in the
"Fair Maid of Astolat" in connection with the degree of the
King's awareness of the adultery: he at first has cause for
suspicion, but subsequent events point contrarywise. The pattern is also apparent in this second subdivision from the passages
concerning the more frequent lack of harmony between the
lovers. Near the beginning, the Queen upbraids Lancelot for
staying behind with her while Arthur has gone to the tournament; in contrast to his completely subservient attitude in the
two preceding instances (802–9, 1047), Lancelot is here sharply
ironic with the Queen; and she is unpleasantly formal toward
him:

> "Have ye no doute, madame," seyde sir Launcelot, "I
> alow youre witte. Hit ys of late com syn ye were woxen so
> wyse! And therefore, madam, at thys tyme I woll be ruled by
> youre counceyle, and thys nyght I woll take my reste, and to-
> morow betyme I woll take my way towarde Wynchestir. But
> wytte you well," seyde sir Launcelot unto the quene, "at that
> justys I woll be ayenste the kynge and ayenst all hys felyship."
>
> "Sir, ye may there do as ye lyste," seyde the quene, "but be
> my counceyle ye shall nat be ayenst youre kynge and your
> felyshyp, for there bene full many harde knyghtes of your
> bloode."
>
> "Madame," seyde sir Launcelot, "I shall take the adventure
> that God woll gyff me." (1066)

Lancelot's decision to fight in disguise against King Arthur presumably results from his annoyance with the Queen. Here, then,
we have the lovers at odds again; and when Guenevere learns
that "hit was sir Launcelot that bare the rede slyve of the
Fayre Maydyn of Astolat, she was nygh ought of her mynde for

wratthe" (1080). She even proclaims to Bors that she does not care if Lancelot is dead. Lancelot finds that Gawain has recognized his shield, and his first reaction is concern that Guenevere will be angry with him (1082); Bors soon makes this concern an actuality for him and urges him to love the Fair Maid of Astolat, but Lancelot cannot forget Guenevere (1084). Then Bors unsuccessfully tries to mollify the Queen (1087). So matters stand until Lancelot returns to the court, at which time Guenevere will not speak to him despite his efforts to see her (1092). When the Fair Maid's corpse arrives, the Queen inconsistently says to Lancelot in Arthur's presence, "ye myght have shewed hir som bownte and jantilnes whych myght have preserved hir lyff." In answer, Lancelot makes a statement which seems his indirect way of warning her that she must cease her unreasonable demands of him:

> "Madame," seyde sir Launcelot, "she wolde none other wayes be answerde but that she wolde be my wyff, othir ellis my paramour, and of these two I wolde not graunte her. But I proffird her, for her good love that she shewed me, a thousand pound yerely to her and to her ayres, and to wedde ony maner of knyght that she coude fynde beste to love in her harte. For, madame," seyde sir Launcelot, "I love nat to be constrayned to love, for love muste only aryse of the harte selff, and nat by none constraynte." (1097)

Apparently the warning has its desired effect, for as soon as the Fair Maid is buried harmony is restored:

> Than the quene sent for sir Launcelot and prayde hym of mercy, for why that she had ben wrothe with hym causeles.
> "Thys ys nat the firste tyme," seyde sir Launcelot, "that ye have ben displese with me causeles. But, madame, ever I muste suffir you, but what sorow that I endure, ye take no forse." (1098)

Again Lancelot and Guenevere are united in adultery. Thus, in this subdivision we have had a repetition of the pattern for suspense which we observed in the "Poisoned Apple": the lovers are at odds and seem headed for a permanent separation which might save the Round Table from ruin; but they resolve their differences and the adultery continues. Though all now seems superficially well in the court, beneath the surface there still exists the cause for future trouble.

The third subdivision, the "Great Tournament," seems almost wholly original with Malory,[13] and there has been a marked lack of discussion of Malory's reasons for including this material. From the analysis of the two preceding subdivisions, we have good reason to suspect that its chief function is to continue the suspense presented by those subdivisions. We are here given an ostensibly happy view of the Round Table engaged in its favorite pastime and training procedure, a large tournament: when the "cry" announces the time and place, "many knyghtes were glad and made them redy to be at that justys in the freysshyste manner" (1103); the King himself takes a vigorous part in the jousting (1108); the Queen sits on the platform as one of the judges (1108); Arthur, in commenting favorably on the events of the tournament, delivers a lecture on the chivalric essentials, ending "And allwayes a good man woll do ever to another man as he wolde be done to hymselff" (1114); and the subdivision closes with the following cheerful paragraph: "So than there were made grete festis unto kyngis and deukes, and revell, game, and play, and all maner of nobeles was used. And he that was curteyse, trew, and faythefull to hys frynde was that tyme cherysshed" (1114).

This entire situation seems to take us back to the early days of the Round Table, before the "Grail" and before the beginnings of the adultery, when Arthur's hopes were high for a brave

[13] *Works*, p. 1578.

new world guided by the chivalric virtues of his utopian fellowship. Nowhere in this subdivision do we find any indication that
Arthur suspects the adultery. But such an ideal impression is
purely superficial, for side by side with this attractive and hope-
ful view, we are again clearly shown the adulterous aspects of the
Lancelot-Guenevere relationship, which is leading the Round
Table to its doom. Shortly after Arthur proclaims the great
tournament to be held "besydes Westemynster, uppon Candyl-
masse day," Guenevere summons Lancelot and says:

> "I warne you that ye ryde no more in no justis nor turne-
> mentis but that youre kynnesmen may know you, and at thys
> justis that shall be ye shall have of me a slyeve of golde. And
> I pray you for my sake to force yourselff there, that men may
> speke you worshyp. But I charge you, as ye woll have my love,
> that ye warne your kynnesmen that ye woll beare that day the
> slyve of golde uppon your helmet."
> "Madame," seyde sir Launcelot, "hit shall be done." And
> othir made grete joy of othir. (1103)

The recommenced adultery is in full progress; Guenevere, pre-
sumably to erase the memory of Lancelot's having worn the
Fair Maid's red sleeve (1068), here demands that he wear her
token. Lancelot has again assumed his completely subservient
role, and carries out her haughty instructions to the letter.
Nothing points toward a permanent separation of the lovers.
The situation contrasts sharply with the impression of the
Round Table that derives from this great tournament itself.
Thus, in this subdivision we find another instance of the pattern
of suspense which Malory is establishing for the entire "Tale of
Lancelot and Guenevere": superficially all seems well, but beneath the surface the situation points toward the coming
disaster.

For source materials in the fourth subdivision, the "Knight of
the Cart," Malory shifted from the *Mort Artu* and *Le Morte*

Arthur, which he had used for the first two subdivisions and to which he returns for the eighth and final division of *Le Morte Darthur.* Here he selected material in the Prose *Lancelot,* from which he had earlier borrowed for his "Tale of Lancelot." [14] This very act of inserting matter from a different source presupposes a careful plan on Malory's part, and it seems clear that this plan resulted from his desire to continue the suspense he had developed in the three preceding subdivisions. That Malory gave careful thought to his presentation of the "Tale of Lancelot and Guenevere" is also indicated by the chronological continuity to be found as we move from subdivision to subdivision: the "Poisoned Apple" begins right after the "Grail" and ends with the court in quiet happiness, which continues until the beginning of the "Fair Maid of Astolat" on "Lady day of the Assumpcion"; this second subdivision ends at Christmas and the "Great Tournament" begins immediately thereafter, ending with a period of feasts and revelry which presumably covers the month of January; at the beginning of the "Knight of the Cart" we are told, "And thus hit passed on frome Candylmas untyll Ester, that the moneth of May was com," and the action in this subdivision covers the period until Pentecost, at which time the "Healing of Sir Urry" begins. Then the "Tale of the Death of Arthur" opens the following May, allowing time for the year during which Lancelot traveled only by cart (1154).

There is also some evidence earlier in *Le Morte Darthur* which suggests that Malory's use in the fourth subdivision of Meleagant's abduction of Guenevere was not a last-minute or haphazard decision. Twice in the "Tale of Tristram" we find apparently foreshadowing touches concerning Meleagant. First, when Lamorak leaves Tristram and stops at a chapel, Meleagant

---

[14] See the article by Wilson, "The Prose *Lancelot* in Malory." Wilson's view that the Prose *Lancelot* is the only source for the fourth subdivision seems to me preferable to Vinaver's claim that Malory also used here a version of Chrétien's *Charrette* (*Works,* pp. 1578–81).

omes to the same chapel but does not notice Lamorak. "And
hen thys knyght sir Mellygaunce made hys mone of the love
hat he had to quene Gwenyver, and there he made a wofull
omplaynte" (485). The next day Lancelot, Lamorak, Melea-
ant, and Bleoberis engage in a discussion of a knight's proper
egard for his lady, and the fact of Meleagant's love for Guen-
vere is made clear to all. Since in the source this fact is kept
ecret from Lancelot,[15] one suspects that Malory's alteration
ere is intentional preparation for the Lancelot-Meleagant ani-
mosity in the "Knight of the Cart." Second, in the course of
he tournament at Surluse we are told that Bagdemagus sends
way "his sonne Mellygaunce, bycause sir Launcelot sholde nat
mete with hym; for he hated sir Launcelot, and that knewe he
not" (658). Here Malory's alteration of his source [16] seems
aimed at preparing for the emphasis which will be placed on
Meleagant's fear of Lancelot in the "Knight of the Cart" (e.g.,
1124).[17]

Malory's presentation in the "Knight of the Cart" is much
shorter than the corresponding section in the Prose *Lancelot*.[18]
In shortening the account, Malory also made a marked alteration in the emphasis emerging from the episode. Whereas the
French prose-writer devoted most attention to the earlier matters concerning Lancelot's use of the cart and his overcoming
various obstacles to reach Guenevere, Malory's treatment puts
heaviest stress on the bloodstained bed and the jeopardy in
which the Queen is placed. In this connection it is important
to note that Guenevere's being in danger of burning at the
stake (1137) is Malory's original addition; this fact suggests

---

[15] *Works*, p. 1458.
[16] *Ibid.*, p. 1491.
[17] This fear is Malory's original conception; in the Prose *Lancelot*
Meleagant defies Lancelot; see H. O. Sommer (ed.), *The Vulgate Version
of the Arthurian Romances*, IV, 203.
[18] Sommer, IV, 154–226.

that Malory's purpose in making the addition was to place this instance in a planned progression of three such situations in *Le Morte Darthur*.[19] First, in the "Poisoned Apple" the Queen, accused of treason for the murder of Patryse, was saved from the stake by Lancelot's defeating Mador; here she was completely innocent of the charge. Second, we have the present instance in the "Knight of the Cart" when Lancelot saves her from the stake by defeating Meleagant; here the question of her guilt is a quibble; she did share her bed with Lancelot, but she is innocent of Meleagant's actual charge that one of the wounded knights was allowed to enter her bed. Third, in the "Tale of the Death of Arthur" Guenevere will be accused directly by Mordred of an adulterous relationship with Lancelot and will be saved by him from the stake through the fighting in which Gaheris and Gareth are killed (1174–78); here the Queen will be undeniably guilty. Thus, we have a climactic progression: Guenevere at first innocent, then directly innocent but indirectly guilty, and finally directly guilty.

The "Knight of the Cart" continues the suspense, present in the three preceding subdivisions and deriving from the two questions concerning the lack of harmony between the lovers and the degree of Arthur's awareness of the recommenced adultery. The subdivision opens with a lengthy discourse, original with Malory,[20] on Maytime and the nature of true love. Here the fresh description of the coming of Spring and the idealistic attitude toward love form an ironic contrast to the covert adultery which Lancelot and Guenevere are conducting. This passage also points forward to the similar material which will ironically introduce the "Tale of the Death of Arthur" (1161), just before the continued adultery brings about the final crisis. Presumably

---

[19] *Works*, p. 1596. Vida D. Scudder earlier suggested this purpose behind Malory's originality; see *Le Morte Darthur*, p. 320.
[20] *Works*, p. 1591.

no evidence at all ✓

motivated by a desire to prevent suspicion of the adultery—a motivation she had earlier stressed (1048, 1066)—Guenevere arranges the Maying expedition with the "Quenys Knyghtes," during which she is captured by Meleagant. When Lancelot receives her plea for help, he comes immediately and soon reaches Meleagant's castle.[21] Then Meleagant, fearful of Lancelot, begs Guenevere to make peace, and she tells Lancelot that there is now no need for fighting. At this point, we find another possibility of a quarrel between the lovers: [22]

> "Madame," seyde sir Launcelot, "syth hit ys so that ye be accorded with hym, as for me I may nat agaynesay hit, howbehit sir Mellyagaunte hath done full shamefully to me and cowardly. And, madame," seyde sir Launcelot, "and I had wyste that ye wolde have bene so lyghtly accorded with hym I wolde nat a made such haste unto you." (1129)

But Lancelot's displeasure rapidly fades and he tells the Queen, "Madame, . . . so ye be pleased, as for my parte ye shall sone please me" (1129). The possibility of a rift is soon over, and Lancelot spends that night in bed with the Queen (1131). There is no further indication of lack of harmony between the lovers, and the subdivision ends with the recommenced adultery continuing after Lancelot slays Meleagant.

Arthur does not appear in the "Knight of the Cart" until the Queen and the wounded knights return to the Court; meanwhile, Lancelot is imprisoned as a result of Meleagant's trick (1135). When told of Meleagant's charging the Queen with infidelity and of Lancelot's challenging Meleagant, Arthur says, "I am aferde sir Mellyagaunce hath charged hymselff with a

---

[21] As has often been observed, Malory almost completely shifts the emphasis away from the Cart episode, which traditionally had been the core of the story.

[22] Malory's treatment is completely different from that in the Prose *Lancelot*; see Sommer, IV, 201–6.

dresn't want to condemn Lancelot, either --he has a "middle ground" stance.

grete charge." Here Arthur is completely noncommittal about what presumably is uppermost in his mind—the bloodstained bed as evidence of the Queen's infidelity—and simply adds that Lancelot will almost certainly appear to defend the Queen. Meleagant's insistence forces Arthur to have Guenevere "brought tyll a fyre to be brente" (1137); when Lancelot does not appear, Lavayne asks the King to allow him to take Lancelot's place. Arthur agrees:

> "Grauntemercy, jantill sir Lavayne," seyde kynge Arthur, "for I dare say all that sir Mellyagaunce puttith uppon my lady the quene ys wronge. For I have spokyn with all the ten wounded knyghtes, and there ys nat one of them, and he were hole and able to do batayle, but he wolde prove uppon sir Mellyagaunce body that it is fals that he puttith uppon my lady." (1137)

Note that this passage—original with Malory [23]—gives evidence of Arthur's having been busy with the question of Guenevere's possible infidelity: he has satisfied himself that no one of the wounded knights shared her bed. Lancelot then arrives and kills Meleagant, and this subdivision, like the three preceding, ends happily: "And than the kynge and the quene made more of sir Launcelot, and more was he cherysshed than ever he was aforehande" (1140). We thus see at the close of the "Knight of the Cart" the same pattern for suspense observed in the earlier subdivisions: all seems well superficially, but beneath the surface the adulterous relationship continues. And here Arthur has good reason to suspect the adultery, for though the Queen has been saved and the disturbance caused by Meleagant has been successfully quieted, the King has had absolutely no explanation for the bloodstained bed. Since he established that no one of the wounded knights was guilty, circumstances point straight toward Lancelot as the culprit.

The fifth and final subdivision—the "Healing of Sir Urry"—

[23] Sommer, IV, 222.

is Malory's original creation. It has been suggested that Malory added this material in order to glorify Lancelot and to present a kind of convocation of the Arthurian worthies just before the tragic eighth division.[24] Be that as it may, there is another explanation of Malory's intention, which fits the pattern we have been examining. As we just saw, Arthur is justified at the end of the "Knight of the Cart" in suspecting that the adultery is again in progress.[25] Then the appearance of Urry and his mother, the circumstance whereby only "the beste knyght of the worlde" (1145) can heal Urry, and the failure of everyone else to heal the wounded knight, present the King with an excellent opportunity for testing Lancelot. In Arthur's mind, the situation would seem to be as follows: If Lancelot can heal Urry, after the King and others have failed, he is "the beste knyght of the world," a title for which he could not qualify if he has broken his promise made during the "Grail" to refrain from the adultery; but if Lancelot cannot heal Urry, Arthur has evidence that the adultery has recommenced. Thus it is that we are told the King's purpose in having Urry searched: "to wyte whych was the moste nobelyste knyght amonge them all" (1149); and thus Arthur is impatient at Lancelot's absence—" 'Mercy Jesu!' seyde kynge Arthur, 'where ys sir Launcelot du Lake, that he ys nat here at thys tyme?' " (1150). Further, Arthur explicitly sets the stage for the testing of Lancelot when he sees the latter approaching—" 'Pees,' seyde the kynge, 'lat no man say nothyng untyll he be come to us' " (1151).

Upon Lancelot's arrival we have the following passage:

> Than seyde kynge Arthur unto sir Launcelot, "Sir, ye muste do as we have done," and tolde hym what they had done and shewed hym them all that had serched hym.

[24] Wilson, "The Prose *Lancelot* in Malory," and W*orks*, p. 1578.
[25] Arthur's suspicion here seems to be the reference when in the eighth division Malory states that the King had "a demyng" of the adultery (W*orks*, p. 1163).

"Jesu defende me," seyde sir Launcelot, "whyle so many noble kyngis and knyghtes have fayled, that I shulde presume uppon me to enchyve that all ye, my lordis, myght nat enchyve."

"Ye shall nat chose," seyde kynge Arthur, "for I commaunde you to do as we all have done."

"My moste renowmed lorde," seyde sir Launcelot, "I know well I dare nat, nor may nat, disobey you. But and I myght or durste, wyte you well I wolde nat take uppon me to towche that wounded knyght in that entent that I shulde passe all othir knyghtes. Jesu deffende me frome that shame!"

"Sir, ye take hit wronge," seyde kynge Arthur, "for ye shall nat do hit for no presumpcion, but for to beare us felyshyp, insomuche as ye be a felow of the Rounde Table. And wyte you well," seyde kynge Arthur, "and ye prevayle nat and heale hym, I dare sey there ys no knyght in thys londe that may hele hym. And therefore I pray you do as we have done." (1151–52)

Two points are noteworthy here. First, the King's manner with Lancelot differs greatly from his customary kindly tone: he gives Lancelot a flat command to "search" Urry, leaving him no way to avoid this test. Second, Lancelot is hesitant to be put in this position, presumably because of his adulterous guilt; he attempts to escape the test on grounds of modesty, but Arthur advances "fellowship" as the reason Lancelot must "search" Urry.

When the other knights and Urry himself beg Lancelot to "search" the wounds, Lancelot clearly states his unworthiness: " 'A, my fayre lorde,' seyde sir Launcelot, 'Jesu wolde that I myght helpe you! For I shame sore with myselff that I shulde be thus requyred, for never was I able in worthynes to do so hyghe a thynge' " (1152). Then he says to the King, "I muste do youre commaundemente, whych ys sore ayenst my harte." Seeing no way out, Lancelot now prays to the Trinity for the power to heal Urry. Included in his prayer is his request "that my symple worshyp and honeste be saved"; apparently, Lancelot understands this situation as a test presented by the King, a test which he fears he shall fail. But he then proceeds to heal Urry. Arthur is overjoyed, and Lancelot weeps like a child with relief because his unworthiness, stemming from the adultery, has not been made apparent by failure to heal Urry.

That Lancelot is able to heal Urry, despite the recommenced adultery, is understandable in accord with Malory's definition of "the beste knyght of the worlde." For him the term means "best worldly knight"; the sections of the "Grail" concerning Lancelot made clear Malory's conception of Lancelot as "the best worldly knight," despite the adultery and his limitations as a spiritual knight. Earlier, in the Elaine section of the "Tale of Tristram," Lancelot as "the beste knyght of the world" had been able to free a lady from boiling waters after Gawain had failed to help her (792). Similarly, this definition in the "Healing of Sir Urry" does not disqualify Lancelot because of the adultery. But his success in healing Urry does not lead Lancelot to consider himself exonerated from the adulterous guilt. When we next see him, trapped in the Queen's room, he makes clear his continued realization that their relationship is "wronge," and he discloses his previous arrangement with Bors and others against just such an emergency (1166).

As the King sees it, however, Lancelot has passed the test; Arthur's suspicion does not have to be followed up, and he happily arranges a tournament and rewards Urry and Lavayne with knighthood (1153). Thus, the subdivision ends with the same situation we have observed in each earlier instance: on the surface all seems well, but the adulterous relationship of Lancelot and Guenevere, which will bring about ruin for all, continues. Though for the time being joy reigns in the court, we are told just before the end of the "Tale of Lancelot and Guenevere": "But every nyght and day sir Aggravayne, sir Gawaynes brother, awayted quene Gwenyver and sir Launcelot to put hem bothe to a rebuke and a shame" (1153); and the

"Tale of the Death of Arthur" will open with Aggravain's deter mination to inform the King of the adultery.

In summary, it would seem that Malory selected, altered, and augmented the materials he used for the "Tale of Lancelot and Guenevere" with the specific intention of giving the seventh division a function as suspense—in the structure of *Le Morte Darthur* as a whole, and in connection with the presentation of the Lancelot-Guenevere relationship throughout the book. The suspense derives from the two related questions concerning the lack of harmony between Lancelot and Guenevere and the degree of Arthur's awareness of the adultery. In each of the five subdivisions we have found the same pattern of suspense: there is a crisis in the affairs of the court; the crisis is seemingly happily resolved, but the continued adultery provides the basis for the future tragedy. In this way the "Tale of Lancelot and Guenevere" serves as preparation for the series of crises in the eighth division, which cannot be successfully resolved and which bring about both Arthur's public awareness of the recommenced adultery and the eventual separation of the lovers.

Finally, if the evidence presented here concerning suspense in the "Tale of Lancelot and Guenevere" has merit, it should weigh heavily against Vinaver's claim that Malory wrote eight separate romances, and for the unqualified acceptance of *Le Morte Darthur* as an intentionally unified work.[26] For when read in this light, the seventh division contributes greatly to the functioning of the other divisions and cannot be adequately understood if considered either completely alone or in conjunction only with Tale VIII.

[26] "The Question of Unity in Malory's *Morte Darthur*," *TSE*, V (1955), 29–39; the references therein cited; the review by R. T. Davies in *RES*, n.s. VII (1956), 330–31; and "Gawain's Miraculous Strength: Malory's Use of *Le Morte Arthur* and *Mort Artu*," *Etudes Anglaises*, X (1957), 97–108.

CHAPTER VIII

"THE TALE OF THE DEATH OF ARTHUR":
CATASTROPHE AND RESOLUTION

BY WILFRED L. GUERIN

I

The essence of the eighth large division of *Le Morte Darthur*, which Malory himself may have entitled the "Deth of Arthur," is tragedy.[1] It is the fall of an ideal society, the collapse of a dream much greater than the members of the Round Table themselves; it is a contrast between what the God-like in man can aspire to, and what his baser self can do. It is a series of deaths and frustrations, caused on the one hand by a conflict of often ironic, yet always supremely human, circumstances, and on the other by an inscrutable fortune or chance which man alone can never dominate. But while the essence of the "Tale of the Death of Arthur" is tragedy, this tragedy occurs in the material world only, for part of its essence is that spirituality which permits man to envision and aspire. Thus, while telling a story of a tragic dichotomy, Malory can conclude with a positive, reassuring view of existence as his protagonists look ahead to the next world.

[1] For the possibility that Malory intended this title, see the *explicit* in *Works*, p. 1260, and Vinaver's related comments on pp. xxxiii and 1646.

Yet this conclusion is by no means the happy ending tha Malory is said to have provided several times for the so-called separate romances.[2] If one sees *Le Morte Darthur* as one book then these earlier supposedly happy endings are only coinci dental with the development of the whole story and are to be considered alongside the elements of tragedy which culminate in the "Death of Arthur," where the thoroughness of the tragic mode is impressive. All the previous "happy endings," the "japes" of Dinadan and Kay, the pleasant disguises of Gareth and Lancelot, serve to emphasize not only the later deaths of everyone of note, but more poignantly the lacerated hearts and minds of Arthur, Lancelot, Guenevere, and Gawain. The great society of the Round Table resolves into nothingness, and the few survivors can only think, "It might have been."

Such a view of Malory's work would be untenable if it is in reality eight separate romances. If this theory is correct, then Malory did not intend a single, unified story, or plan an epic of a society rising from chaos to glorious order only to fall back to its original state. Nor did he project a tragedy with cosmo-logical and sociological significance, making manifest a causative relationship between vices sometimes rampant, sometimes hidden during the early and middle periods of Arthur's reign, and the less glorious and finally disastrous events of the later periods.

But, as the preceding chapters have shown, the whole of the book up to the "Tale of the Death of Arthur" serves as founda-tion for Malory's tragedy. From sourceless additions to his story, from adaptations and even radical changes of his sources, and even from deletions, Malory's intent can be seen. He fashions one work which moves toward the tragedy of the last division.[3]

[2] *Ibid.*, pp. 1361, 1416, 1431, and 1432–35.
[3] Contrast Vinaver's comment, ". . . as the action moves from Arthur's court to Joyous Gard, thence to besieged Benwick and finally back to Britain where Arthur dies bereft of his fellowship, one feels less and less

He provides motifs and themes that permeate the book; he makes characters generally consistent from division to division; he includes numerous specific links between the first seven divisions and the last; he interconnects these seven divisions and employs foreshadowing within the eighth. In short, he gives a unified story which persistently gravitates toward its conclusion. Without the first seven, the eighth is like a silent, isolated fossil, unable to tell of the forces that have brought it to its final situation.

As the tragedy draws to its end, the style shifts to careful use of an elegiac tone. After the suspense provided by the "Tale of Lancelot and Guenevere"—the happiness of the Great Tournament, the healing of Sir Urry, and the rescues of Guenevere [4] —Malory opens with a passage on the joys of May, "whan every harte floryshyth" and "gladith of somer commynge with his freyshe floures." But this passage includes the ominous suggestion of "a grete angur and unhappy that stynted nat tylle the floure of chyvalry of the worlde was destroyed and slayne." Malory continues, often without source authority, this tone of sorrow,[5] which culminates in Ector's eulogy at Lancelot's burial (1259). The tone indicates circumstances not unlike those found in Old English poetry, which W. P. Ker called "the transience and uncertainty of the world, the memory of past good fortune, and of things lost";[6] the very phrases can as well be applied to *Le Morte Darthur*. Indeed, in the same paragraph with these phrases, Ker makes this comparison explicit: "*Beowulf* is invaded

---

the need for any reminder of what happened earlier on" (*The Tale of the Death of King Arthur* [Oxford, 1955], pp. xvii–xviii).

[4] R. M. Lumiansky, "Malory's 'Tale of Lancelot and Guenevere' as Suspense," *Mediaeval Studies*, XIX (1957), 108–22.

[5] Notable and generally sourceless passages are Lancelot's conferences with his followers (1169–73, 1202–4), Gawain's reminder to Arthur of the debt they owe Lancelot (1174–75), much of the scene of Lancelot's defense before Arthur (1196–1202), Gawain's death scene and his letter (1230–32), and Guenevere's funeral (1256).

[6] W. P. Ker, *Epic and Romance* (London, 1922), p. 215.

by pathos in a way that often brings the old English verse very nearly to the tone of the great lament for Lancelot at the end of the *Morte d'Arthur*. . . ." [7]

But while the tone of the "Death of Arthur" is dominantly sorrowful, the division is singularly alive as narrative art. Much of this vitality comes from the dramatic nature of its movement. As in a play, this "Tale" presents that part of the story resulting when antecedent stresses have so generated tension that open conflict results. The dramatic nature of the "Tale" results partly from the materials Malory had before him, for in his sources he found sharp opposition of forces, both in external battle and in internal or psychological problems: the ambush at Guenevere's chamber; her rescue from the fire; the sieges at Joyous Garde and Benwick; the single combats involving Lancelot, Arthur, Gawain, and Mordred; the war against Mordred. These events are balanced by the more subtle conflicts within Lancelot, Arthur, Guenevere, Gawain, and even Bors, and the debates between Lancelot and his followers, between Gawain and Arthur, and between Lancelot and the combination of Arthur and Gawain. There is great variety here, and Malory skillfully alternates the kinds of opposition by original use of conferences and debates to interrupt the battles and the open quarrels provided by his sources. Furthermore, Malory makes great use in this "Tale" of dialogue, as he has done throughout the book, a dramatic device quite different from the monologues and narrative pattern of the Old French *La Mort le Roi Artu*, or the choppy, episodic account in the Middle English stanzaic poem, *Le Morte Arthur*.[8]

[7] He compares the same lament also to a passage in the Old French epic *Garin le Loherain* (p. 307).

[8] The use of dialogue can be illustrated by the scene in which Gawain learns of his brothers' deaths at Lancelot's hands. In 123 lines (1183–86), some of which are narration, there are twenty-five separate speeches. The comparable French passage has nine speeches in a total of 138 lines, and the English poem has five in a passage of forty-eight lines. References to

II

These two works are now generally considered the sources for the "Tale of the Death of Arthur." The Middle English poem exists in a single manuscript and dates possibly from the late fourteenth century.[9] The Old French *Mort Artu* exists in many manuscripts and dates probably from the early thirteenth century.[10] But acceptance of this view of the source relationship is relatively recent.

In 1891 H. O. Sommer said, "The twentieth and twenty-first books ["The Death of Arthur" in Caxton's divisions] are a prose-rendering of the English metrical romance, 'Le Morte Arthur,' as given in the Harl. MS. 2252; the 'Lancelot' [that is, the *Mort Artu*] may occasionally also have been used." [11] Later he said of the twentieth book that "The source which [Malory] used . . . stands in close relation" to the prose *Lancelot*.[12] Still later, "a minute examination of [Malory's] twenty-first book compared with the last ten folios of P. L. [prose *Lancelot*] discloses many and great differences, but also here the ground-plan of the two accounts is the same, and the incidents common

---

Malory's French source in this chapter are taken from *La Mort le Roi Artu*, ed. Jean Frappier (Paris, 1956); the pertinent passage in this illustration is on pp. 128–32. This work will hereafter be cited as the *Mort Artu*, and references usually will be to this edition by page (not paragraph) number, with occasional reference to lines: thus, (p.) 118. (line) 22. References to Malory's English source in this chapter are to *Le Morte Arthur*, ed. J. Douglas Bruce, *EETS-ES*, No. 88 (London, 1903); the passage concerned in this illustration includes lines 1966–2013.

[9] Bruce, *Le Morte Arthur*, p. xxv.

[10] In addition to the edition by Frappier, others are by J. D. Bruce (Halle, 1910), and H. O. Sommer, Vol. VI in *The Vulgate Version of the Arthurian Romances* (Washington, 1913).

[11] *Le Morte Darthur by Syr Thomas Malory*, Vol. III: *Studies on the Sources* (London, 1891), p. 11.

[12] *Ibid.*, pp. 250–51.

to both establish beyond doubt an intimate, though indirect, relation between the two versions; this fact points out either that the sources of both are derived from a common source, or that P. L. itself is the source of the French romance" used by Malory.[13] J. D. Bruce, differing with Sommer, argued that the Middle English poem and Malory are related only insofar as they have a common French source.[14] Of this debate Vinaver wrote in 1929, "On the whole Bruce gave a more satisfying solution of the problem, and there is little doubt that the MS Malory used for his Death of Arthur was French." [15]

Then in 1939 Robert H. Wilson maintained that there are "correspondences with the narrative of MH [stanzaic *Morte*] in Book XVIII of [Malory] and verbal resemblances in Books XX–XXI," and that Malory used both the French and the Middle English texts.[16] In other words, Wilson found it more difficult to believe in a common source for Malory and the latter part of the poem, than to believe that Malory had made use of both works and had also added original material.[17] But Wilson still considered the French Malory's primary source for the "Death of Arthur": "Malory's use of the two sources can most easily be understood on the assumption that he at first followed MA [*Mort Artu*] (or some modification of it responsible for rearranging the events of Book XVIII as well as inserting those of Book XIX) rather systematically. But he likewise drew on his memory of MH and in time consulted a copy—on occasion

[13] *Ibid.*, p. 265.
[14] "The Middle-English Metrical Romance 'Le Morte Arthur' (Harleian MS. 2252) . . . ," *Anglia*, XXIII (1901), 67–100, and the introduction to his edition of the poem (pp. xiii ff.). Sommer answered in "On Dr. Douglas Bruce's Article . . . ," *Anglia*, XXIX (1906), 529–38. Bruce then published "A Reply to Dr. Sommer . . . ," *Anglia*, XXX (1907), 209–16.
[15] *Malory* (Oxford, 1929), p. 150.
[16] "Malory, the Stanzaic *Morte Arthur*, and the *Mort Artu*," *MP*, XXXVII (1939–40), 134.
[17] *Ibid.*, p. 136.

following it closely where, in Books XX–XXI, its version of the story is strikingly different, yet still always keeping MA before him as his primary source." [18]

In 1947 Vinaver established more certainly Malory's direct debt to the Middle English poem, mainly by pointing out verbal parallels (1600 ff.). He, like Wilson, concluded "if one is to judge hypotheses by the degree of their probability, one cannot escape the conviction that the only reasonable one in the present instance would be that which made Malory responsible for the simultaneous use of the *Mort Artu* and *Le Morte Arthur* and for the invention of each of the passages untraceable to either" (1609). Since 1947 other scholars have either accepted or extended the theory of simultaneous use of both sources. E. Talbot Donaldson employed Vinaver's method to show Malory's use of the Middle English poem in Book XVIII.[19] Wilson argued that one need not seek a hypothetical source for Book XVIII any more than for Books XX–XXI.[20] R. M. Lumiansky saw in Lancelot's request to be buried at Joyous Garde a "use of material found in both" sources,[21] and he claimed similar derivation for the passage on Gawain's miraculous strength.[22]

Critics thus have differed markedly in their attitude toward the stanzaic *Morte* as source for Malory's "Death of Arthur": Sommer's view of it as principal source, with Malory borrowing occasionally from the *Mort Artu*; Bruce's refusal to accept it as at all pertinent; Wilson's acceptance of it as only auxiliary to the *Mort Artu*, the supposed primary source; and, finally, the idea of Malory's simultaneous use of both texts not only for the

---

[18] *Ibid.*, p. 137.
[19] "Malory and the Stanzaic *Le Morte Arthur*," *SP*, XLVII (1950), 460–72.
[20] "Notes on Malory's Sources," *MLN*, LXVI (1951), 22–26.
[21] "Two Notes on Malory's *Morte Darthur*," *Neuphilologische Mitteilungen*, LVIII (1957), 150–52.
[22] "Gawain's Miraculous Strength: Malory's Use of *Le Morte Arthur* and *Mort Artu*," *Etudes Anglaises*, X⁰ Année (1957), 97–108.

"Death of Arthur" but also for the "Tale of Lancelot and Guenevere."

Contrary to recent critical opinion, my view is that Malory used *Le Morte Arthur* as *primary* source for the "Tale of the Death of Arthur," and the French *Mort Artu* as *secondary* source. My conclusion is based for the most part on a collation of the entire "Death of Arthur" with the two possible sources.[23] The complete collation reveals that a great majority of the lines of the poem, and a still greater percentage of the stanzas, are identifiable in the "Tale," though often in truncated form. Of approximately 2,300 lines in the pertinent part of the poem, I found only about 700 lines not traceable in the "Tale." More to the point, the sequence of details and episodes in the "Tale" is generally like the straightforward narration of the Middle English poem, not like that of the digressive Old French *Mort Artu.*

This aspect of the narrative sequence can be illustrated in several ways. For example, in the scene of the return of Guenevere to Arthur, Malory (1196–1202) uses the French source somewhat more than he normally does, but he picks and chooses from various, non-sequential passages, while at the same time he follows (with two exceptions) the narrative line of the English poem. In Malory the lines of the poem are reflected in the following sequence: 2352–74, 2379, 2382–87, 2398–2403, 2390–91, 2407, 2024–29, 2449–52. But the sequence in which Malory uses French passages is as follows (four citations are not even certain): 158, ?157, ?158, ?159, 160, 190–91, ?158, 163, 158. The point here is that although Malory borrows considerably from

---

[23] The complete record of my collation of the "Death of Arthur" with the sources forms Appendix One to my dissertation, "The Function of 'The Death of Arthur' in Malory's Tragedy of the Round Table" (Tulane, 1958). This study is available from University Microfilms, L. C. Card No. Mic 59–614.

the French, he grafts these borrowings on to the framework taken from the English poem.

Another type of evidence is to be observed when Malory momentarily stops using the English poem, adds a passage from the French, but then goes back to the poem at the point from which he left it. For example, Gawain's death scene (1230–32) is largely from the French (212, 220); in order to use that source Malory leaves the poem at or near line 3133. He next includes some two pages of original material and borrowings from the French, and then (1232) he returns to the poem at line 3137 for Gawain's burial at Dover. After that sequence, he uses the poem from line 3137 to line 3211, adds (1234) to Arthur's dream of Gawain the detail from the French prose that ladies have interceded for the dead Gawain (225), and then returns to the poem at line 3220. Next, he follows the poem closely (to page 1238) for over 220 lines, at which point he slightly reflects the French again (247).[24]

The primacy of the poem as source can also be shown from general consideration of the third, fourth, and fifth subdivisions of the "Tale." Beginning with the third, the "Siege of Benwick," we observe less and less use of the French *Mort*: with Frappier's edition as reference, we see that Malory took details or passages from the following pages: 165, 167, 166, 194, 195, 198–99, 197, 200, 204, 171, 175–76, 179, 214–16 (with rearrangements), 212 and 220 (in alternating, recurring use), 225, 247, 248, 249, 252, 261, 263. The heavy omissions and the frequent rearrangement of sequence show Malory's freedom in his handling of the French source. Of the passages cited, he makes extended use of only two: pages 212 and 220 give him about two pages of his version of Gawain's death scene (1230.11–1232.15), and page

[24] For indication of Malory's use of the poem in the next scenes, where Arthur awaits and boards the fairy boat and where his tomb is described, see R. M. Lumiansky, "Arthur's Final Companions in Malory's *Morte Darthur*," *TSE*, XI (1961), 6–8.

252 gives him the first page of the fifth subdivision, the "Dolorous Death and Departing." In each of the other instances, he borrows lines, not pages. When we turn to his use of the English poem, we find some transpositions in the sequence of lines, but these changes result in various improvements; they do not represent Malory's adoption of the French narrative line. The comparable part of the poem has approximately 1440 lines, of which Malory seems to reflect all but about 330. From this example, Malory's preference for the Middle English poem as narrative guide is obvious.

On the other hand, whenever Malory finds the poem inadequate for his purpose in the interpretation of the tragedy, he resorts to his own invention or he borrows from the *Mort Artu*.[25] Since much of the "Death of Arthur" is devoted to the dilemmas of choice and decision, Malory sometimes makes use of the psychological perceptions of the French. When Lancelot, having routed his assailants, leaves Guenevere, the poem has no speech at all (*ca.* 1864). Though Malory has just used the poem (1854–63) to describe Lancelot's success, he turns to the *Mort Artu* (117.50–62) for the subsequent dialogue (1168–69). Then, in a passage that for the most part seems to be original with Malory, Bors advises Lancelot to rescue the Queen (1171); but for Bors' explanation of the problem Malory may be indebted to the *Mort Artu* (118.88–100). When Guenevere is being led to the fire, most of the scene derives from the poem; but Malory does not wish to use the poem's statement that "lordyngis was there many and good/And grete power" (1952–53). Instead, he says that many lords and ladies wept and wailed; and instead of

[25] Vinaver considers the place of "character and motive" and Malory's contribution to the genre of the later novel in *Works*, pp. lix ff. In his earlier book, *Malory*, Vinaver stated that Malory concentrates on "the psychological elements" rather than on the "adventurous aspect," "the chief motive of the *roman d'aventure*" (p. 43).

"grete power," he writes that "there were but feaw in comparison that wolde beare ony armour for to strengthe the dethe of the quene" (1177). The changed sense of the passage comes close to the grief expressed in the *Mort Artu:* "Lors lieve le criz et la noise par la cité de Kamaalot et font si grant duel com se la reïne fust leur mere" (122). After the stress on the emotions of the lords and the ladies, Malory returns to the poem for the battle scene. In another instance, Lancelot debates with Arthur from the walls of Joyous Garde, and there delivers one of the longest speeches in *Le Morte Darthur* (1188). Though Malory borrows from the poem both before and after the speech, the first half of it seems to come from Lancelot's charge to the damsel who is to be his emissary in the *Mort Artu* (140–41); the rest seems to be original with Malory. For a later and similarly long defense before Arthur, Malory again uses portions of the *Mort Artu;* the poem has a much shorter, less argumentative speech.[26] Lancelot's offer to "founde and gar make" houses of religion and his farewell to the "moste nobelyst Crysten realme" also derive from the French.

For the fast-moving subdivision called the "Siege of Benwick" Malory holds generally to the poem. But when, in the next subdivision, he deals with Gawain's death and his pathetic letter to Lancelot, much of the inspiration comes from the French. Immediately after the death scene, Malory returns to the poem and holds to it generally thereafter, though he makes original additions. Among these are Lancelot's reaction to the death of Guenevere (1256–57) and Ector's threnody (1259). For such passages and for many shorter ones,[27] Malory seems indebted in

---

[26] *Works,* p. 1198.1–6 and p. 1198.21–27; *Mort Artu,* p. 159.92–108 and p. 160.117–24; stanzaic *Morte,* lines 2398–2403.

[27] "So whan she had tolde her tale the watir ran oute of the kyngis yen" (1213); "So the damesell wepte and departed, and so there was many a wepyng yghe" (1213).

spirit if not in fact to the emotional and psychological tone of the *Mort Artu*.[28]

Such evidence points to the conclusion that Malory turned to the English poem as narrative guide, but desired greater elaboration of the thoughts of his characters and deeper analysis of their emotional reactions than the poem provided. For this material he turned either to the French or to his own invention. By such methods Malory avoided the excesses of the French—such as the reactions of Arthur and Gawain to the deaths of the latter's brothers (128–35)—as well as the extensive detail of certain scenes: the rescue of Guenevere, the siege of Joyous Garde (143–57), and the siege of Guanes (181–95).[29]

III

Although critics have praised highly both sources for the "Tale of the Death of Arthur," and although many of their best attributes are reflected in the "Tale," close study indicates that much of the high caliber of the "Tale" is the result of Malory's own efforts. This situation can best be seen by further examination of (1) his treatment of his primary source, (2) his supplementary use of his secondary source, and (3) his own additions. The pattern that emerges indicates that Malory chooses, synthesizes, even deletes according to a deliberate plan. The result is something much different from the sources, and—for his purposes—much superior to them. As a matter of fact,

[28] See Jean Frappier, *Etude sur La Mort le Roi Artu, Roman du XIII*ᵉ *Siècle* (Paris, 1936), especially Chapter Five, "Un Romancier psychologue dans le deuxième quart du XIIIᵉ siècle."

[29] Mention should be made here of the alliterative *Le Morte Arthure*, for while it is not a source of the "Tale of the Death of Arthur," its vigorous, epic-like qualities compare with the quickness of movement and directness of phrase that characterize the "Tale." Cf. *Le Morte Arthure*, ed. Edmund Brock, *EETS-OS*, No. 8 (London, 1865).

Malory is so different from his sources that earlier scholars, as can be seen from the Bruce-Sommer dispute, based their arguments on the confident assumption that Malory must have been using a "lost" source for the "Death of Arthur." Vinaver more reasonably argued that Malory's originality lies in those modifications and additions which give a "new direction, a new colour, and a new meaning" to the story.[30] The conclusion to be accepted is that the felicitous merging of the two sources and the deliberate alternation between them, as well as the insertion of original matter, very likely resulted from Malory's governing purpose for this "Tale" as a part of *Le Morte Darthur*.

Let us first look at some examples of how Malory condenses material taken from the Middle English poem. When Aggravain and his group begin their attack on Lancelot in Guenevere's chamber, the poem devotes an eight-line stanza to the queen's first speech. Malory achieves a much more natural outburst by suppressing the poem momentarily and adapting the French; Malory has the Queen say simply and credibly, "Alas! now ar we myscheved bothe!" [31] Later, when Sir Bors has an opportunity to kill King Arthur at the siege of Joyous Garde, Malory is again drawing generally from the poem. But the poem uses a whole stanza of eight lines when Bors seeks Lancelot's permission to kill Arthur; wanting a more natural and emphatic dialogue, Malory turns to the French and draws from it Bors' simple speech: "Sir, shall I make an ende of thys warre?" [32] Then Malory returns to the poem. Since the poem was probably recited orally, the filling out of stanzas is perhaps understandable; but Malory adapts for a reader—and for better effect as well. That same guiding hand is visible in the treatment of

[30] *Malory*, p. 41; *Works*, pp. lix ff., 1602 ff.; *The Tale of the Death*, pp. xiii ff.

[31] *Works*, p. 1165.22–23; cf. *Mort Artu*, pp. 115–16.

[32] *Works*, p. 1192; cf. the stanzaic *Morte*, lines 2170–96 and *Mort Artu*, p. 152.128–29.

longer passages. Malory suppresses one of the two very similar embassies sent by Lancelot to Arthur.[33] He also omits a twelve-line repetition (2258–69) of the Pope's orders to the warring factions. For brevity, and to point up the dilemmas of personal conflicts in *Le Morte Darthur*, he suppresses the formal truce between Lancelot and Arthur, which occupies over thirty lines in the poem (2318–51), and simply substitutes Lancelot's statement of his great trust in Arthur, a statement which takes less than three lines (1195). Much later, the inconsequential battle between the forces of Arthur and Mordred at Bareon Downe uses thirty-two lines in the poem (3090–3121); Malory condenses it to six (1232).

While Malory generally follows the order of the poem's material, some of his alterations in sequence seem designed for special effects. One of the most interesting comes after the siege of Joyous Garde, when Lancelot ceremoniously returns Guenevere to Arthur. By the transposition of lines taken from the poem and by the addition of some original passages, Malory heightens the internal struggle of his characters, stressing Arthur's silence as Lancelot leads Guenevere to him. Malory first sourcelessly says that the king "seyde no worde" (1197). Then he draws from two separate speeches in the poem (2382–87 and 2398–2403) and adds a passage to give Lancelot a long speech before the silent Arthur. When Arthur does speak, it is the paternal vexation of "Well, well, sir Launcelot, I have gyvyn you no cause to do to me as ye have done. . . ." Arthur's speech apparently derives from a passage in the poem (2390–91) which was *between* the two sets of lines used for Lancelot's speech. A similar alteration with comparable results occurs in the section presenting the siege of Benwick. There, when Lancelot's emissary brings to Arthur a request for peace, the poem presents the responses

---

[33] Malory retains the second (*Works*, pp. 1212–13; cf. the poem, 2608 ff.), but omits the first (2048–81).

first of Arthur, then of Gawain, and then of the lords (2668–89).
Malory reverses the sequence of the lords and Gawain, so that
in his version Gawain sees his chances for revenge dwindling and
frantically cries, "My lorde, myne uncle, what woll ye do?"
(1213).

Probably the most notable transposition is in Malory's version
of Guenevere's death and burial. Not only does Malory avoid
the anti-climactic effect of the poem, where Guenevere's funeral
is the final action (3946–69), but his version has positive aspects
as well. For example, Malory heightens the degree of holiness
in the last years of both Lancelot and Guenevere. Only in his
version is Guenevere shown with the gift of prophecy, evident
from her knowledge that Lancelot is coming to bury her
(1255–56); similarly, Lancelot is granted a vision of her death.
Because of the altered sequence, Malory can also create an objective connection between the now saintly lovers, whereby Lancelot's body is carried in the same bier that was used for Guenevere's body, and a "hondred torches" are mentioned in both
cases (1256, 1258). Further, in Malory's version the prior death
of Guenevere lends added motivation for the death of Lancelot.
The treatment of Lancelot's request for the last rites is analogous
to the passages just considered because in Malory the request
is the first Lancelot makes of the bishop when he realizes that
he is dying (1257). In the poem he first asks to be buried at
Joyous Garde, then goes to his deathbed, and finally receives
the rites (3842 ff.). Such transpositions of the source material
for the deaths of the lovers seem to stress the characters' spiritual
orientation, and, through better sequence and climax, clearly
emphasize the tragedy of the love affair. As with Malory's abbreviations and deletions, the transpositions reveal his reasons
for changes—sometimes for clearer thematic statement, sometimes for stylistic and artistic purposes.

Some of these changes clearly are associated with Malory's

French source, the _Mort Artu_. Though I consider this source secondary, I do believe that Malory had it before him as he wrote, and that he drew much of the spirit of his own work from the French. Thus at times we find Malory drawing directly from the _Mort Artu_, and at times fusing its material with his own, or the poem's, or both.

A typical example of verbal similarity with both the French and the English is Lancelot's request to Guenevere when Aggravain attacks: "Madame, ys there here ony armour within your chambre that myght cover my body wythall?" (1165). Half of the sentence is like the poem's "Bot is here any Armoure inne" (1826), and the other half like the French "dont ge poïsse mons cors armer" (116.26). Guenevere's answer has elements from both the French and the English; for that matter, the whole scene shows traces of both. One more detail may suffice here: Lancelot's fight with Collegrevaunce of Gore, though largely original with Malory, juxtaposes a passage from the poem ("Bot Launcelot gaffe hym soche A dynte"—1842) with one from the French ("qui estoit chaoiz a l'uis de la chambre par dedenz"—117); thus in Malory: "gaff hym such a buffette uppon the helmet that he felle grovelyng dede wythin the chambir dore" (1167). Similar parallel use of the two sources is evident in the next several scenes, especially in the deaths of Gareth and Gaheris at Lancelot's hands (_Works_, 1177–78; stanzaic _Morte_, 1941, 1962; _Mort Artu_, 124.53–55).

Much of the following subdivision, the "Vengeance of Sir Gawain," derives from the _Mort Artu_, for in numerous passages there is evidence of Malory's joining the French to his primary source.[34] Two of the most important not only show the use of the French but also demonstrate how Malory deliberately chooses his materials. Lancelot's moving offer to do penance for the deaths of Gareth and Gaheris (1199–1200) derives from a passage in the _Mort Artu_ (190–91) some thirty pages beyond

the current action of the story. Again, to incorporate Lancelot's
heartfelt farewell to England into this already intensely emotional scene, Malory anticipates by some three pages the comparable action and speech in the French, adding at the same
time some of his own material (*Works*, 1201; *Mort Artu*,
163.1–14).

Parallel phraseology with and evidence of the borrowing of
details from the French can be seen in the third subdivision, that
concerning the siege of Benwick, and again in the early parts
of the subdivision treating Mordred's rebellion; clearly, however,
Malory continues to follow his primary source (here, 2780–
3138), fusing the French passages with it. I pass over several
uses of the French[35] to stress the scene of Gawain's last hours

[34] Malory's use of the French can be seen in the following:

Works	Mort Artu
1186.13–15	135.37–42
1186.17–19	136.63–67
1186.20–22	135.56–60
1186.29–1187.7	136–37
1188.1–17	140.21–141.49
1191.23–24	150.44–47
1191.26–30	149 (cf. the poem, lines 2158, 2167, 2174)
1193.3–13	150.43–57 (cf. the poem, lines 2208–22)
1194.26–1195.7	153.26–154.30
1197–99 (*passim*)	158–60 (*passim*)
1199.28–1200.24	190–91
1201.7–22	163.1–14
1202.6–8	158.35–38

[35] Passages not commented upon include the following:

Works	Mort Artu
1216.21–30	195.2–196.48
1216.31–1217.1	198–99
1217.10–15	197.6–12
1217.15–18	200.1–5
1227.4–25	175.1–5 and 13–19, 176.38–43, 179.78–81, and 214.1–4

For a full treatment of Malory's version of Lancelot's first single combat
with Gawain (*Works*, pp. 1216–17), see Lumiansky, "Gawain's Miraculous
Strength."

and death. Obviously Malory was attracted by the pathos and tragic motifs he found in the French, and by skillfully rearranging, even reusing certain speeches, by adding the letter that Gawain writes to Lancelot, and by adding significant lesser items, he has fashioned an important episode in Arthurian literature. He uses two passages from the French (212–13 and 220–21) and merges materials originally separated by several pages devoted to Mordred's preparations for war and Arthur's arrival at Dover. Contrary to the situation in the English poem, where Gawain is found dead, in Malory Arthur finds him "liynge more than halff dede" (1230). After this necessary modification Malory adds a lament by Arthur and then follows with an adaptation from the French of a speech by Arthur (212.21–34) when his forces arrive at the shore of the sea. Malory enhances Arthur's lament for his personal loss of Gawain and Lancelot and plays down Arthur's fear of the military consequences. Though at this point in the French Gawain says, "je sai bien que je ne vivrai ja quinze jours," Malory jumps ahead to the actual death scene in the French, where Gawain says, "ge me muir" (220). From the latter passage Malory takes Gawain's blaming himself for his death, and the motif that the wound given by Lancelot causes his death (1230). For the next several lines of Gawain's speech, Malory reuses the speech Arthur just made—taken from the *Mort Artu* (212.21–34)—though now Malory stresses the military consequences which he previously played down. Thus, in Malory Arthur is less selfish than in the French, and Gawain is more solicitous. Malory then adds the device of Gawain's letter to Lancelot, but for its contents (1231) he draws from the already used sources, reworking them for this new setting. The early part of the letter (to line 23) derives from Gawain's last speeches to Arthur in the French (220–21), while the latter part compares with Gawain's earlier request to Arthur that he send

for Lancelot (212.4–213.13 and 213.23–28). Malory then includes Gawain's castigation of his treacherous brother, and the
close of the letter. Gawain's written request that Lancelot visit
his tomb is found in the French as an oral message (220.20–23).
Next, Malory adds Gawain's receiving the last sacrament. When
Gawain asks that Arthur send for Lancelot, Malory is apparently
using directly the French passage which he used indirectly just
a few paragraphs earlier. Once the emotional matter of the
French has given Malory all it can, he returns to the poem for
his narrative, and Gawain, as in the poem, is buried in Dover
Castle (*Works*, 1232; stanzaic *Morte*, 3137–38). With few ex-
ceptions, Malory holds to his primary source for the rest of *Le
Morte Darthur*.

Finally, some passages are best considered as additions by
Malory with no dependence upon either source. I have already
mentioned some of those which are fused with source-derived
material. Many others function simply as introductory or transi-
tional comments, or provide practical details and explanations.
More important are those which further the development of
Malory's characters. A simple example is Malory's stress on the
divided opinion between Gawain and his two evil brothers.[36]
Perhaps even more significant is his development of the dilemmas that beset his protagonists, for these problems he apparently sees as fundamental to the tragedy. Arthur finds himself condemning to death his wife and fighting her lover, for
both of whom he still feels deep affection.[37] Lancelot must fight
the forces of the honored king who made him a knight, return
the woman he loves after he has risked his life for her, and
fight in single combat with one of his most respected fellow

[36] *Works*, pp. 1161.24–32; 1162.1–2, 11–20, and 23–29.
[37] *Ibid.*, pp. 1163.12–19, 1174.12–18, 1175.27–33, 1194.21–22, 1196–99
(*passim*), 1213, 1218.

knights.[38] Gawain is caught between the opposing forces of his loyalty to Lancelot [39] and his monomaniac desire for vengeance against Lancelot.[40] In each case—Arthur, Lancelot, and Gawain —Malory adds six or more passages to emphasize the individual's dilemma. For similar purposes Malory adds two rather formal conferences between Lancelot and his followers (one before the rescue of Guenevere—1170 ff., and one before the departure for France—1202 ff.), and a less formal conference between Arthur and his nephews when Arthur must decide whether or not to execute Guenevere (1176–77). He adds at least seven conversations which stress personal relationships and conflicts.[41] In these and in related speeches, incidentally, we can often see Malory's own forceful and rhythmic style, the most often quoted passage being Ector's eulogy over Lancelot (1259).

A number of Malory's additions strengthen the importance of religion in the lives of his characters. Some, such as requests for prayers or the reception of the last rites, may seem at first mere traditional devices, but Malory uses them sourcelessly.[42] Elsewhere (1234.6–7, 9–15) Malory stresses the idea that God's mercy is extended to Arthur when he is granted the warning vision in which Gawain appears. Malory intensifies the sorrow and repentance of Guenevere and Lancelot,[43] especially stressing their saintliness by means of Lancelot's sourceless vision of Guenevere's death (1255–56), the mysterious warning of Lancelot's own death (1257), and the odor of sanctity about his corpse (1258).

Among Malory's additions, interestingly enough, is evidence of his caution, even of his skepticism, about Arthur's death and

---

[38] *Ibid.*, pp. 1172 ff., 1188, 1193, 1213–14, 1215–16, 1253.

[39] *Ibid.*, pp. 1161, 1162, 1174–75, 1176, 1230–32.

[40] *Ibid.*, pp. 1186, 1191, 1200, 1200–1, 1213 ff.

[41] *Ibid.*, pp. 1166–67, 1185, 1189–90, 1193, 1195–96 (in part), 1236–37, and 1253 (in part).

[42] See, e.g., *Ibid.*, pp. 1166, 1184, 1202, 1218, 1231, 1249.

[43] *Ibid.*, pp. 1243, 1252, 1254–56 (*passim*).

burial and future return, a caution possibly motivated by his stress on the Christian rather than the mythological aspects of Arthur's death.[44] In any event, Malory is interested in "bokis that bene auctorysed" and "verry sertaynté" (1242). When such caution is compared with other original additions and with careful adaptations of source material which develop characters and theme, I think it fair to say that while Malory may have questioned the historical authenticity of at least some of his material, he had no doubt whatever of its poetic and psychological truth.

IV

Another view of Malory's originality in the "Tale of the Death of Arthur" can be observed from his use of preparation, foreshadowing, and linking devices. Vinaver has claimed that there are no links between the "Death of Arthur" and the preceding seven "Tales": "Nowhere perhaps is Malory's comprehension of [the principle of 'singleness'] more apparent than in his remodeling of the story of Arthur's death and of the destruction of the Round Table. The central theme is disengaged from all concomitant elements and freed from links with the other branches of the cycle. The events leading to the downfall of Arthur's kingdom are no longer interwoven with others, and the tragic destiny of Arthurian knighthood is divorced from the earlier account of how the 'worldly' knights failed in the quest of the Grail." [45]

[44] R. M. Lumiansky also believes that Malory "was concerned by the conflict between Arthur's stating that he was going to Avalon to be healed —with the result that men say he will return—and the midnight burial by the ladies in a tomb marked as Arthur's." He suggests that "it is Malory's effort to reconcile the conflicting statements and to allow for the possibility of both events having occurred which leads him to conclude that Arthur 'changed his life' here in this world." See "Arthur's Final Companions," p. 9.

[45] *The Works of Sir Thomas Malory* (Oxford, 1954), p. ix; cf. also p. viii and *Works*, pp. xxx and lxxx.

Among the more forceful challengers of this theory is D. S. Brewer, who has argued that there is a definite "connectedness" in *Le Morte Darthur*.[46] Brewer does not go into great detail, but it is not difficult to find in the eighth "Tale" many instances of linking and continuity of the kind he discusses.[47] I shall not be concerned here with the pervasive elements that run throughout the book, or through large divisions of it, such as the theme of treachery, the character of Morgan, the development of Lancelot as the tragic hero of the "Death of Arthur," or the Lancelot-Guenevere liaison. But there are many specific links in addition to these pervasive ones; in fact, such links may even be more to our point, for the pervasive links conceivably could exist in separate stories. For the purposes of illustration, I shall relate to the eighth "Tale" one such specific link from each of the first seven.

1. When Malory is creating his own, sourceless version of Arthur's final journey before his death, he says of one of the ladies in the boat: "Also there was dame Nynyve, the chyff lady of the laake, whych had wedded sir Pellyas, the good knyght; and thys lady had done muche for kynge Arthure. And thys dame Nynyve wolde never suffir sir Pelleas to be in no place where he shulde be in daungere of hys lyff, and so he lyved unto the uttermuste of hys dayes with her in grete reste" (1242). Seemingly digressive, this summary of the story of Nineve and Pelleas, stressing marital bliss, indicates their role in the connectedness of *Le Morte Darthur*. The function and the character of Nineve are important throughout Malory's book; also, she has a place in Arthurian tradition in her own right.[48] But it

---

[46] "Form in the *Morte Darthur*," *Medium Aevum*, XXI (1952), 14–24. See also his review of *The Tale of the Death of Arthur*, *Medium Aevum*, XXV (1956), 22–26.

[47] See Chapter Three of my dissertation.

[48] Cf. A. B. Taylor, *An Introduction to Medieval Romance* (London, 1930), pp. 76–77.

is through her relationship with her husband that Malory's purpose here is more easily seen. Only in Malory does Pelleas play a role beyond the material covered by the "Tale of King Arthur"; [49] in the *Morte* he appears in eight subsequent passages. Only in Malory does Pelleas love and wed Nineve (170–72 and note). Malory carefully builds the reputation of Pelleas as a knight, as a faithful lover, and as a husband.[50] In the first "Tale" he provides a synopsis of Pelleas' career that compares in phraseology with that in the last "Tale." Several other, and of course sourceless, passages continue this characterization of Pelleas, including still another synopsis in the "Healing of Sir Urry." Thus, before the important synopsis in the "Death of Arthur," two summaries and several mentions of Pelleas and his happy marriage with Nineve present or refer to Malory's original use of their story, a use which clearly links the "Death of Arthur" to the first "Tale," and stresses the thematic import in this happy marital relationship, which stands in such sharp contrast to the less happy relationships between men and women that contribute so markedly to the collapse of the Round Table.

2. One of the clearest indications that Malory wrote or revised the "Tale of King Arthur and the Emperor Lucius" with a knowledge of what was to come in the "Death of Arthur" is the preservation of Bedwere.[51] In the alliterative *Morte Arthure*, the source of Malory's second "Tale," Bedwere dies near the middle of the poem (2238–41). But Malory has Lancelot and Lovell rescue this knight (223). Bedwere appears in intervening sections of the book, but in each case before his participation in the final battle at Salisbury his appearance seems unparalleled

---

[49] See *Works*, p. xxxviii and note 5.
[50] Sourceless passages that indicate Malory's purpose are evident in *Ibid.*, pp. 162.1–5, 167.18–29, 168.8–18, and 179.16–25.
[51] This matter was only briefly mentioned by Mary Dichmann, "Characterization in Malory's *Tale of Arthur and Lucius*," *PMLA*, LXV (1950), 891.

in the sources.[52] Malory obviously is preparing for Bedwere's important role during Arthur's last hours.

3. A key episode in the "Tale of Lancelot" is Lancelot's fight with Tarquin (265 ff.), which Malory found in the prose *Lancelot* (cf. *Works*, 1400). In the "Death of Arthur" there are two separate references to this fight (1162, 1198), neither of which is in the sources. The second bears verbal resemblances to a passage near the end of the third "Tale," when Lancelot returns to court. During the general rejoicing, "now and now com all the knyghtes home that were presoners with sir Terquyn. . . ." Gaheris tells Arthur "how hit was and how sir Terquyn was the strongest knyght that ever he saw excepte sir Launcelot; and there were many knyghtes bare hym recorde, three score" (286). In the "Death of Arthur" Lancelot echoes these details when he tells Gawain, "I founde your brothir, sir Gaherys, and sir Terquyn ledyng hym bounden afore hym; and there also I rescowed youre brothir and slew sir Terquyn and delyverde three score and four of my lorde Arthurs knyghtes oute of hys preson" (1198). Lancelot adds, "I mette never wyth so stronge a knyght nor so well-fyghtyng as was sir Carados and sir Tarquyn, for they and I faught to the uttermost."

4. In the "Tale of Gareth" Malory provides the original motif that Lancelot knighted Gareth. The dubbing is directly alluded to in the "Death of Arthur" by Gareth (1162), by Gawain (1189), and by Lancelot (1199); necessarily, all three passages are sourceless.

5. Of many connections between the "Tale of Tristram" and the "Death of Arthur" one of the clearest and most important

[52] Malory brings Bedwere into the "Tale of Gareth," the subdivision concerning the Maid of Astolat, the "Great Tournament," and the subdivision concerning Sir Urry; and he makes him one of the negotiators with Mordred. Arthur's love for Bedwere, mentioned twice in the second "Tale" without source authority (223, 224), also seems a preparatory link with the sourceless emphasis on that love in the "Death of Arthur" (1239).

is the change that Malory effects in the conclusion for the story of Tristram: Malory has made this aspect of the story complement rather than compete with or detract from the conclusion of his entire book.[53] In the eighth "Tale" Malory concludes the Tristram story with a sourceless recollection by Lancelot of the manner of Tristram's death and the possibility that he, Lancelot, may suffer a similar fate (1172–73).

6. During the "Tale of the Sankgreall" two sourceless passages allude to Lancelot's lack of stability,[54] his tendency to "turn again" to Guenevere (897, 948). Two significant references to the matter occur in the "Tale of Lancelot and Guenevere" (1045–46, 1119). Then in the eighth "Tale," when Lancelot seeks out Guenevere, learns of her intention to remain in the nunnery, and tells her that he will follow the same destiny, her reply is very similar to the sourceless words of the hermit Nacien in the "Grail" (948): "A, sir Launcelot, if ye woll do so and holde thy promyse! But I may never beleve you, but that ye woll turne to the worlde agayne" (1253). Her answer is virtually original with Malory. The steadfast penance that Lancelot undergoes in the rest of the story not only causes Nacien's prophecy of a holy death to be fulfilled but also gains for Lancelot the virtue of stability. Thus the allusions to his instability by the hermits during the "Grail," by Lancelot himself in the "Tale of Lancelot and Guenevere," and by Guenevere and Lan-

[53] In addition to Chapter V above, see Thomas C. Rumble, "The *Tristan* Legend and Its Place in the *Morte Darthur*," unpublished dissertation (Tulane, 1955), especially pp. 115–30.

[54] It would appear that Vinaver does not interpret in this way the frequent use of the word *stability*; see his note to p. 948.19–28. Cf. pp. 897.29–31; 948.19–28; 956.2; 1035.12; 1045.10–1046.14; 1119.14–21; 1253.7–9, 19–22. With the exception of p. 1035.12, the passages are all associated with the qualities of chastity and dedication to virtue. Similarly Gawain admits during the quest for the Grail that Lancelot would not fail of pre-eminence "if one thynge were nat" (941). Vinaver's note to this passage again suggests his failure to see certain thematic implications of *Le Morte Darthur*.

celot in the final "Tale" closely connect the "Grail" to the "Death of Arthur," where the fault is finally conquered.

7. Malory connects the "Tale of Lancelot and Guenevere" with the "Tale of the Death of Arthur" by such parallels as the sourceless addition of the colloquy between Lavayne and Lancelot when the latter wishes to visit Guenevere (1130–31). Here is a clear parallel, even in phraseology, with the similar colloquy between Bors and Lancelot in the "Death of Arthur" (1164–65). The thematic importance of this parallel is that it helps to show Lancelot's inability to profit from experience when his love of Guenevere is involved.

V

As the preceding sections of this chapter have indicated, Malory shows a deep concern for the full and detailed development of his situations and characters, and an equal concern for avoiding any slowing of the dramatic movement of his plot. He also deliberately fosters the connectedness of his story. But character and plot development are only two of the three great components of storytelling: with the third, theme, Malory is of course equally concerned as he develops the tragic significances of his story. Tragedy needs a system of philosophy to give it weight and cogency; this context is provided in the "Death of Arthur" by a sense of religion. It is not true that Malory finds "no comfort" in "religious explanations," as Vinaver asserts (lxxxv), just as it is not true that the "Grail" has no significance for the "Death of Arthur" (lxxv, lxxx). On the contrary, most of the seven deadly sins are identifiable in the "Death of Arthur" and earlier as contributing causes to the fall of the Round Table; and the protagonists die holy deaths, after which important secondary characters die fighting the infidels.

Tragedy, with its focus on human emotions, its dependence

on rational decisions, and its relation to the moral order, necessarily concerns people as individuals first, and people as members of society second. It is understandable, then, that however much Malory was concerned with the story of an ideal society in a non-ideal world, he chose to build his tragedy around the central personalities of Arthur, Lancelot, and Gawain. Through these characters, and others like Guenevere, Bors, and the brothers of Gawain, Malory shows the tragedy simultaneously in human terms and in its social implications. We cannot say that one level is more important than the other; but the larger implications of the story are better considered only after the characters themselves are discussed.

Lancelot is an unusual and complex blend of good and evil. Malory seems to conceive of him as having the highest potential virtue of all the knights—the Grail knights not excluded; his sensibilities and passions are equally great. The combination of good and evil makes him a representative man, but the caliber of his personal attributes raises him to heroic levels. It is in this context, so much like that described by Aristotle, that he suffers a change of fortune that first lowers, then raises him; that he experiences a conflict of emotions in his actions and the tragic irony that besets those actions; that he gradually increases in knowledge of self and in resultant repentance. These characteristics make him Malory's tragic hero.

Such a pre-eminent role in the "Death of Arthur" necessarily had to be prepared for, and—as we have seen in preceding chapters—in the earlier development of Lancelot's character Malory clearly had in mind his hero's later importance. Lancelot displaces Gawain as the chief knight in the Roman campaign; [55] he becomes the protagonist of a careful selection of episodes that form the "Tale of Lancelot"; [56] he sponsors and dubs the noble

[55] Dichmann, "Characterization," pp. 881–86.
[56] Vinaver, *Works*, pp. 1398–1402; Wilson, "Notes on Malory's Sources," 22–26. See also Lumiansky, "The Relationship of Lancelot and Guenevere in Malory's 'Tale of Lancelot,'" *MLN*, LXVIII (1953), 86–91.

Gareth; [57] and he nearly assumes the status of an achiever of the Grail.[58] Yet while adding such favorable passages as those in the "Grail" and in the "Healing of Sir Urry," Malory also adds within the "Grail" the important qualification, "And if one thynge were nat, sir Launcelot he had none felow of an erthely man . . ." (941 and note). The paradox of Lancelot's moral character is strongly brought out by a hermit shortly after this passage, again in an addition by Malory. The hermit not only is aware of Lancelot's great spiritual worth and his love for Guenevere, but also is aware that Lancelot "ys lyckly to turne agayne" to Guenevere and that "yett shall he dye ryght an holy man . . ." (948 and note).

Both prophecies come true in the "Death of Arthur," where Lancelot's change of fortune combines with discovery and instances of reversal or peripety, the very combination which Aristotle found so important to tragedy. To be sure, the total catastrophe of *Le Morte Darthur* causes Lancelot to share the fall from weal to woe with all other principals of the story; but only in the case of Lancelot do we find so total a change of fortune for which the character is himself responsible. His fortune progressively falls in the "Death of Arthur" until it reaches its lowest point in his inability to help Arthur in the King's greatest need; it is tragically ironic that Lancelot, who has hitherto always been able to bring victory to his chosen side—even when defending an adulterous woman—is unable to save Arthur from a traitor. He is aware of his direct contribution to his change of fortune, his "unhappiness":

[57] See Chapter IV above and the relevant sections of my M.A. thesis, "The Functional Role of Gareth in Malory's *Morte Darthur*" (Tulane, 1953).

[58] *Works*, pp. 1523–24. Cf. p. 1571, where Vinaver says that Malory's object in adding a key passage at the end of the "Grail" "is to make Lancelot appear at the end of the Grail adventures as their main protagonist." Cf. also pp. lxxvii–lxxviii.

Alas, that ever I shulde lyve to hyre of that moste noble kynge that made me knyght thus to be oversette with hys subjette in hys owne realme! . . . And in an unhappy owre was I born that ever I shulde have that myssehappe to sle firste sir Gawayne, sir Gaherys, the good knyght, and myne owne frynde sir Gareth that was a full noble knyght. Now, alas, I may sey I am unhappy that ever I shulde do thus. And yet, alas, myght I never have hap to sle that traytoure, sir Mordred! (1249)

Unhappy, myssehappe, unhappy, hap: Malory clearly points to the change of fortune.

But unlike Arthur's, Lancelot's change of fortune is not yet complete, for Malory turns the wheel full circle. After a false start in the interview with Guenevere, Lancelot successfully seeks a new life in the hermitage, after which Malory stresses his increasing saintliness. He is granted a vision three times, charging him, in remission of his sins, to go to Almesbury, where he will find Guenevere dead (1255). Later he has an apparently divinely granted premonition of his own death, a communication unfit for other ears (1257). The comparable passages in the sources have nothing of the supernatural.[59] Malory's sourceless description of Lancelot's corpse mentions the traditional odor of sanctity: ". . . he laye as he had smyled, and the swettest savour aboute hym that ever they felte" (1258). The Middle English poem simply says that the corpse was "Rede and fayer of flesshe and blode" (3888).

With this change of fortune we may link the reversals and the pattern of discovery Lancelot experiences. Among the reversals, or actions which have ironic results, are his rescue of the Queen (when Gareth is killed), the delay in fighting Arthur at Benwick (which gives Mordred time to rebel), and the death of Gawain (in part from the wound inflicted by

[59] *Mort Artu*, p. 261, and the stanzaic *Morte*, lines 3834–41.

Lancelot). The pattern of discovery is lengthy and complex. Certainly Lancelot is always conscious at a rational level of the significance of his sins, but only gradually does he become purged of his predilection for illicit love.[60] The full discovery, the complete *emotional* appreciation of what he is and of what he has done, comes after Guenevere is buried beside Arthur. His speech at that point (1256) clearly shows that at the moment of his enlightenment he is both at the lowest and at the highest levels. In short, with great originality Malory has presented a progression in which change of fortune, reversal, discovery, and responsibility for actions combine to make Lancelot protagonist and tragic hero of the "Death of Arthur."

Although Lancelot is clearly the tragic hero of this "Tale," Arthur himself is also presented in tragic perspective. He is less than Lancelot in this respect because he is less the prime mover in the "Tale." "More sinn'd against than sinning," Arthur faces betrayal in Lancelot's adultery and in Mordred's rebellion, and is pushed into war by Gawain. Malory also keeps Arthur removed from the role of tragic hero simply by keeping him out of the final subdivision of the story. On the other hand, he plays a more prominent role in the eighth "Tale" than he has played since the war with the Emperor Lucius. The prominence is not attributable only to the fact that Arthur dies in the "Death of Arthur"; what matters is that his characterization has new life, his actions new importance. In the middle divisions of the book, Arthur is something less than the person seen earlier. But this situation does not detract from—it may even result from—Arthur's central position in Round Table society,[61] since as head of an estab-

---

[60] For passages in the progression, see *Works*, pp. 270, 898–99, 1046, 1152, 1170 ff., 1187 ff., 1212 ff., 1249, 1252–53, 1254.

[61] Cf. Vida Scudder, *Le Morte Darthur of Sir Thomas Malory: A Study of the Book and Its Sources* (London, 1921), pp. 276–77, 371. See also Taylor, *An Introduction to Medieval Romance*, pp. 66–67; Vinaver, *Malory*,

lished empire and a thriving society of knights, his primary concern is to preserve the status quo: respect for the King and unity of the Round Table.

The loss of that Round Table, a loss partly attributable to Arthur himself, constitutes the tragedy of Arthur. More than a symbol for him, the society is the practical means of governing his empire; it provides good fellowship; it is the source of great pride and personal satisfaction. After Lancelot has rescued Guenevere, Arthur says, "And much more I am soryar for my good knyghtes losse than for the losse of my fayre quene; for quenys I myght have inow, but such a felyship of good knyghtes shall never be togydirs in no company. And now I dare sey, there was never Crystyn kynge that ever hylde such a felyshyp togydyrs" (1184).[62] As in the case of Lancelot, a system of tragic devices informs Arthur's last actions. In killing Mordred, he himself is mortally wounded. That he has gained tragic self-knowledge is clear when he tells Bedwere, "Comforte thyselff, and do as well as thou mayste, for in me ys no truste for to truste in." And although he hopes to go to Avalon to heal himself of his wound, he suspects, rightly, a different fate: "And if thou here nevermore of me, pray for my soule!"

Arthur's knowledge or lack of knowledge of his own cuckoldry is important for an estimate of him as a tragic character. His "demyng" of the liaison (1163) is, in my understanding of Malory's purpose, of long standing.[63] But he has carefully

---

pp. 91 ff.; and Nellie Slayton Aurner, *Malory: An Introduction to the Morte D'Arthur* (New York, 1938), pp. xxiv–xxvii.

[62] For another allusion to Guenevere's secondary place in Arthur's affections, see p. 1187.33, where the word "also" relegates her to a position below the Round Table and Arthur's blood relatives. For comparable speeches on the fellowship of the Round Table, see *Works*, pp. 864–67, 1174.14–16, 1183.7–14, 1187.29–35, 1201.20–22, and 1236.

[63] Arthur's suspicions can begin to increase at least as early as the "Tale of Tristram." See *Works*, pp. 554–55, 557, 617, 832–33; this last, significantly, is sourceless. Cf. Lumiansky, "Arthur's Final Companions," pp. 13–15.

maintained the fiction of ignorance, deceiving even the scheming Aggravain. The reason for such concealment tells us something of Arthur's wide vision, his magnanimity, and his self-restraint. For Arthur the greatest good is the preservation of his empire and the correlative stability of the Round Table. To insure these ends he needs the sympathy and respect of his followers and the strong hands of Lancelot and his kin. At first he can retain these aids only by ignoring what he knows; then, after the public accusations are made, only by publicly repudiating the adulterers. His weighing of the situation, unlike Othello's outraged feeling that an adulteress must not blight the earth, dictates that the adultery shall continue, and his decision is determined by concern for the greater good that will come to his empire and the Round Table. When action is forced upon him, his conflicting emotions are clear.[64] Under similar stresses others might escape into insanity; Arthur tries to preserve what is left to him. He follows Gawain's advice, joining to it his own reluctant permission to execute Guenevere and his temporary anger at Lancelot; thus, he furthers his own tragedy while seeing it thrust upon him.[65] That Malory's Arthur himself condemns Guenevere to death—contrary to the sources, in which the barons do so [66]—Vinaver attributes to Malory's "conception of kingship [which] tends to transform a feudal overlord into a fifteenth-century monarch." But we should note that such a change increases Arthur's responsibility for the following events and immeasurably adds to his personal, inner struggle. Both effects make Arthur more of a tragic figure.

The third tragic figure in the "Death of Arthur" is Gawain.

[64] *Works*, pp. 1163, 1174, 1192, 1196 ff., 1201, 1211, 1213.
[65] For passages showing Arthur's perplexity and the nature of his dilemma, see the following in *ibid.*: 1190.17 ff.; 1194.21–22; 1196.8; 1197.1, 32–34; 1199.1–4; 1213 ff., 10 ff., 18 ff.; 1218.22–27; 1230.11–17.
[66] Cf. p. 1174.18, 28–29, and note.

To be sure, Gawain's literary history includes both a "good" and a "bad" Gawain,[67] and this ambivalence continues in *Le Morte Darthur*, even into the "Death of Arthur," where Gawain's attitude toward Lancelot is sometimes strongly favorable, sometimes violently antagonistic. But Malory turns this ambivalence to his advantage; it is not the simple blunder some have thought. Especially significant is the motif of vengeance. Throughout the book Gawain is of great importance, but not always blameless, at least partly because of the "conducions" that Gareth is aware of: Gareth "wythdrewe hymself fro his brother sir Gawaynes felyship, for he was evir vengeable, and where he hated he wolde be avenged with murther: and that hated sir Gareth" (360). Although the siege of Benwick is motivated by Gawain's desire for vengeance in the Middle English stanzaic poem as well as in *Le Morte Darthur*, Malory specifically adds the phrase "thorow the vengeaunce of sir Gawayne" (1211) when Arthur begins burning and wasting Lancelot's lands. The long-standing feud with the family of Pellinore, culminating in the treacherous slaying of Lamorak, also helps to show the pattern of vengeance in which revenge for Gareth has a place. Thus the motif, especially as personified in Gawain, is important in the "Death of Arthur": vengeance for the death of Gareth is the motivation of Gawain's last actions, and contributes greatly to the destruction of the Round Table. In Malory's view the bad in Gawain stems from his emotional and instinctual characteristics, the good from the civilizing and Christian influences around him. Gawain's tragedy is that the opposing forces within him come into strong conflict,

[67] B. J. Whiting, "Gawain: His Reputation, His Courtesy and His Appearance in Chaucer's *Squire's Tale*," *Mediaeval Studies*, IX (1947), 189–234. Cf. Taylor, *An Introduction to Medieval Romance*, pp. 57–58, and *Works*, p. 1423. For a view of Malory's "artistic purpose for the contradictory behavior which Gawain exhibits," see Barbara Gray Bartholomew, "The Thematic Function of Malory's Gawain," *CE*, XXIV (1963), 262–67.

and the baser side prevails long enough to have catastrophic effects.

The clue to this conflict is in Malory's original handling of Gawain's monomania after the death of Gareth, the intensity of which helps to raise him to the level of a tragic character. Unlike his feud with the House of Pellinore, it is not mere loyalty to his own clan that motivates his rage against Lancelot. Love of his sons, for example, is not enough to spur his vengeance when Lancelot kills them and Aggravain (1175–76). Only in Malory do Gawain's sons participate in that fatal ambush; Malory seems thus to point to the importance of Gareth in Gawain's emotions, and at the same time he explains that the deaths of Aggravain, Florence, and Lovell impress Gawain still less because Gawain feels that they sought trouble against his advice and are not deserving of his vengeance.[68] But Gareth is his "good brother," the epitome of his family's best parts, an innocent victim. His death carries Gawain over the brink which separates insanity from a gnawing conflict between the pagan and instinctive desire for vengeance and the checkrein of Christian principles.

The change from one to the other is easily seen. Gawain's caution and his attempts to forestall the growing break with Lancelot are clear,[69] and Malory's original efforts here are followed by his original preparation for the change (1183). When Gawain is finally convinced that Lancelot has killed Gareth, he swoons; when he wakes, he is the Gawain who carelessly

---

[68] Gawain can overlook Lancelot's adultery much more easily than the alleged treachery against Gareth; see pp. 1189.9–15, 1191.12–15; cf. also p. 1194.24.

[69] Cf. Lancelot's speech at p. 1168.3–10 with Gawain's at pp. 1174.31–1175.18. Gawain compares himself with Lancelot at p. 1184.18 ff. Both believe that some knights whom Lancelot endangers would defect to Lancelot if possible (pp. 1172.30–32, 1185.3–5); Gawain specifically refers to Gareth. The bulk of the scene of Gawain's remonstrations with Arthur (pp. 1174–77) is original with Malory.

slew a lady on his first quest, the Gawain eager to revenge King Lot's death, the enemy of Lamorak, the knight for whom the spiritual heights of the Grail were boring. He runs to tell Arthur what Arthur already knows, swoons again, and swears vengeance in a speech much stronger than its sources in the stanzaic poem (2010–13). Gawain's oath at this point in the book contrasts markedly with his speech just before he learns of Gareth's death (1184), in which he asserts that Lancelot's rescue of Guenevere is only "as I wolde have done myselff and I had stonde in lyke case." It is not merely that love for Lancelot is turning to hate.[70] Rather, in the volatile mixture of good and evil that is Gawain, that part which is primitive and violent boils so high as to dominate all other sentiments. Thenceforth, numerous passages attest Gawain's monomaniac desire to revenge his beloved brother.[71]

But the other Gawain, the magnanimous and regretful Gawain who befriends Lancelot in the early part of the "Death of Arthur," returns to command his last scene. Part of the change is surely attributable to Gawain's knowledge that he is dying. Like Guenevere, like Edmund in *Lear*, he means to do some good before he dies. The deeper reason for the return of the other Gawain, however, lies in the combination of change of fortune, reversal, and discovery, the same combination that makes tragic figures of Arthur and Lancelot, and, to a lesser degree, of Guenevere. In his hope to revenge Gareth's death on a supposed traitor, he has enabled a real traitor to mount a rebellion against his uncle and king. In trying to kill Lancelot he has received his own death blow, and Lancelot lives. With

[70] E. K. Chambers, "Sir Thomas Malory," The English Association Pamphlet No. 51 (January, 1922), p. 11: ". . . Gawaine's love is turned to hate." For a similar oversimplification, see Aurner, *Malory*, p. xxviii.

[71] The list of passages which either use the phrase "traitor knight" and the like or otherwise show Gawain's intensity of purpose is imposing—over twenty-five between p. 1189 and p. 1231. See especially pp. 1190, 1197, 1201, 1213, and 1216.

the realization that he has brought these reversals upon himself, he achieves a spiritual regeneration: he confesses to his "owne hastynes and . . . wylfulnesse," and to the pride that has caused "all thys shame and disease" (1230). He regrets that he refused to come to terms with Lancelot, whom he praises and whose superiority he admits. Surely it must be with full realization of the irony of events and with full humility that he requests the alleged traitor to rescue Arthur from that "false traytoure whych ys my halff-brothir, sir Mordred." He applies the now familiar phrase "false traytoure" again to Mordred a few lines later. After Gawain finishes the letter to Lancelot he asks Arthur "to sende for sir Launcelot and to cherysshe hym aboven all othir knyghtes"; it is a speech much different from the earlier "My lorde, myne uncle, what woll ye do?" Though he had said at the height of his anger that he could never forgive Lancelot (1200), he now not only forgives Lancelot for the earlier deaths but blames himself for his own (1231). Meek and humble, of contrite heart, Gawain receives his sacrament; significantly, the detail is original with Malory.

Brief mention must be made of three others—Guenevere, Gareth, and Bors—who contribute to the context of tragic characters. Guenevere, like Lancelot, is a virtual saint at the end of *Le Morte Darthur*. But she becomes one only within the "Death of Arthur," for, unlike Lancelot, she has earlier shown little evidence of spiritual depth. And since she loses less than Arthur, Lancelot, or Gawain while gaining much, she is the least tragic of the central characters. Bors' most difficult problem, that which places him among the tragic figures of the "Death of Arthur," is that he, a Grail Knight, finds himself so closely allied to the greatest of the adulterers, Lancelot. Here, as in the other figures, is a conflict of emotions. It is never a violent conflict; Bors is not usually given to violence. Rather it is the ever-present knowledge that he must live in a world of sin, must—as a vassal—do his overlord's bidding, must—as one trusted and depended upon—aid his beloved kinsman. Bors, like Gareth, suffers from the conflicting forces of his society; he does not generate them, he is not to blame for them. Instead, he suffers from them and becomes a projection of the society's inherent tragedy. Gareth's death may not be considered tragic in the same sense as those of the central characters because he is not truly responsible for it, and it does not come as a logical development of the action. But however much chance plays a role in his death, the death is still related to the evil around him, and the stark contrast between the worth of his character and the senselessness of his death points to the tragic confusion at this time in the moral order of the Round Table society.

VI

The fall of this society comes as the climactic and artistic conclusion of a unified epic-romance, a tragedy which results, however, from the sins and errors of the characters as individuals over a lengthy period of time. The tragedy gains cogency from the ideals of the Round Table, formulated as early as the first "Tale" of *Le Morte Darthur,* and from the constant, medieval sense of religion, of man in relation to God, to good, and to evil. Through his excellently conceived and well-executed treatment of his central characters, Malory shows the change of fortune that they bring upon themselves, upon each other, and upon their society. Yet their tragedy and the failure of the Round Table society are not unrelieved, for Malory sincerely accepts the medieval view of salvation. Accordingly, most of the principal characters achieve a spiritual catharsis and sanctification; however, they achieve this state not as parts of the

Round Table society, but as individuals following the path described in Dante's comedy.[72] Malory is thus able to develop a synthesis of what he had come to know as experience with what he had come to believe as an idealist. From the discrepancy he had found, Malory had come to see the tragedy inherent in men and their society. Accordingly he writes a tragedy of the Round Table, a human device intended to weld king and vassals into an ordered society, but one which fails through human error.

Whatever harmony Malory achieved between the ideals of the Grail Quest and the terrestial ideals of the medieval world is achieved in the final pages of the "Death of Arthur." This point is insufficiently stressed by Vida D. Scudder, though it is not lacking in her book (407–9). Lancelot and Guenevere die as ascetics; they are the embodiments at the end of *Le Morte Darthur* of the same spiritual forces which Galahad represents during the "Grail." The "Tale of the Sankgreall" thus bears a twofold structural relationship to the end of Malory's book, in that while it causes the action to fall toward its catastrophic conclusion in the "Death of Arthur," it also reaches its own full resolution only within the "Death of Arthur," where the "life of penitence," the "one life only which ensures the freedom of the sons of God," is "the note of hope" upon which the story closes (Scudder, 408). In the postponement of the full resolution of the Quest motif until the "Death of Arthur," Malory is following a principle analogous to that which causes the "Tristram" also to be concluded only within the eighth "Tale." In both cases the drawing together of motifs within the "Death of Arthur" greatly enhances the artistic pattern of *Le Morte Darthur* as a whole.[73]

[72] For a similar emphasis in the *Mort Artu*, see Frappier, *Etude*, p. 235.
[73] Another kind of connection between the "Grail" and the "Death of Arthur" is seen by P. E. Tucker, "The Place of the 'Quest of the Holy

The tragedy of the Round Table as a social unit is in its unsuccessful attempt to create on earth an idealistic state. Since the Round Table is a society flourishing in the midst of medieval Christianity, its characteristics are steadily seen against the backdrop of otherworldly philosophy where the function of man is to aspire to an eternal reward. And since the Round Table exists in an era when the historicity of original sin and the reality of the seven deadly sins are accepted, its members find it difficult always to live in accord with the strictest dictates of their consciences. Thus the tragedy of the Round Table as a society exists in the discrepancy between its idealistic aspirations to fulfill a great potential, and the realistic understanding that reliance upon human beings must necessarily and ultimately defeat its purpose. Furthermore, in the spiritual orientation of the medieval mind, salvation, the pre-eminent goal, is an individual matter. Society, at best, can only facilitate that salvation; at worst, it must suffer the catastrophic tendencies to evil.[74] But the Round Table society is magnificent in failure, for it helps many of its members to reach their ultimate goal, and its aspirations stand—somewhat ironically—as a monument to the great potential in every man: his ability to desire and to seek perfection.

When Vinaver turns his attention specifically to the "Tale of the Death of Arthur," he continues to find no moral, universal, Christian theme but only a human tragedy in psychological terms. Of Lancelot he says, "It is not as a Christian,

---

Grail' in the 'Morte Darthur,'" *MLR*, XLVIII (1953), 391–97. But Tucker gives less importance to the Quest than I do.

[74] Miss Scudder views sympathetically this medieval religious orientation, especially its mysticism and asceticism (*Le Morte Darthur*, pp. 259–64). For a short but clear statement of the ethical orientation of Malory's book and the "discrepancy between the lofty religious idealism [of his sources] and the wantonness of the stories inherited from the age of courtly love," see Ernest A. Baker, *The History of the English Novel: The Age of Romance* (London, 1924), pp. 193–94.

but as a lover that he mourns the queen; he repents, not of the
sins he has committed against God, but of the grief he has
caused his lady and King Arthur. . . ." [75] In Malory's "account
the downfall of Arthur's kingdom appears neither as a retribu-
tion for a sinful life nor as a necessary sequel to good fortune.
. . . Implicit in the story and its characters, though never fully
expressed in any previous version, was the great mediaeval
theme of divided allegiances." [76] These allegiances are the
"heroic loyalty of man to man" and "the blind devotion of the
knight-lover to his lady." Consciously or not, Vinaver here
echoes what Miss Scudder said years earlier, with one significant
difference, a difference basic to the consideration of the tragedy
of the Round Table society: for there is a third loyalty in
Le Morte Darthur properly read, the loyalty to God. Miss
Scudder, considering Malory's book "as an integral work of
art," says, "The aim . . . is to present the controlling interests
of the Middle Ages—love, religion, war—in their ideal sym-
metry and their actual conflict. Malory's way of doing this is to
tell the story of the rise and fall of chivalry, with its three
loyalties, to the overlord, to the lady, and to God, as symbol-
ized in the fate of that fair fellowship, the Table Round." [77]
Even more significant for the present consideration is her comment on the final episodes of the book: "Thus it comes to pass
that the conclusion of the *Morte Darthur* presents, not merely
the tragic death of Arthur and his queen, but the death of the
Middle Ages. The epoch witnessed a great experiment in living;
and it failed, through the ancient failure to harmonize factors
good in themselves but evil if stressed in isolation" (353).

This larger view of the theme of *Le Morte Darthur* seems
thoroughly defensible. Malory is concerned with the Round

[75] *The Tale of the Death,* p. xxiii. Cf. *Works,* pp. 1642–43.
[76] *Ibid.,* p. xii. Cf. *Works,* pp. lxxviii–lxxxv, and 1606–8. Chambers,
"Sir Thomas Malory," p. 9, has said much the same thing.
[77] P. 185. Cf. pp. 268, 276, 278, 291, 309, 314, 335.

Table as the attempt to embody on earth spiritual as well as
human virtues, an attempt to keep God in England so that all
may remain right in the English world. But earth is not heaven,
and men on earth are not yet saved, as any medieval author
knows. Dante shows how man can successfully progress toward
paradise by degrees of purgation, and the result is a comedy.
Malory shows how human society can only fail in trying to
bring paradise down to earth, and the result is tragedy. Like
Dante, Malory shows, however, the way out of this tragic state:
the path to salvation can be trod by individuals alone, and its
summit can be reached only after death. But Malory's method
of presenting this view of man and his society is not an attempt
to exhort, to preach, or to teach; it is in the failure to realize
this indirect method that Vinaver's refusal to use the word
"moral" in connection with *Le Morte Darthur* seems singularly
shortsighted. Malory seeks not to be hortatory but to be dramatic, to display the tragic shortcomings of earthly life while
dramatizing the final solution to them. In this connection, it is
crucially important to recall that early in his book (119–20)
Malory added a set of principles with which Arthur charged
the member knights; to these principles the Round Table an-
nually swears at Pentecost.[78] At the foundation of the society,
Arthur was aware of the vices that could destroy it. Malory's
adding this set of principles is also significant because of its
concern for spiritual, not just moral or human matters; further,
it is an oath for society, not just for individuals. In thus showing that Arthur was trying to fashion a society which would up-

---

[78] Similar—and also apparently original with Malory—is Arthur's oath
when he is crowned king. Arthur is "sworne unto his lordes and the comyns
for to be a true kyng, to stand with true justyce fro thens forth the dayes
of this lyf" (16). According to Vinaver's note (1285), Arthur's "first duty"
in the French "is to the church. He swears 'd'aidier Sainte Eglyse et es-
sauchier, et tenir loiauté en terre et païs.'" For specific allusions to the
oath of knighthood, both apparently sourceless, see pp. 177.1–6 and
269.21–24 and Vinaver's notes.

hold the Christian ethic, Malory deliberately calls attention to the human failings inherent in the society from its inception.

Once these human failings have caused the disintegration of the Round Table, have destroyed it as a successful society, decisions must be made on an individual basis. For just as Arthur knows that the days of the successful Round Table are gone, so he knows that only as individuals can we pass through death into another life: "Comforte thyselff, and do as well as thou mayste, for in me ys no truste for to truste in. For I muste into the vale of Avylyon. . . ." Vinaver has said that this "is a scene not of mourning but of triumph"; [79] insofar as the Round Table has been Arthur's means of triumph, this is a scene not of triumph, but of abject dissolution. The various individuals may find the triumphant path to salvation, but for the noble order of the Round Table it is the tragic death of a mighty world.

[79] *Malory*, p. 92.

INDEX

H